SKIING W

THE MORZIN

SKIING WITH DEMONS

THE MORZINE CHALET PROJECT

CHRIS TOMLINSON

www.skiingwithdemons.com

YOUCAXTON PUBLICATIONS

OXFORD & SHREWSBURY

ISBN 978-190964-466-3
Printed and bound in Great Britain.
Published by Chris Tomlinson 2015
YouCaxton Publications

Cover illustration by Daniel House

CONTENTS

Authors Notes   i

1. The Journey Home   1
2. The Chalet Project   12
3. The Wall & The Couloir of Certain Death   20
4. The Après Aliens   29
5. Baptism of Snow   43
6. Cougars and Manthers in Manzine   52
7. The Ski Nazis   56
8. Morzine Mary   61
9. The Vallée Blanche   65
10. Summer of Discontent   79
11. Je Suis un Moniteur de Ski   88
12. Come Dine With Me (in the Alps)   96
13. Is Skiing a Sport?   106
14. Breakfast of Skiing Champions   110
15. The Ski Club of Great Britain   118
16. Languid at Luton Airport   124
17. No Friends on a Powder Day   126
18. Fear on the Fall-line   135
19. Girlfriend Skiing   149
20. The Avalanche   154
21. Lad Skiing   162
22. The Leaders' Course – Week Two   173
23. What does a ski bum do in the Summer?   187
24. New Year's Eve in the Alps   191
25. The Bacon Run   200
26. Half-Term Hell Week   211
27. Everything is Easier Second Time Around   218
28. The Big Brother Chalet   223
29. No Change Without Loss   231
30. The Blue Jacket   234
31. Living the Dream?   244
32. The Final Descent   248

Appendix – Ski Terminology   249

DEDICATION

To Debbie: I'm loving angels instead

"There is nothing to writing.
All you do is sit at your typewriter and bleed"

Ernest Hemingway

AUTHORS NOTES

1.2 million Britons go skiing every year and most of them come back. Around thirty die through misadventure. Only a dozen or so are killed by avalanches, a few from crashing into immovable objects or each other, however the majority die in what are known as 'alcohol related incidents' - usually by freezing to death. This book is my skiing memoir and includes one fatal avalanche, a few crashes and numerous alcohol related incidents. It documents my transition from a city-living adman to a garage-dwelling ski bum and rookie ski instructor over four ski seasons in the French alpine town of Morzine. More importantly, it documents the price I paid for living my dream.

I also try to answer some difficult questions: what constitutes a 'proper job', what do ski bums do in the summer and what does being a 'good skier' actually mean? I explore skiing phobias and exorcise a few demons of my own, primarily a morbid fear of avalanches and an infamous run called the Swiss Wall.

I describe some of the people, from different nations, who have been my guests along with their domestic and gastronomic habits, and some notable French traits. I recall some memorable skiing adventures with the Ski Club of Great Britain and some of the guides and instructors I've skied with – some of whom were even more mentally unstable than me.

Currently the names of those mentioned in this book have *not* been changed, but probably should be, in order to protect against the loss of friendships and possible litigation. However, everything described in this book, to the best of my recollection, actually happened.

1. The Journey Home

Waking up had become problematic. Not because my body was shattered or my brain had started to filter out my alarm clock. Neither was it because the room was often spinning, my head thumping and my mouth dry - these were problems I'd become accustomed to solving.

The problem that was becoming increasingly hard to solve was working out *where* exactly it was I had woken up. This was starting to take a worrying amount of time too. The conclusion that 'it had happened again', that I'd been abducted by aliens and deposited in a strange bed, was getting hard even for me to believe in.

On one unforgettable morning in April 2012, I woke up alone in what, this time, looked distinctly like a hospital room. My second season as a ski bum in the French Alps had been completed without significant injury, despite some seriously kamikaze skiing, but that morning I'd woken up in a hospital in Reims - a very long way from the Alps.

After the usual morning roll call - phone, wallet, keys, shoes, coat, dignity - and noticing that all but the last were present on the chair next to my bed, I started the now-well-practiced mental debrief, to figure out what had happened the night before.

I asked myself the usual 'W' questions. What had I been drinking? Who had I been drinking with? What had I done and said? Who might my inappropriate behaviour, which I always took as a given, offended? What, in my drunken bravado, had I agreed to do - usually ski some impossible slope. Most importantly, where had I left 'Landie' – my battered Land Rover Defender?

I pulled an IV drip out of my arm, thinking it a bit excessive for a hangover, and wondered if I'd been out with my medical student friends again? A young woman entered the room, I recognised her face as that of the nurse from the night before, and it all came flooding back to me.

She'd insisted that I stay in the hospital overnight. I'd argued with her, in my pigeon French, that my injuries were no worse than I'd previously incurred on a rugby field and that my English skull was made of thicker stuff. She'd summoned the other staff to block my exit and told me she would call the gendarmes if I attempted to leave. When I protested further, she made me stand in front of a mirror. I peered into it and a bulky, unshaven, bald man looked back. He was somewhere in his late forties although facial abrasions, a black eye and a broken nose prevented more accurate dating. He was wearing a blood stained T-shirt that had the words 'Powder to the People' written on it around a symbolic clenched fist. The skiing pun obviously didn't work in French and he looked like some sort of militant you'd cross the street to avoid. After wobbling my head a couple of times to confirm the reflection was mine, I'd agreed it was not sensible to let me loose on the good people of Reims until I was sober.

I'd stopped for the night in Reims while returning from my winter residence in Morzine, a town in the Haute-Savoie department of the Rhône-Alpes region of France. Spring had sprung and I was heading back to my home in Birmingham where I knew I had left a lot of trouble in store. I had managed to alert my long-suffering wife, who was resident in Birmingham all year round, to my unexpected delay in Reims by text. She'd wanted to send a rescue party but, before my phone battery had run out, I'd convinced her I was capable of making it home under my own steam. I just had to convince myself.

'The Chalet Project', as I liked to call it, had been my latest attempt to escape the rat race, the latest in a sequence of midlife crises that my wife had vicariously endured. Over the preceding winter we'd become even further estranged. The previous morning, I'd loaded my ski gear and enough red wine to last a summer (or so I thought) into the back of Landie and had started the long journey home. The night before, I'd had a farewell drink with my Morzine crew and had mercifully woken up in my own bed. The journey had been uneventful despite Landie not being the trustiest of steeds, especially on long motorway journeys.

It had become late and I'd diverted into the centre of Reims for the night and found a hotel. That night, being my last night in France for seven months, I'd decided to venture out on foot to seek some local colour in the historic French city. I'd found a cosy bar, not far from the hotel, and ordered *'un plat de charcuterie'* and *'un verre de vin rouge'* to wash it down. But by the end of the evening I'd added my own colour to the town, that of claret, to its pavements.

Reims is famous for Champagne, not Claret, and I had been persuaded to drink a fortified derivative of the stuff by some locals who'd attached themselves to me. My new friends had suggested I try their local hooch but warned me it was a mind-altering liquid. I wasn't the sort of person to shirk an international drinking challenge so I agreed to try some. Besides which, I'd had a lot of drinking practice during the preceding season so I felt match-fit. After that, my recollection of the evening got a bit sketchy.

I recall chatting to the lead singer of a band called the 'Bewitched Hands' – I know this because I made a note on my phone to look them up on Facebook when I got back. His friend turned up, who had much more English at his disposal, although I'd made a good stab at explaining my reason for being in *'Rans'*, as they told me it should be pronounced. It's amazing how much braver you get at speaking a foreign language after a drink, although, after several more glasses of their hooch, speaking English became the challenge.

The lead singer's girlfriend had turned up, bizarrely carrying a bunch of daffodils, and I distinctly remember being mesmerized by their colour. She was disgruntled that her boyfriend had not returned home earlier. He'd introduced me as 'a ski instructor, on his way home from the Alps.' I could blame my French for giving him the wrong impression or, more likely, I'd embellished the truth just a little. At that stage in my skiing career, I was trying to qualify as an instructor but had not yet accomplished it. I remember thinking 'what the hell, I might as well go with it and see what it feels like to be one'. This was certainly better than admitting the truth – that I was an online marketing consultant.

Ski Instructor was also a lot easier to say in French *'je suis un moniteur de ski'*. Besides which, I was hardly going to be found out in the Ardennes, one of the flattest regions in France, if someone asked me to prove it.

I remember going outside to smoke with my new friends, something I hadn't done in years and a telltale sign that the evening had, once again, 'gone large' on me through no fault of my own. I then vaguely recalled lying on the pavement leaking claret from my face. Had there been a fight? Was I hit? Or did I just pass out and hit my head? Bruises on my knuckles could have been caused in either scenario.

The personal debrief proved inconclusive. I'd had many a UBI[1] before, but had never woken up in a hospital. There hadn't been any UFO sightings reported over '*Rans*', so I couldn't blame alien involvement, as had become my practice in Morzine. One thing I was certain about was that my drinking had become problematic and I made a mental note to contact Alcoholics Anonymous when I got back home. As it turned out, it was a different AA (the Automobile Association) I was in more urgent need of later that day.

---

1   *An Unexplained Beer Injury (**UBI**) is usually a bruise, scratch or burn that is discovered the morning after being drunk. The sufferer will have no recollection of how or when the injury was acquired because no pain was felt at the time.*

It's hard to tell if you've got a drinking problem or not when you work in a ski resort. Binge drinking and skiing are inextricably linked sports. In Morzine, no-one bats an eyelid if you fall off a barstool. Perhaps that's why we Brits love 'skiing' so much; despite being terrible at the actual skiing part, we excel at the après-ski.

Meanwhile I had a ferry to catch and, first, I had to convince my captor, the on-duty consultant, that I was *'sain d'esprit' (sane)* enough to leave the building. He insisted I had to wait for a CT scan to make sure, so I hatched an escape plan.

While no-one was looking, I got dressed and made my first bid for freedom. I wandered through a labyrinth of corridors looking for the sortie (exit). I went through an automatic door that closed behind me, preventing me from retracing my steps. I started to wonder if I'd made a mistake and had doomed myself to wander the corridors of this hospital forever – 'The Ghost of Reims Général'. I bumped into my favourite nurse. Fortunately I'd wandered in a big circle back to the casualty ward. She told me I was a *'très naughty boy'* and that I couldn't leave until I'd had *'my brain checked'* and that the hospital porter was waiting to take me to the scanning machine.

I'm not sure why, but apparently it's international practice for hospitals to ferry patients around in wheelchairs even if they're perfectly capable of walking. I assume it turns the patient into a more manageable commodity - and keeps the porters in a job. It does have a decidedly pacifying effect, I'll admit.

Having had the escape equipment (my shoes and coat) confiscated, I was wheeled off deeper into the labyrinth wearing only a hospital gown and left in a corridor outside radiology. After fifty minutes of sitting facing the wall (which, bizarrely, had a picture of the Mary Rose on it, now indelibly committed to my memory), I flagged down a passing white coat. I explain in pigeon French that I'd been abandoned and needed reuniting with my clothes, and that I had a ferry to catch and was quite capable of walking.

Whatever I *actually* said in translation, combined with my Rocky VI appearance, only confirmed to the coat that I'd escaped from the psychiatric ward and that maybe my wheelchair needed restraints. The white coat smiled, rotated my wheelchair to face away from the wall and continued down the corridor. I was ignored for a further thirty minutes before finally being wheeled into the scanning room.

My second attempt at freedom, an hour after being wheeled back to my room, was more successful. I was starting to get the lay off the land. I'd found my shoes and coat, which they'd foolishly left in the wardrobe and I actually made it outside. It was nice to see the sky but where exactly in Reims was I? In which direction was my hotel? I hadn't intended travelling far from the hotel, so I hadn't really noted its location or indeed its name. The room key was an anonymous electronic one - so of no help. This time I *really* didn't know where I'd left Landie!

In a flash of genius, inspired by desperation, I remembered the hotel was next to a train station. I jumped into a taxi outside the renal ward, *'La gare, s'il vous plait'*, I triumphantly requested. *'Non'* he replied, a phrase I'd encountered a lot while living in France. He explained he couldn't take a fare unless the hospital had booked him.

Now in France, *'non'*, the default response to any request, really means, 'I'm thinking about it, so persuade me'. In this case I didn't succeed. Sheepishly, I returned to the casualty ward where the duty nurse leapt out of her chair, delighted to see me again - the feeling wasn't mutual — she told me my scans were back and *'zee brain was intact'* and I could leave after the *'paperassière'* (paperwork) was done.

The French love paperwork. If I've learnt anything from living in France it's that the *paperassière* usually takes longer than the work it relates to. I was definitely going to miss my ferry. Finally, after forty or so minutes, I was handed a report to give to my GP by the consultant. It confirmed there'd been precious little blood left in my alcohol system when the ambulance had dropped me off. I had in fact broken my eye socket, an injury that has left me with a permanent lump – which I now put down to a 'skiing accident'.

When the consultant gave me a judgmental look over the top of his glasses, I felt no shame. These guys and their ancestors had dedicated their entire region to the production of the world's most famous alcoholic beverage – Champagne - and I was merely an over-indulgent fan. At last, he gave me the all clear. I had a Glasgow Score of fifteen, which was apparently good for someone who'd recently been unconscious. Amused that Glasgow should be the origin of an international system used to calibrate head injuries, I thanked him and the nurse and asked if she would call a taxi. I was finally free.

I sat in the front seat of the cab. The driver, who assumed I had been through one windscreen already that day, insisted I put my seat belt on lest it happen again. He looked at me, a bandage wrapped around my head and one eye partially closed by swelling, and asked '*d'accord?*' (okay) To which I replied '*J'ai un mal de tête*' (I have a headache). He chortled, presumably at my typical English understatement, and I politely chortled back. 'You're not getting a tip', I thought. He took me to the train station and my hunch was right, Landie was parked outside the hotel next door.

I went up to my room to grab my washbag and clean shirt. They were still lying on the unused bed, having had a less eventful night than their owner. I checked out; it had only cost me €80 to store them there overnight. I jumped into Landie; Calais was just three hours away. She started first time, which was always a bonus, but when I went to depress the clutch pedal, horror of horrors, it lay limp on the floor. Could the day get any worse? Landie was seemingly going nowhere.

Over the last two seasons, like many Defender owners, I'd developed an emotional relationship with mine – a blue and white 110 TDi almost as ancient as me. Equipped with old-fashioned bench seats in the back it can accommodate up to ten adults in a tolerable amount of discomfort for short trips. There are few vehicles that make me anthropomorphize, usually motorbikes and boats, but Landie is one of them and despite being a pile of junk by modern standards, Landie has a soul.

Whether it's a female or male soul is still up for debate. Despite its ruggedness and unrefined strength, Landie does have many female qualities. Landie always plays up at just the wrong time and definitely hates the cold. It regularly needs money spending on it, which soon amounts to more than its original value, responds to pleading and needs to be told she is loved before and after every ride.

Its male attributes include making unusual noises and unpleasant smells from time to time. It's scruffy and unkempt and belches toxic fumes in the morning when it's first woken up. It also drinks a lot. But men always refer to the vessels they love as 'she' so 'la' Landie *it* is.

She is superbly suited to the job of running skiers around mountains and superbly unsuited to crossing a continent on motorways. I'm often asked why I don't sell her and buy something more modern that would do both jobs but nothing can do the former in such patriotic style. There's nothing that symbolises Britain's former engineering prowess and our nation's stoic traits than a Defender - with the exception of a Spitfire perhaps but that would be less practical to park and would have significantly less room for passengers, although the machine guns could prove handy.

Many of my guests feel the same. Especially men, of a certain age it has to be said, who enjoy jumping in and out of 'the beast', chests swollen with jingoistic pride. I'm usually wearing wellington boots, another great British invention, and a cloth cap, to complete my man-about-Yorkshire ensemble. In any case, Landie and I have been through too much together, both good and bad, to part now. For better or for worse, in sickness and health, we'll stick together − 'til death do us part.

But that day, my love affair with Landie seemed over. At that moment, I would have swapped her for anything - even a Renault. I was tired and hungry and my head felt like I was wearing an internal balaclava. I gave Landie a piece of my mind. A woman hurried past, averting her gaze, while I ranted in 'franglais' at the *putain de merde'* (whore of shit).

With hindsight, I suspect Landie knew that returning to the UK meant that she would be locked in a shed all summer and was probably reluctant to continue. What she probably didn't know, because neither did I, was that I faced an equally grim fate on our return. I would end up living in a box that summer too, a tiny bedsit in fact. But you can take anthropomorphism too far; the clutch had gone and no amount of expletives would fix it. To add to the horror, I then discovered my AA European Road cover had run out the week before. I'd stayed longer than initially planned in the Alps. After the season had ended in Morzine, I'd gone over to Chamonix for a few days. I'd put off what seasonaires call 'returning to reality' but had forgotten to extend my cover.

I decided to see if it was possible to drive Landie without a clutch. The answer was 'almost', if you crashed the gears and concentrated on never coming to an absolute stop. After rolling through many a red light, I made it on to the motorway, got up into fifth gear and then up to cruising speed, which is about 60 mph in a Defender. 'Calais here I come', I shouted. If I could get Landie on the ferry, I could literally roll her off at Dover, where the AA would be obliged to tow me home under my UK membership.

Unfortunately I had to stop completely at passport control before boarding the ferry. Landie spluttered and stalled more or less at the kiosk window. I handed over my passport and explained to the customs officer that I'd recently had a 'skiing accident' and that my face bore little resemblance to the passport photograph. He joked 'nobody's does mate,' in a reassuringly English accent. I bunny hopped up the ferry's boarding ramp willing the car in front of me not to stop. It didn't and I made it aboard.

Any relief I felt at being back on UK soil was lost when I realised I would hit the M25 at rush hour. That would involve a lot of stopping and starting and, in my case, crunching of gears. While spending three miserable hours on that circular embodiment of hell, I had time to reflect. I remember looking down on some sharp-suited city type, chain-smoking in his Mercedes. At least I was only passing through. He probably had to do this every day to afford that car and his fancy suit. He could keep them both; I'd keep Landie and my jeans. He would probably have a heart attack over the next stock market crash. I'd take my chances with the avalanches – if the aliens didn't get to me first!

I made it onto the M40 and headed north to Birmingham, from where I'd departed almost four months previously. Landie and I were now running on hope, the gearbox was mashed and the swelling over my left eye had closed in over the eyeball. Having charged my phone from the cigarette lighter, I called my wife to tell her I was alive and a few hours from home and that I loved her very much. An unusually emotional outburst from me, but it was true. I remember stumbling through the door expecting a warm homecoming. I felt like a polar explorer who'd been lost for months in Antarctica, about to be reunited with his loved one. However, she didn't seem that pleased to see me. After a small embrace, dinner was served. I found it strangely hard to find anything to say, so much had happened and we had so much to discuss but there was no obvious place to start.

The familiar surroundings were a comfort at least and I remarked that it was 'nice to be home', the biggest understatement of my life. Although, glad I was safe, my wife wasn't so pleased. She'd not changed her mind over the winter - she still wanted me to move out permanently!

The next morning was another problematic one. Once again, it took me a while to work out where I'd woken up – sadly, I concluded, I was in my own spare room.

2. The Chalet Project

On the 4th of January 2010, I woke up in a garage surrounded by skis. It was the beginning of 'Season 1', to use the American nomenclature, my first full skiing season in the Alps. 'The Après Aliens', as I'd started to call them, had not really started their abduction campaign at that point so the location of the garage, and how I'd ended up sleeping there, were not mysteries to me.

The term 'gap year' hadn't been invented when I left university but, at the age of forty-seven, I thought mine was well overdue. At least, that's what I thought the first time I found myself without a job. Actually I hadn't had a 'proper' job in years; I don't think anyone who works in marketing actually has a proper job. I'd recently held the disembodied job title 'Head of Digital' and more latterly that of 'Social Media Consultant' – clearly these were not proper jobs.

I'd started my working life in a proper job, working as a software engineer, but thanks to the rise of the World Wide Web I'd somehow ended up working for an advertising agency. During the halcyon dotcom era, I'd set up a website development company and then sold it, along with my soul, to the agency for a bag full of cash and a lot of unfulfilled promises. Most expats in Morzine have a how-I-escaped-the-rat-race story to tell, about how they decided to 'live the dream' and move to the Alps.

The seminal moment in my story happened in an office in Sutton Coldfield, the most nondescript of suburban commuter towns, a place that was as random to me then as it probably is to you now, but it seems to crop up a lot in the story. The headquarters of the agency I'd sold out too was in Sutton and

I'd agreed to work there for three years. Late one evening, while sitting in a brainstorming session or 'thought shower' as the agency's creative director cringingly liked to call them, I had an epiphany. We were trying to think of ways to make a brand of pre-washed lettuce stand out on the supermarket shelf.

The main thoughts going through my mind were: how had I ended up in this room with these vacuous people and who actually cared about how their pre-washed lettuce was packaged? Not me. I concluded that I was having a midlife crisis. I recognised the symptoms – because I'd had several before.

I had my first crisis in my thirties when I moved to the Middle East, only to return three months later due to an unfortunate misunderstanding with a sheikh. I returned with a fatwa and the Python lyric 'never be rude to an Arab' ringing in my ears.

Since my Arabic odyssey, I'd tried less radical cures for subsequent midlife crises. I'd bought a sports car, toured Europe on a Harley Davison, ran with the bulls in Pamplona, been to Glastonbury, got married in Vegas, but mostly I just got drunk a lot. My long-suffering friends will probably point out that these crises have actually been a continuum rather than a series of discrete events and that most middle-aged people are dissatisfied with their lives. I then like to point out that this is largely thanks to people who work in marketing.

Marketing is the process of finding, or better still creating, dissatisfaction amongst consumers then presenting a product as the solution. It is the art of making people want things they previously never knew they needed. I'm willing to admit that I might be bitter and twisted, but that's what working in an agency does to you!

This midlife crisis was different. I was now actually middle-aged - so this was the real thing. This time I wasn't going to just treat the symptoms; I was going to cure the problem and start a completely new career; I'd had enough of helping companies promote products I wouldn't buy myself. Furthermore, I swore I'd never take a job that required me to wear a suit or use Microsoft Power Point ever again. I was going to find something I loved doing and work out how to get paid for it. Advice someone should have given me when I left school.

The Careers Officer at my school neglected to mention that you needed to like your job, because you'd probably be doing it for a long time. Since he helped me choose mine, I've discovered that there are lots of really interesting careers he failed to mention: arctic explorer, pyro technician, rollercoaster engineer, marine biologist and, of course, ski instructor. Frankly, why I took careers advice from a man who had settled on 'Career Adviser' for himself, I don't know.

The truth is, like most people, I'd never really had a vocation. I'd basically made career decisions based on which jobs would provide me with the most money in the shortest space of time. Once caught in that particular gravitational field, you're naturally pulled towards sales and marketing and slowly become just another whore for capitalism.

But thanks to the sale of my company, I'd paid off my mortgage and my new career was not going to be determined by salary expectations, pensions, company cars, health insurance and all those unimportant considerations. This time I was going to do something I loved. So what did I love doing and how could I get paid to do it?

I loved skiing and, more importantly, I loved being in the Alps. After a dodgy start in my twenties, I'd taken up skiing properly at the late age of thirty-four. By the time I was forty, I was well and truly hooked and went skiing at least three times a year to get a fix. Each year, I would have one week doing what I call 'girlfriend skiing' with my wife and mutual friends and at least one 'boys trip' with my single mates, some of whom were technically female but I digress.

However, at my age, training to be a ski instructor seemed a little unrealistic and it overlooked the more obvious barrier - my skiing ability. So what else could I do for a living in the Alps? Maybe, I could get a management job with a ski company? But I had no experience in tourism and I didn't speak a foreign language which most of the resort managers and ski-reps' job ads seemed to mandate. Maybe I could be a chalet host? But I didn't know anything about catering or housekeeping either. I certainly didn't fancy being a chalet girl; for starters I was the wrong sex, besides which, I'd stayed in many luxury chalets and knew that working as a 'seasonaire' for a tour operator was akin to slavery. I was also too old to share grotty accommodation with immature youths or have a simpleton as a boss. During my so-called 'career' I'd spent enough time with both.

Even though I would rather clean toilets in the Alps than work in marketing, I had to be realistic. At my age, no tour operator would give me a job at either end of the employment ladder. No, to get a job in the Alps I would have to be self-employed. I'd have to do the one thing I did have experience of - setting up and running a business. The trouble was, I was devoid of business ideas.

It was on a lad's trip to Morzine that my entrepreneurial light bulb finally came back on, while talking to a bartender in The Farmhouse, one of Morzine's more up-market chalet hotels. James, who'd left a proper job in financial services to be a ski bum, offered some information around which an epic 'thought shower' precipitated. It seems obvious now, but he told us that most tour operators don't own the chalets they sell holidays in - they rent them.

My companions that trip, fellow entrepreneurs Jon and Andy, found this fact interesting too. We'd all been on ski holidays run by some pretty amateur outfits and if they could make money, so could we. We ignored the fact that most of them probably didn't make a success of it, let alone make any money, and quickly went bust. However, to amuse ourselves, we set about the academic exercise of creating a business plan for the 'best skiing holiday company - ever'. Unhampered by reality our entrepreneurial spirits flowed along with the whisky and Guinness. If only this collection of similarly stimulated minds could have been unleashed on the problems of marketing pre-washed lettuce, we would have easily quadrupled my former client's sales, I thought.

The problem with having fantastic ideas when drunk is they almost always seem ludicrous the following morning. Ernest Hemingway advised to 'always do sober what you said you'd do when drunk, to teach you to keep your mouth shut'. I'd taken the so-called 'Hemingway Oath', many years back, to avoid letting down people who took my drunken promises seriously but, even when sober, I still thought the 'best skiing holiday company - ever' was a good idea!

When I got home, I created a more considered business plan and fiddled with my spread sheets until I convinced myself that, 'The Chalet Project' as I renamed it, would actually work.[2] The business plan was relatively simple: I needed to find a luxury chalet, get a large discount for renting it for an entire season, then persuade around one hundred people to come skiing with me.

I had to get the proposition, as we marketing types called it, right too: what were people looking for in a skiing holiday that (more importantly) was hard to find elsewhere? I needed a unique selling point (USP) as we call it.

---

2   *The purpose of a **business plan** is to convince yourself and possible investors that you're not taking a large financial gamble, when invariably you are. After that, they're never read again.*

The best market research is done on a sample set of one - yourself. So what did I look for when choosing a skiing holiday? I liked staying in luxury chalets near the slopes. I wanted an en-suite room - surprisingly difficult to find in old French chalets - and I wanted a cooked breakfast, preferably one involving proper bacon (equally scarce in France) with some form of eggs.

More important: what did I *not* want? I hated having to eat with the same potentially boring strangers every night and I didn't want a three-course evening meal included. I wasn't fussed about having an afternoon cake either, albeit a chalet tradition. I also didn't want to be forced to arrive on a Saturday and have to stay for a full week - a week is far too long to survive a boys' ski trip! Chalet-based short ski-breaks were almost unheard off - so there was my USP.

But which resort was best? I'd skied in many of the famous alpine resorts, each had their own attraction, but I'd been to Morzine more often than anywhere else. My friends kept organising trips to the place and, much as I liked exploring new mountains, it was more important I had people to ski with so I went with the flow. Morzine and its ski area were already familiar to me and I knew it was popular with my target audience - the Brits. So I didn't really choose Morzine, it chose me.

Morzine sits near the Swiss border in a small nook of France below Lake Geneva. It is part of the Portes du Soleil, arguably the largest skiing area in Europe.[3] Being just over an hour from Geneva Airport, it's ideal for short-stay ski trips so it suited my proposition.

More importantly, I knew Morzine's biggest fan, Siobhan (Shiv), a fellow skiing enthusiast, we'd been on many skiing boys' trips together. Although technically not a boy, she was a fellow hedonist

---

3   The **Portes du Soleil** *is arguably the largest ski area in Europe, claiming to have 650 kilometres of piste. It connects the French resorts of Les Gets, Avoriaz, Châtel, Morzine and a handful of Swiss ski stations.*

and a hardcore après-skier. She knew lots of other Morzine regulars, mostly from her hometown Liverpool, along with many expats who owned chalets there and even a few Morzinenois.

Being of a similarly adventurous disposition to me, Shiv thought the Chalet Project was a fantastic idea and wanted to be my partner in the project. My years in marketing had made me very good at selling ideas - especially bad ones. Her enthusiasm gave me the courage to go for it. I knew that a risk shared was a risk halved and that her Morzine contacts would be invaluable. Her wide circle of skiing friends would swell the ranks of potential guests too - which they did in large numbers.

Frustratingly, before saying yes, Shiv sought consent from my wife before joining the project - which she got. I'm not sure why she asked for it; she was being offered a partnership in a serious business venture − or so I kidded myself. Previous business associates hadn't felt the need to check it was okay with my wife to work with me. I wasn't running away with Shiv or, indeed, running away at all. She intended to keep her proper job in Brussels and to visit Morzine as often as possible. I was going to be there all season but intended keeping my proper life in the UK too; honouring my domestic and financial commitments. I rather hoped my wife would be a frequent visitor as well.

Shiv found a suitable chalet via her Liverpool connections, more importantly the owner was interested in off-loading a lot of hassle by renting it to one person for the entire season. I visited the imaginatively named 'Chalet Neige' (Chalet Snow) the following summer. It was perfect for our requirements. It wasn't next to a piste but that made the rent all the more affordable; it also meant we would need to ferry guests to and from the lifts. My BMW Six Series, left over from a previous midlife crisis, wasn't really going to cut it.

I had to procure a more suitable vehicle. While deciding what to buy, I became over-nostalgic about Defenders. I'd owned a matchbox model of one as a child and they symbolised intrepid exploration and adventure in my adolescent psyche. Many of my early skiing experiences involved being carted around in one too. So I fulfilled a schoolboy dream and bought one (Landie) knowing little about their true nature and nothing about their maintenance.

After a good deal of haggling, the chalet was secured and I set about finding guests for the forthcoming season. I spent the rest of that summer badgering anyone I'd ever met or seen on a pair of skis to book a few days at the chalet. Finally, I was using my marketing skill for a product I believed in. By December, we'd taken a reasonable amount of bookings and on the 3rd of January 2010 I found myself heading to Dover in Landie on the inaugural 'Bacon Run', as my winter migration became known.

In order to maximise guest occupancy, I'd decided to sleep in the chalet's garage. It had an entrance from the chalet and a heated floor, which kept it cosy as long as no-one opened the garage door itself. I turned it into a bachelor pad, adding a TV, sofa bed, microwave, toaster, kettle, minibar and ski repair bench - what else did a man need? I even had an iPod docking station so I could listen to 'garage music'.

On that first night, while lying in the garage, I did wonder if I'd made a very big mistake. I kept repeating the words 'living the dream', 'living the dream', 'living the dream' to reassure myself that I hadn't. It was a mantra that I would utter more often in sarcasm than sincerity over the next three months and indeed the next four seasons.

3. THE WALL

&

THE COULOIR OF CERTAIN DEATH

As far as I'm aware, nothing frightening has ever come out of Switzerland. Graham Greene famously wrote: '500 years of democracy and peace, and what did they [the Swiss] produce – the cuckoo clock!' For me, more notable Swiss achievements are the invention of the zip, Velcro and the triangular chocolate bar (Toblerone). None of which are particularly frightening, I think you'll agree.

Why the Vatican chose the Swiss to guard the Pope, I do not know. You need only look at the camp uniform of the Swiss Guard, or, indeed, the tiny folding knives the Swiss army take into battle, to realise they wouldn't make very formidable foes. Given that nothing frightening begins with the word 'Swiss', it's ironic that the most intimidating ski run in the Portes du Soleil and arguably the Alps should be called the Le Mur Suisse - The Swiss Wall.

'The Wall', as the run is commonly referred to, is located at the top of the Fornet Valley, just above Avoriaz. Officially called Le Pas de Chavanette, it's often mentioned in newspaper articles with titles such as 'The World's Scariest Ski Runs' or 'Steepest Pistes in the Alps'. It usually comes in at second or third on such subjective lists. Less subjective are its vital statistics.

It's 1km long, during which time it drops 400 metres. The top of the run has an incline of 76%, so steep that you can't see the face of the slope while standing at the top. It's often covered in moguls the size of VW Beetles.[4] These monster moguls have claimed lives

---

4   *Moguls* are bumps that form on steep slopes when many skiers make sharp turns in the same places. They grow slightly larger every time someone skis around them. *Mogul* Skiing requires advanced skills and has even been made into a sport for masochists.

but largely before the wearing of helmets became ubiquitous. It's often closed due to the risk of avalanches, much to the delight of those who otherwise might be pressured into skiing it.

Given the unthreatening nature of the word 'Swiss', its use in this context must be for purely geographical reference, the top of the run being in France and the bottom being in Switzerland. The word 'wall' is more informative because walls are usually vertical, hard and generally unyielding.

Most large ski resorts have a so-called 'signature run'. The one run every testosterone filled twenty-five-year-old wants to ski to prove his manhood. In my younger days, when I knew no better, I used to collect signature runs too. I have skied down La Fave (Val d'Isère), the Tortin (Verbier), the Hahnenkamm (Kitzbuhel), the Hari-Kari (Myrhofen), the Grand Couloir (Courchevel), the backside of the Valluga (St Anton) and The Widow Maker (Breckenridge), to name just a few.

Actually, I made that last one up, to illustrate my forthcoming point. The comparative difficulty of signature runs depends almost entirely on the snow conditions they're attempted in, although, in some cases, the name of the run is important too. With a suitably foreboding name a run can build a reputation - one that gets embellished by those who have skied it, in order to underline their achievement. Comments such as 'Yes, I skied the Widow Maker - but I don't want to talk about it,' followed with a vacant gaze into the distance, is the classic way to do this.

Give a ski run a name like 'The Wall' and you give it an auspicious notoriety. It automatically becomes ten degrees steeper than it actually is. It's true people do die on the Wall, but usually through medical complications, head injuries and avalanche.

I had one guest who, unknown to me (and himself at the time), had a rather dodgy ticker despite being an outwardly fit twenty-eight-year-old. A collector of signature runs himself, he persuaded me to ski the Wall with him. Half way down he had, what turned out to be, a heart attack! Luckily for me, he fell the rest of the way into Switzerland where assisted suicide is legal - for that is surely what I might have been accused of had he not survived.

❦

The truth is you don't need a death wish to ski the Wall. Dozens of not especially accomplished skiers get down it each day without significant incident and live to embellish the danger they faced in the bar the same evening. Taking on the Wall, like most skiing, is a mental challenge rather than a physical one. I'll agree that a certain level of ability and fitness are needed, but technique can triumph over the lack of the latter and the former comes with experience. Remember, skiing is an activity you can do well into your eighties.

The most important ingredient for a successful descent of the Wall is confidence. If you think you're going to fall – you will fall. In this respect, skiing can be a self-fulfilling prophecy and the main prophets of doom are the Ski Demons.

The Ski Demons are the voices in my head that feed on my self-doubt. They tell me I'm going to fall. They tell me, 'Frankly Chris, you're not capable of completing the skiing challenge ahead.' They doubt my ability, my fitness and especially my courage. If I pause too long at the top of a slope they drag me into a debate about the difficulty of the terrain below. 'It looks a bit icy Chris' or 'it's too steep for you Chris.' They give me plausible excuses I can use for wimping out. 'I'm nursing an injury', 'The avalanche risk is too great' or 'I brought the wrong type of skis.'

Once I've manned up and dropped in, the demons proclaim every turn to be my last. I usually silence them by making those all-important first turns successfully. But if I fall they immediately pipe up again with 'We told you so.' If things go completely pear-shaped, and I suffer a sequence of falls, exhaustion sets in and their voices become deafening. 'This time Chris you've started a descent you're not going to finish - you'll need a helicopter to get out of this one!'

We all have Ski Demons that feed on our mortal fears. Sometimes the fear is rational: fear of injury or death. Sometimes it's primeval: fear of heights or being buried alive. Sometimes the fear is emotional: fear of failure, fear of embarrassment or fear of fear itself – panic. Skiing is a veritable buffet for demons if we let them eat.

Many Ski Demons take residence during our childhood, manifesting as phobias and compulsions, but only reveal themselves when we first put on skis. For instance, I battled with panic attacks as a young man. Psychologists would probably blame an early childhood trauma or my parents – it's always your parents' fault, right? Attacks would occur in amusingly benign situations: On trains, in traffic jams, in churches (especially while attending weddings) and on one memorable occasion in the Sistine Chapel. The attacks hampered my early skiing trips, although they were mostly induced by alcohol and nicotine abuse. I've since learnt how to function and think rationally when panic strikes. Despite inner turmoil I can now usually maintain a calm exterior. Thanks to the Chalet Project, I've had a lot of practice at looking calm while panicking.

The route over to the Wall from Morzine is a long one, giving plenty of time for people's skiing demons to surface. When people take their first look at its steep and icy entry point, the Col de Chavanette, many audibly swallow. The slope seemingly vanishes into mid-air and is often shrouded in mist for dramatic effect. On busy days, the Col can be blocked with skiers, peering over into the abyss, straining their necks like meerkats to see the extent of the slope, some obviously wishing they hadn't taken the Hemingway Oath. Those who back out of the Col can watch their more courageous friends descend the Wall from the Chavanette chairlift, which runs down its side. The chair makes an excellent viewing and camera platform. I jokingly call it the 'Chairlift of Shame' because it's ridden by those who've wimped out of skiing the Wall.

Goaded by a so-called mate, I first found myself on the Wall far too early in my skiing career and grew to hate what became an annual pilgrimage to it. Some years I'd be lucky and the run would be closed for the entire duration of my holiday. If not, the best strategy was always to ski it on the first day of the holiday. You might think it a good idea to practice on some easier runs first and build up to skiing the Wall on the last day but, actually, it was better to get it over with before the accumulative effects of skiing fatigue and compounded hangovers kicked in. It also meant that, once you'd skied it, you could then enjoy the rest of the holiday unstressed.

Back then, to leave Morzine without doing the Wall or indeed to leave any resort without doing its signature run seemed like failure. Nowadays, with less to prove and more sense, I avoid the Wall unless the conditions are favourable. I'm more selective about whom I ski it with too. These days my golden rule is: never ski with a group if you're the slowest skier. I've learnt the hard way that if you end up being 'Tail End Charlie' you'll find yourself in a world of pain.

T. E. Charlie will be constantly out of breath trying to catch the others up. They will occasionally stop and wait for him, but frustrated with all the hanging around, will set off again the minute he catches them up. They'll stand at the bottom of difficult slopes shouting helpful, yet patronizing, advice at Charlie.

They'll have a sequence of long rests while watching Charlie, but he will have no such breathers – Charlie will hate them all by the end of the day.

No matter how many times I'd successfully skied the Wall, I still got a knot in my stomach whenever I approach the wretched run, such was the terror it had engraved in my psyche as a beginner. The Ski Demons often won their argument at the top and I'd jump on the Chairlift of Shame. Until one day an ESF guide cured me of the problem.[5] I'd foolishly ignored my golden rule. Well, more accurately, the people I was skiing with that week had fooled me into thinking I wasn't the weakest skier. We'd hired the guide for their final day of the week to take us off-piste, but when the going got tough the, the tough got going, christening me T. E. Charlie.

Our guide was typical of his species. His chiselled facial features were darkly tanned from spending a lifetime in the mountains. His faded, red ESF jacket, with a gold medal hanging from the breast pocket, were signs that he'd reached the highest ranks in the organisation. He was also wearing a white, knitted sweatband that only an ESF guide could wear without looking gay. This head garment was clearly a fashion accessory; he was never going to break into a sweat skiing with '*Les Anglais*'.

All ESF guides have eyes installed in the back of their heads. Before taking you off-piste, they will usually take you down a couple of easy red runs first. You'll never catch them looking over their shoulder, using their front eyes, to see how you're skiing – not once. Using their back eyes, they will determine your ability, the off-piste

---

5   To be an **ESF** *(École du Ski France) guide or instructor you have to be an exceptional skier - or at least you were once. After they awarded you with your red ESF jacket they can never take it way.*

terrain you can cope with and make route plans accordingly. Or maybe they will just go where they had planned anyway.[6]

It's a big mistake to ski really well on those critical, first, red runs. A mistake we obviously made on that day. We must have skied like gods because, several sweaty and exhausting hours of mogul skiing later, we found ourselves at the top of a narrow couloir looking down at the Wall. 'He never mentioned a *couloir*, did he?' I said to my companions.

The word *couloir* is one of those skiing words that demand attention. Simply translated it means 'corridor'. It's a benign word, if say, you're receiving directions to the toilet, but a much more significant one, if you're talking about the route off a mountain. In which case, it means a long, narrow, steep strip of snow between two exposed rock faces. You may not have been paying much attention when the day's itinerary was discussed, but you *will* remember if the word 'couloir' had been used. I didn't and now I was looking down at the 'Couloir of Certain Death' – as it was surely named.

Most people, whether they know it or not, subconsciously hire guides to take them out of their comfort zone, to make them take on slightly more adventurous skiing than they would on their own - but only slightly.

On occasion, when I'm leading the skiing, I too can inadvertently take people out of their comfort zone. There's a fine line between adventure and terror on the mountains and that line is not always in the same place for everyone in the group. If I get it wrong and commit my groups to a run that someone is unhappy with or, indeed,

---

6   *I suspect ski **guides** prejudge clients before they've even mounted their skis. Their appearance, their attire, their equipment or just the way they carry their skis, tells them all they need to know about their client's skiing ability.*

get it really wrong and the entire group is in open revolt, I often get what I call a 'First Refusal'. This is where someone, usually Charlie, will pass the point of commitment (no practical way of going back) and then freeze with terror at the top of the run. My method for dealing with this is to talk them through their various options:

1. Try and ski down.
2. Climb back up. I point out that this would be very physically demanding and that we are carrying all the right equipment (skis) for a descent, not an ascent (crampons).
3. Dig a snow cave and wait for summer, then walk down. It's always good to introduce an element of humour into stressful situations.
4. Call a helicopter. I explain that, unless they're incredibly rich, this is not a viable option. They could, however, deliberately injure themselves then claim back the immense cost of a helivac from their insurance. But that would be no less painful than getting injured using option 1.

Most will take option 1 and thank me for the little pep talk when they eventually get to the bottom. Of course, some hold a grudge and never come skiing with me again - but you can't win them all.

That day we too had hired a guide to take us out of our comfort zone and he had spectacularly succeeded. He didn't flinch when we exhibited the telltale signs of a First Refusal - probing the snow in front with our poles and adopting an ostrich-like stance — but his technique for dealing with this was very different to mine. He assured us that it was an easy couloir, well within our capabilities, and that it was an important part of the ESF's *esprit du corps* that guides always returned with the same number of clients as they'd left with. Not wanting to blot his record, we dropped in. I tentatively picked my way down using little jump turns, stopping to congratulate myself after successfully completed each one. He was right; it was within our capabilities since most of us made it down without falling.

One foolhardy comrade chose 'route one'. He pointed his skis directly down the couloir and accelerated past me like a missile. Presumably he hoped to find somewhere flat enough at the bottom to lose the immense speed the manoeuvre would accumulate, or at least he hoped to find somewhere soft to crash. In this case, because the couloir exited onto the Wall, neither option presented itself. So, once again, I found myself watching a human body ragdolling its way into Switzerland. He survived the Wall – but didn't want to talk about it.

After my own less spectacular exit from the couloir, I found myself perched on a mogul halfway up the Wall. While catching my breath with the other survivors, I spluttered, 'Never thought I'd be so happy to find myself on the bloody Wall.' They all laughed, but I wasn't joking.

Now, whenever I find myself panicking on the Wall, I look up at that seemingly un-skiable couloir, now renamed the 'Couloir of *Almost* Certain Death', and consider myself to be in a comparatively safe position. The Chavanette may or may not be the most difficult run in the Alps, but its notoriety increases with every skier who conquers it. I still enjoy being a witness to those who take on this rite of passage. I love to enjoy their elation vicariously after they succeed, knowing that they will be leading the drinking and bragging in the bar that evening.

Once I'd got over the Wall, so to speak, no marked piste would hold any fear. Conquering the off-piste, especially in deep powder, would be the next challenge – a challenge that proved significantly harder to meet.

4. The Après Aliens

Statistically, you're more likely to be abducted by aliens in the USA than France. This, I suspect, has more to do with the respective mental health of the two nations than extra-terrestrial disinterest in Gallic life forms. Whatever their nationality, abductees usually claim their abductors returned them to the place and time from which they were taken, conveniently explaining why no-one noticed their absence. Most abductees, despite being able to recall prolonged ordeals, usually involving humiliating medical experiments, discover that on their return no actual 'earth-time' has passed.

My abductions were different. I was being returned to seemingly random places often some distance from the bar where the abduction occurred and usually after quite a lot of earth-time (of which I had no recollection) had elapsed. By the end of Season 2 the correlation between extended après sessions and abduction events became hard to ignore: either these were specialist *après* aliens - or I had a drink problem.

The phrase 'après-ski' (after skiing) was no doubt invented by the French to describe the tradition of having a *vin chaud* (hot wine) after a long day's skiing - a civilised aperitif, taken at the bottom of the last slope, before heading back for dinner. However the beer drinking Northern Europeans, encouraged by the Austrians, have hijacked the term to legitimize binge drinking, although the British don't need much of an excuse. The Alps are now littered with specialist après bars that offer free shots and slightly dodgy music to drink them to. Sadly, French youth is now in on the act, although they call it '*alcool défonce*' which literally translates as 'alcohol trapping'. I'm not sure that the word 'trapping', which implies a degree of cunning, is really the right word for the activity, since alcohol is not that difficult to 'trap' in a ski resort.

Traditionally après-ski should be done at the bottom of a slope while still wearing your ski gear. Theoretically it should only last an hour or two, until the sun goes down then the sensible people will go back to the chalet to shower and change, have dinner and then go to bed replete. A few young singletons might go back out for a few more drinks and a dance but we all know what one drink leads to (another), then the Après Aliens turn up and your evening and possibly the next day are ruined.

There's a good reason to après in your ski gear. Firstly, if you're outside, as a lot of après venues are, it's cold; secondly, at some point the urge to take off your ski boots, which are torturous to walk and stand in, will supersede your desire for more drink, thus bringing your après-ski to a reasonably early close. Unfortunately for my guests, I pride myself on preventing them from having to walk anywhere in ski boots. So I meet them at the bottom of the slopes, or even in the bar itself, carrying their shoes. But I'm not really doing them any favours because I'm enabling them to après too long. The more experienced après-skier, like Shiv, rent their skis from a shop near the slopes. They leave their soft shoes in the shop so they can abandon their ski boots the minute they stop skiing. Having said that - Shiv seldom makes it home for dinner.

Many Brits, knowingly or not, enter into a binary system when they go skiing. They alternate between two states: State One is recovering from a hangover and State Two is acquiring a new one. For all but the most dedicated, this 'binary-living' is unsustainable for more than six days, which is why skiing holidays seldom last more than a week. Unlike almost any other binge-drinking holiday, athletic and sometimes life-threatening activities need to be undertaken during the day while in State One - fortunately help is at hand.

There is simply nothing like alpine air to cure a hangover. Some people think this is because, at altitude, the air has reduced oxygen content. Why less oxygen should make you feel better is not entirely clear to me and, since most skiing is done below 2000 metres, I suspect the oxygen reduction is negligible. It might just be that being up in the mountains makes you generally feel better about everything – it does for me. Whatever the reason, once you've take a few deep breaths of the clean, crisp elixir, you immediately start to recover from State One and you'll soon be back in State Two. I've put it through extensive field tests and compared it to dozens of other hangover tonics but none compare, except one that is: 'the hair of the dog'. Which is why binary-living is so popular on any holiday.

Like most people who are learning to ski, I initially enjoyed the après-ski more than the actual skiing – although I'll admit my enthusiasm for the former often impairs my improvement in the latter. During my early skiing holidays, I even used to advocate taking a day off from skiing midweek to recover. However, learning to ski is a painful, exhausting and emotional experience, not to mention thirsty work, and most beginners feel they've earned a drink or two after a hard day's toil on the mountains, so it's easy to slip into binary-living. Whatever the reason, the atmosphere and camaraderie during après can be very special; everyone seems to be in a hedonistic mood or simply just glad to be alive.

Back then, I had a fairly hedonistic lifestyle in the UK too. I had few responsibilities (no kids), I lived in the centre of a vibrant city and had plenty of disposable cash to enjoy it with. I worked in a youthful industry where, along with other substances, alcohol abuse was associated with creative thinking. I also encouraged this drinking culture amongst my subordinates. The pub was often the venue for many a thought-shower, and when we moved offices to Sutton Coldfield, one of the meeting rooms was converted to a fully stocked free bar to make up for the lack of a decent local. By the end of my career I was pretty much binary-living 52 weeks of the year, so skiing holidays were no different.

By Season 3, my abductions were becoming problematic. Not only did they start to affect my work (running the chalet and skiing) but also they were getting me into some tricky situations - even forcing me to avoid people in the street. I was often waking up in the presence of complete strangers!

One morning I woke up, not for the first time, in the wrong chalet. This time I was in a basement room with what looked like a young teenage boy in the bed opposite. Worryingly, I couldn't identify him and prayed some parental consent had been granted for me to crash in the lad's room. I set about my well-practiced extraction routine whilst trying not to wake my roommate.

I'd learnt that it was always best to leave answering the 'W' questions (Where, Why, What, Who etc.) until after a successful extraction. First, a roll call for the limbs: were they all still attached and responsive to instructions? Next, establish time, date and location and relate this information to where I was supposed to be and what I was supposed to be doing: Next, the equipment check: phone, wallet, keys, coat, hat, gloves, fleece - the loss of any two of the latter three, I deemed acceptable. On this occasion I had them all, which was a result.

I looked at my watch. My guests would soon be waking up at Chalet Neige expecting breakfast. I had time to get back to the right chalet and not disappoint them. I crept out of the room and started looking for a front door. It was a large and somewhat shabby chalet that, for the life of me, I could swear I'd never been in before. After a few wrong turns I found the front door and the good news was it wasn't locked. I'd had to exit even my own chalet via a window before now - why guests can't leave keys in doors I don't know.

Closing the door quietly behind me, I looked around and recognised the street. I was still in Morzine, which was encouraging, although I was on the other side of town from my chalet. I must have driven there so where had I left Landie? I looked up and down the street but there was no sign of the beast. I took a deep breath of the clean freezing air and pondered the question. The alpine air got to work and memories of the previous evening started to trickle back. I took another look at the chalet behind me and recognised it.

I'd been invited there for a drink by new acquaintances. They knew my family back home and I'd wanted to make a good impression. I should have been on my best behaviour, but then the Après Aliens must have turned up and inconveniently abducted me. I took another breath then remembered leaving Landie in the underground car park near the Pleney Lift to prevent the diesel freezing, a perennial problem in February.[7] I reunited myself with Landie and drove her back to Chalet Neige.

Having done it so many times before, I can cook and serve breakfast with little cognitive effort. A guest enquired why I was wearing my clothes from the night before and my sunglasses indoors. I explained I had an eye infection and was behind with my laundry. After breakfast, I flicked through my historic text messages. This was always a good way of piecing together what had actually happened prior to an abduction event. I've discovered that Après Aliens often

---

7   *Regular **diesel freezes** at -18c. But the temperature never falls lower than zero below ground. Thanks to the Chalet Project, I have learnt many other ways to keeping a Defender rolling in arctic conditions.*

use their victim's phone to send random text messages to people in their contacts list, often in some sort of intergalactic code I've yet to decipher. But a few of the earlier messages were decodeable.

Apparently, I'd agree to lead my new friends to my favourite mountain restaurant for the day. I'd arranged to meet them at 10am outside the Le Tremplin Bar. Remembering the Hemingway Oath, I pulled on my ski gear, jumped back in Landie and raced to the Tremplin, wondering if I'd recognise any of them. I did, particularly my roommate from that evening. My snoring must have disturbed his night but he didn't seem to be bearing a grudge.

The adults looked hung-over too. They at least had an excuse; they were on holiday and had pushed the boat out. Unfortunately it was a ship I set sail in almost every night that season. Luckily, a hangover shared is a hangover halved and despite mild bouts of nausea, paranoia and self-loathing (the usual stuff that follows an abduction event) the morning was uneventful. I judged their skiing ability well and took a route that didn't unduly trouble them, or indeed me while I was in State One. We were all back on the beer at lunchtime and by 5pm back in Le Templin for après drinks.

A binary-living cycle was completed and another one was about to begin. They could go home after seven days; I could not. I had a fresh set of binary-livers to compete with - my next set of guests; I was stuck in a skiing version of Groundhog Day, they were not.

Abductions were most likely to happen on my nights off (usually Wednesday) or on any night that the chalet was empty and I had no guests to look after. If friends were staying in the chalet abductions were less likely, or at least I'd a better chance of being returned home. However, I was always very wary when notoriously boozy friends from home came to stay – which, now I come to think of it, was most of them.

Their familiar faces could lull me into thinking it was safe to 'go large', but they didn't have to get up, make breakfast and drive in the morning, or indeed later that night. At least, if friends were staying with me, it meant there would be a collective will to return to the correct chalet to sleep. Generally speaking, to hit the town on my own was the most dangerous option because this usually meant that there were no constraints. I would invariably bump into some cronies and be persuaded into a larger evening than I'd planned.

Making sure I was driving and therefore, theoretically, not drinking, helped reduce the chance of abduction but, because drink-driving laws are largely self-enforced in Morzine, it didn't always prevent them. After a couple of close calls with other vehicles steered by similarly impaired drivers and, on one notable occasion, with black ice, the aliens became more insistent that I abandoned Landie and walked back with them. Finding Landie badly parked outside the chalet one morning, with a human shape imprinted in the snow directly below the still-open driver's door, convinced me they had a point.

If a family had taken the whole chalet, I would often be needed to ferry them to and from restaurants in the evenings, which *did* prevent me from drinking because 'mum', unfamiliar with the local drink and driving customs, was usually monitoring my alcoholic intake and I would have to order a soft drink whenever she was looking.

However, walking home inebriated in arctic conditions can be as foolhardy as drinking and driving. Getting lost or falling asleep on a bench can lead to hypothermia and 'death by misadventure' as the words would read on the coroner's report. Teenagers are most prone to suffering this fate because they generally lack the ability to find their way back to the chalet or wear appropriate clothing to survive the walk. If I had a bunch of youths staying, I knew I'd probably be called out when the bars started closing

(2-3am) on a search and rescue mission to find them and bring them home. If I was on 'extraction duty' as I called it, I had to remain reasonably sober, which also prevented abductions.

On one especially cold night a friend, who'd agreed to be on extraction duty in my place, took pity on a random herd of drunken English youths while driving past them in Landie. They were aimlessly wandering around in the snow inappropriately dressed and, after dropping off my guests, he went back to pick them up. His motives for doing this may not have been entirely altruistic; given the lack of clothing he described on some of the girls.

Once he'd worked out from their cryptic clues where their accommodation was, he drove them to it. Then he found a similarly distressed herd on the way back and decided to save them too and then a third lot on his return. I don't know how many young lives he saved that night, but I do know he used nearly all my diesel. Magnanimously, he refused all payment from the frozen urchins!

After the Reims incident, if I'm staying in a strange town I always make a note in my phone of the name and location of my digs. I try to make sure even the most responsible-looking teenagers who stay at Chalet Neige do the same so, if the aliens get them, at least any benevolent strangers will know where to return them. That having been said, most young guests assume, whatever hour it is, I'll just come and get them (modern youth is not keen on walking anywhere I have discovered).

I would often be invited out with groups of younger guests as their après-ski guide which lead to many an 'age-inappropriate evening' as I now classify them. I suspect many of them just

4. THE APRÈS ALIENS

wanted me along as backup, to make sure they could find their way back to the chalet. However, by the end of Season 3, I wasn't enjoying my age-inappropriate-evenings very much. Hanging out in bars rammed with twenty-somethings, listening to drum and bass, might seem like fun, but there are a finite amount of times you can relive your youth – it's never as much fun as you thought it was the first time.

Besides being inappropriate, 'hanging' with youths less than half your age is also problematic because there are few common points of reference. After you've asked about their A-level results and where they went to 'Uni', conversation soon dries up. There's always skiing to talk about of course, assuming they're not snowboarders, but no matter how 'down with the kids' you think you are, you always feel a bit tragic. After a while, you also stop taking the comment 'you're fit for your age' as a compliment.

When I started the Chalet Project I had aspirations to be a ski guide and lead people around my favourite mountains but, as yet, I'm not qualified enough to get paid for it, so I had to settle for being an après-ski guide - something I am supremely qualified to do. I've always taken my après-ski guiding duties very seriously. If guests have a few memorable nights out, or indeed in, they are more likely to come back next year. I pride myself on finding the best age-appropriate bars for them. However, assessing people's mental age and musical tastes and then determining how hardcore an evening they are actually after, can be tricky. Often the middle-aged guests want to relive their youth too.

Sadly, most intermediate skiers will remember and rate a resort by its après scene rather than the actual skiing area, and I feel it's important they get the right guidance off as well as on-piste in order to enjoy Morzine.

There's no effective late night taxi service in Morzine for obvious reasons. What Frenchman would want to stay up all night trying to extract money and sense from vomiting foreigners?

Most drunks will end up staggering down the middle of the road trying to find their accommodation and hoping to find a non-existent kebab shop on the way. If I've agreed to be on extraction duty I often find it hard to navigate through the melee of intoxicated pedestrians. It can be reminiscent of a scene from a zombie movie, especially if it's chalet night-off. [8]

During 'Zombie Hour' (2-3am) as I call it, I've had several of the walking-dead jump on Landie's bonnet and one even tried to get in the back while I wasn't looking. In the dark, I sometimes find it hard to identify which of the zombies are my guests if they only arrived that day. I've thought about giving them tabards with 'Chalet Neige' printed on the back, but I suspect they would object to wearing them and, in many cases, I wouldn't want people to know they were associated with my chalet.

By Season 4, the après-ski guide part of my job had become a chore and (thanks to the Après Aliens) a very dangerous one at that. So I developed some successful strategies for avoiding abduction, primarily by not going out with guests in the first place unless they were particularly funny, interesting or good-looking of course. I also made a set of après guidelines to keep me sober, or at least significantly more sober than them - which I discovered wasn't that hard, if I did the following:

1. Avoid Rounds. It took me a while to be comfortable with guests buying me drinks and not returning the favour. I try not to take the micky, but I do accept the odd alcoholic

---

8   *Wednesday is traditionally '**chalet night-off**' in Morzine and guests are forced to eat out. This means that staff, liberated from kitchen duties for the night, swell the ranks of the binge drinkers.*

drink from them to be sociable. I feel this is better than ordering a soft drink because having non-drinkers around me, when I was on holiday, always made me nervous. If you're not in a Round, you can drink at your own pace.

2. Avoid drinking pints. Some guests, especially if they're friends from home, can be very insistent that you match their drinking volume. I try to order *'une petite bière'* (½ pint) whenever possible, although some guests will return with a pint anyway – Northerners in particular, hate to see a man drinking halves. But not only do pints double your alcoholic intake, they also double the number of trips to the loo. French bars don't have the toilet capacity to deal with a pint-drinking culture and women, in particular, will spend half their night queuing, if they insist on drinking pints.

3. Refuse all shots. For some reason (some sort of altitude sickness?) après-skiers often unilaterally buy a round of shots that nobody wants. Usually they are shots of Jägermeister or toffee vodka, two substances that I'm not sure were originally intended for human consumption and are mostly unheard of at sea level. Almost without exception, no evening that starts with shots ends well.

4. Never drink Mützig. This beer is named after, and originates from, an area in Alsace. It's unusual for a region in France to be more famous for its beer than its wine, but this tells us something about the notoriety of the beer. It comes in two versions, a 5.5% and 7% ABV. Needless to say if you confuse them or worse still, ignore Guideline 2, you'll be away with the aliens before you can say – well anything. The famous Morzine après bar, *Robbos*, sells only the latter version. It opens at 4pm and closes at 8pm presumably for safety reasons.

5. Avoid first and last nights. Most guests get over enthusiastic on their first night. I think there is an English law stating that you must get especially shit-faced on the first and indeed the last night of a holiday. So guests who have just arrived or are leaving in the morning, are particularly dangerous drinking companions. Especially with my regulars, I feel a lot of pressure to celebrate their arrival or to give them a traditional alpine leaving present – a hangover. Unfortunately, during January when I offer short breaks, guests are coming and going all the time and nearly every night is someone's first or last. January is therefore regarded as high season by the Après Aliens.

6. Avoid going into any bar between 7pm and 8pm. I call it 'Alien Hour' because it's when the Après Aliens are at their most dangerous. It's noisy and often smelly so I'm tempted to drink to make the bar feel less hostile. By 8pm, those who've managed to place a meal and a shower between them and their après session will return and the ambience becomes significantly less lairy.

7. After 8pm, always avoid anyone in a bar still wearing skiing gear - especially ski boots.[9] They have opted to drink-on instead of eat and aren't going be capable of conversation. They will continually repeat themselves and not comprehend anything you say, if indeed they have enough remaining attention span to listen. It's incredibly boring being the only sober person in a room and I'm often tempted to get drunk too, just to make other

---

9   *It's very hazardous to stand next to a drunk wearing **ski boots**, particularly if you're in soft shoes and they are trying to dance. With one accidental stomp they can end your entire ski season.*

people interesting. 'An intelligent man is sometimes forced to get drunk to be with his fools', Hemingway once pointed out.

8. Never go clubbing. Frankly, if you haven't had enough to drink or you haven't pulled by 2am when the après bars have closed, you're never going to. Ski resort nightclubs are predominately full of men who've been abducted by the Après Aliens. It's safe to say that, if you find yourself at 'The Opera' (Morzine's only nightclub), your evening and possibly your life have gone horribly wrong.

When I stuck to the above guidelines, the Après Aliens would ignore me and I could then observe them at work. I discovered that they would possess a victim prior to abducting them. First they would seize control of the abductee's voice - effecting volume and pronunciation. Then they'd target their motor neurone pathways and start controlling their movements – Après Aliens must have a different physiology to humans because they find it difficult to simultaneously control four limbs.

When in full control, rather than take the victim back to their ship like normal aliens, they would conduct their medical experiments in the bar. Some seemed designed to measure a human's capacity for liquid. Others to test the effects of alcohol on the female's desire to reproduce and the aggressive effect it has on the male. Once the experiments were in full swing, the bar would become a very unpleasant place to be sober in, and often a very dangerous one too.

When entering a bar with guests, I'd always stop and chat to the bouncer. I'd let him know I wasn't a punter but, like him, I was 'working'. This way, if he felt it was time for one of my guests to leave; he would know whose shoulder (mine) to tap on first.

This working relationship also helped him decide whose face not to thump if it all kicked-off. If it did and I didn't get hit, I always reiterated to him on they way out that I'd disowned my fellow countrymen and that's why I lived in France. If he muttered something first, '*Zee bloody Dutch*' for instance, I'd not let on that the protagonists where actually from Liverpool.[10]

By Season 4 'staying in' had become the new 'going out'. Having learnt to cook, I discovered that throwing a dinner party for my guests could be more fun than going out and considerably cheaper for them. Staying in significantly reduced the chance of alien abduction and reduced the risk of death by misadventure too (other than from self-inflicted food poisoning of course).

It had taken me a while, but by then I had finally worked out that I wasn't actually on an extended ski holiday myself and that the best après-ski guide was a sober one. Many of my regulars didn't seem to agree but, despite their best efforts, I had finally left the Morzine binary system. By then my summer lifestyle had changed beyond all recognition. Hedonism had been replaced with suburbanism and there were far fewer reasons to get drunk. By the end of Season 4, the Après Aliens finally stopped abducting me. Presumably, they moved on to other galaxies in search of more interesting life forms, their experiments on me complete. I can't say I miss them.

---

10   *Thank goodness for the **Dutch** who make the Brits look like amateurs when it comes to après-ski.*

5. Baptism of Snow

I first went skiing at the age of twenty-eight and absolutely hated it. The tale of my first abortive attempt at skiing serves well as a warning to other debutants. It illustrates the folly of listening to so-called mates, who can already ski, and why skipping ski school is a big mistake. It involved five Geordie lads and a week of hell in St. Anton.

❖

The best age to learn to ski is five. At five you have no fear of falling over because you're only three-foot tall and the ground isn't really that far away. Also, because you only weigh three stone, it's easier to get back up. Generally, falling over when you're five isn't that big a deal and, having only just learnt to walk, you've had a lot of recent practise. Skiing is also much easier when you're five because your centre of gravity is a mere one-foot-six above your skis and it takes little effort to keep it there. But, most importantly, at five you're prepared to put your body on the line and explore the laws of Newtonian physics. You don't have to teach a five-year-old to ski, they work it out for themselves.

❖

I wasn't born to rich parents, which was generally disappointing and, specifically, meant skiing was not on the cards when I was five. In 1968, skiing was still the preserve of the upper classes, a bygone era before cheap package holidays had made skiing accessible to Northern oiks like me.

At 28 I finally made it to the Alps and fell in love with everything alpine - except skiing. I particularly loathed my first skiing instructor, a stocky Austrian girl called Ingrid who lacked patience, a sense of humour and, as far as I could tell, any humanity at all. I can still hear her shouting '*benz zee nees*' with ever-increasing frustration, at me. I've since met many a charming Austrian and discovered that my first instructor was not typical of her race. Austrians, with one notable historic exception, are on the whole a very friendly bunch - as long as you keep them off the wheat beer.

I'd met the Geordies as a student in Newcastle. They were the less academic pals of my flat mate and all of them had skied before. They were a fine body of working-class, rather-hard lads, very untypical of the largely hooray-henry English skiing fraternity.

This was in the days before the budget airlines took off, so we travelled to the Alps by train. The Snow Train, as it was called, was actually a twelve-hour drink-fest that set the blood alcohol level that would be maintained for the rest of the week. We'd booked a cabin in the couchette car, a deceptively attractive name, given it described a tiny room with six bunk beds crammed three-high either side of a narrow window. The dimensions of the cabin turned out to be unimportant because nobody used it, on the way out at least. The Geordies left their '*scratchas*' (beds) empty, preferring to spend the '*neet*' standing up in the disco carriage drinking '*beeah*' and chain-smoking '*tabs*'.

As we approached the Alps, the tracks meandered and the train increasingly lurched from side to side. The conversation turned to whether it might be a '*canny ideah*' for me, the '*beginnah*', to skip ski school and go up the mountain with them on my first day. They would kindly '*larn*' me to ski. They had a very flattering theory that because I looked quite athletic, I might just be a '*natural, like*', a theory that my alcoholic modesty found hard to argue with. Under their expert guidance, I might just pick it up from them and save myself a '*lowda dosh*'.

The train journey turned into a rollercoaster ride as we wound our way up into the Alps. It was hard to tell who was drunk and who wasn't because the Geordie accent doesn't change when its owner is inebriated, it just gets more excited and higher pitched towards the end of each sentence. Those attempting to dance were flung from side to side, making it an almost impossible pursuit but hysterical to watch. No one in the car was going to bed; everyone seemed far too excited for that. This was clearly my sort of holiday, why had I not been skiing before?

Now, whenever departing for skiing, I always vow not to overdo it on the first night, but I invariably wake up with a hangover borrowed from an elephant. This is something a beginner can really do without when taking their first tentative steps on the slopes. Had I known then what I know now, I might have headed to the couchette before midnight or at least thought about reducing the drinking rate. Even more importantly, I might not have agreed to skip ski school and go up the mountain with the Geordies in the morning.

Blokes who have mastered skiing will soon appoint themselves as experts and offer unsolicited advice, especially when they're in a bar. But a 'good skier' (whatever that means) doesn't always make a 'good ski instructor'. The truth is that even extremely accomplished skiers find it hard to explain what they're doing with their limbs when skiing. Being a ski instructor is a teaching challenge, not a skiing one. There are many different approaches deployed by professional instructors. The idiosyncrasy of a particular methodology will often match that of the personality delivering it. There are often linguistic barriers to learning if English isn't the instructor's first language too. It's hard enough comprehending instructions spoken in English – let alone in Geordie.

The Geordie School of Skiing apparently involved taking students to the highest peak in one of the Alps' toughest resorts and pushing them off the top to see if they were '*a natural - like*' – after that they were pretty much out of ideas.

It was soon obvious, even to the Geordies, that not only was I not '*a natural - like*' but actually I was a hopeless skier. Unfortunately this discovery was made shortly after they had committed me to a 3 km long piste.[11] So I spent most of the day ragdolling down that run, sweating what smelt like neat alcohol, travelling only as far as I could fall. Why the Geordies couldn't have taken me to a green run first, to see if I was indeed a natural, I don't know. Possibly because St. Anton doesn't have any real green runs, possibly because they didn't like me - being a '*sootherner*' from Hull. Sometimes a 'good skier' (whatever that means) forgets just how exhausting constantly falling can be, because they seldom do it themselves. Well, more accurately, it's not the falling over but the getting back up that saps your energy. Falling over (a lot) is a good way to learn if you're five, but adults soon run out of energy and most get demoralised if they spend too much time face-planted in the snow.

Which is what happened to me. By midday I'd given up trying to learn how to ski and focused on learning how to fall. I developed a system to extend the distance of a fall in order to reduce the number needed to get me to the bottom. Once I'd hit the snow and my skis had come off, I'd curl into a ball and roll as far as possible down the slope. The Geordies would collect my skis, dust me off and put me back on them. Then I would start the prelude to the next fall – point my skis down the hill.

My second rookie skiing mistake, after going to Geordie ski school, was using borrowed boots for the trip. Why did the Geordies not tell me the importance of well-fitted ski boots? An entire holiday, and in my case almost a skiing career, can be ruined by badly fitting boots. The pair I borrowed were older

---

11   *I've returned to **St. Anton** on numerous occasions and every time I visit that run I wonder how I ever survived my first alpine descent – although the majority of it was done without skies.*

than me and had probably tortured many generations of feet before mine. They were the old back-loaders that clamp the heels in like a vice. After the holiday, I did what their previous victims should have done; I destroyed them and reported their owner to the police.

When I first tried them on and protested at the pain they caused, I was assured they would feel better when I was actually skiing in them. This advice was hard to evaluate given it was offered to me in a Birmingham living room. I tried crouching over my knees, in the tuck position that I'd seen the racers do on Ski Sunday, but the boots didn't seem any less painful. I know that no-one, on their first encounter with ski boots, thinks they are anything other than devices of torture - but wearing second hand ski boots is almost an act of self-mutilation.

Along with the boots, I'd also borrowed some equally well-fitting goggles that kept misting up, rendering me almost blind for long periods of time. My borrowed ski jacket proved less than waterproof although most of the moisture was probably being generated by me - from inside. Beginners always get people's inferior cast-offs because they see little point in investing in expensive gear until they know they're going to like skiing and want to go every year. Unfortunately, not having effective gear can be the reason they end up hating it.

I finally fell my way to the outskirts of St. Anton. I was an exhausted, bruised, sweaty mess with what turned out to be a broken collarbone, a cracked rib, crushed feet and some serious dehydration issues. I found myself looking at a bar called the Krazy Kanguruh (KK), which was fortuitous because I had a rather large thirst on.

The KK is often referred to as the birthplace of modern après-skiing and one of St Anton's most famous après bars. It's now been usurped by the MooserWirt bar opposite, which reportedly serves 2500 litres of beer in an average afternoon. The bar's owner, a (now-not-so) poor farmer, claims to sell more beer per square metre of floor space, than anywhere else in Austria, which is amazing considering it's halfway up a mountain and closes at 8pm!

At that time, après at the KK seemed to involve the playing of loud rock music and the pouring of schnapps by particularly nubile waitresses, straight from the bottle into punters' mouths. Communal singing, the playing of drinking games, and dancing on the tables in ski boots seemed to be encouraged too.

Despite the previous night's excesses, I decided to join in. Not because I had a thirst on but mainly because I needed anesthetising and, well - it was my kind of party. The Geordies took the drinking games seriously, because national pride was apparently at stake. This was a little counterproductive because they became totally incomprehensible to the point where it was hard to determine which nation they were actually from - although that often happened when they were sober too.

The melee outside the KK at closing time is equally as famous as the bar. Hundreds of pissed revellers try to locate and mount their skis to travel the last 500 metres to the bottom of the piste. The more sensible don't even bother and try to walk down but the Geordies were having none of that defeatist attitude and, for the first time that day, I wasn't the only one trying to cover most of the distance while prostrate.

I signed up the next day for *proper* ski school and went to my class with a shattered body, a compounded hangover and a really bad attitude towards skiing. The ski instructor, Ingrid, wasn't too happy that I'd joined a day late, although the others in the class were only too pleased that, finally, the class idiot had turned up to take the pressure off them. I wasn't too happy with Ingrid either; even though she'd just qualified, she seemed rather pissed off with life. Being at the bottom of the instructor pecking order meant she was condemned to teach beginners all season. To her I was just this week's class idiot, one in a long line of idiots she'd have to endure that season.

After a day on the beginner slope and in my case failing to learn to snowplough, the most elementary of skiing techniques, Ingrid introduced the class to our first T-bar, which I also failed to master.[12] I found the T-bars in St Anton particularly traumatic. Being dragged, feet spasming, through terrain I had no effective way of skiing out of should I fall off, caused me great anxiety, especially when I neared the top. If I fell off near the bottom, I could at least walk back down to try again. To add to my problems, the next day St. Anton had a whiteout where I discovered the importance of wearing functioning goggles. There were some advantages to being partially sighted – I couldn't see the terrain I was being dragged through.

It now seems preposterous that an instructor, even a really pissed off one, would take a second-day beginner on a T-bar but this was St. Anton in the eighties and not the most beginner-friendly of resorts. The Geordies had put me straight on a cable car to the top, avoiding any unnecessary need to learn how to use a draglift or indeed snowplough, which in hindsight was actually very thoughtful.

The cycle of drinking to excess every night, falling off T-bars all day while being shouted at by Ingrid, continued for six days until, mercifully, the so-called holiday was over. I could go home to, literally and metaphorically, dry out.

---

12 A **T-Bar** *is an outmoded form of draglift still very common in Austria and Switzerland and is especially difficult to master. Many accomplished skiers carry deep psychological scars and in some cases physical ones from early encounters with* **T-bars**. *Mercifully, there are very few still running in the Portes du Soleil.*

The train ride home was a somewhat more sombre affair than the one out. The operators hadn't even attached the disco carriage, experience having obviously taught them not to bother. The train felt and looked like a hospital ship evacuating wounded from the front line of some great conflict. The carriages were filled with shattered bodies, many with limbs in plaster. I lay on my stretcher-like couchette bunk, whimpering every time the train jarred against the rails. I felt like crying out 'Please nurse, more morphine'. While lying there for twelve hours, I wondered if all beginners experienced the same painful baptism of snow. If so, why did so many of them go back? I suspected that debutants who are not five years old or 'naturals' go skiing a second time to make sense of their initial suffering, 'lest it be in vain'. I wouldn't be going back – or so I thought.

Over a decade later my ski-parents, Val & David, persuaded me I should return to the Alps and lay the Ghosts of St Anton to rest.[13] Both accomplished skiers, they pointed out just how badly the Geordies had managed my debut while trying not to wet themselves laughing at my horror story. Over dinner one night, after much wine, I agreed to go skiing again with them – and Hemingway did the rest. I've skied with them every year since. With their guidance, learning to ski a second time was a very different experience to the first, not without fear, pain and frustration, or indeed alcohol, but with more manageable quantities of each. It seemed I was a bit of a natural after all and I soon started to find large periods of skiing actually enjoyable!

13 *You're allowed to adopt supplementary skiing parents (**ski-parents**), if your biological ones don't ski. It helps if they're rich too.*

While lying in my couchette all those years ago, listening to five Geordies fart and snore, if you'd told me 'One day you'll be a qualified ski instructor, Chris' I would have broken another rib laughing. But that was indeed my destiny and I'm not sure who to thank or, indeed, who to blame the most: the Geordies for showing me the mountains, even though they got it horribly wrong, or my ski-parents for persuading me to try again. Ironically, despite being an ineffective instructor, it was probably Ingrid who motivated me the most. If I ever saw her again, I wanted to be able to say, 'Look bitch, I *can* ski!'

Now, whenever a beginner turns up at Chalet Neige, I like to tell them my St Anton horror story in the hope that they will have one less drink on their first night and not skimp on equipment hire or professional instruction, and, most importantly, not go up the mountain on their first day with friends who can already ski – or indeed anyone from the North East.

6. Cougars and Manthers in Manzine

Like most resorts, Morzine's après scene goes through several distinct phases during a ski season. In January (considered low season) the bars are full of men. I think blokes favour January because the snow conditions are usually good and accommodation prices low. Often it's the only time many married men are allowed to go skiing without their wives.

Shiv, my fellow garage-dweller, and her female friends like to stay at Chalet Neige during January too. They've humorously renamed the town 'Manzine', for that is surely what Morzine becomes in January.

During February (considered high season) Morzine becomes overrun with families. Although the snow is often good then too, the slopes get crowded and during the middle of the month, infested with school kids. It becomes difficult to get into restaurants without booking; the après bars empty relatively early then fill up again with teenagers who have escaped their parents after dinner.

Then in March the 'girls trips' start to arrive. Despite the 'Spring Snow'[14] conditions, women seem to favour the higher temperatures and the sunshine that causes them. Most seem to favour sunbathing, long lunches and après more than skiing – well, at least the ones that stay with me do.

Some women have worked out that going skiing is a great way to meet men and Morzine can turn into Cougar Town in March. Although for a truly target-rich environment, cougars should visit in January. To get chatted-up in 'Manzine' all you need to be is: female, have a pulse and be there in January.

---

14 **Spring Snow**, *ice in the morning and slush in the afternoon, is caused by high daytime temperatures. Leaving only a small midday window for enjoyable skiing, when most girls choose to have lunch!*

I met one set of early-season cougars who had clearly worked this out. The skiing conditions were of no concern to them; they hadn't bothered to buy ski passes and had no intention of wasting any of their time actually skiing.

However, cougars do need to be aware that ski resorts attract a lot of 'manthers' too. The younger, more predatory male equivalent of the cougar, the manther often stalks cougars, picking on the weakest; the drunk straggler at the back of the herd - usually the ugliest one. During the winter months Morzine can sometimes start to look like the Serengeti, I've noticed.

For Shiv and her mates it's Morzine's après scene, and their familiarity with it, not its ski area, that is the biggest draw. Frankly, at their ability level they would be happy skiing anywhere, but in Manzine, they know where to go for the best action on any given night. Shiv is an excellent après-ski guide and taught me all I know.

It's easy to see why they are frequent visitors to Morzine. An attractive bunch, they soon become the centre of attention in most bars they walk into. I like to après with them and observe the different approaches deployed by their would-be suitors – and rate their chat up lines too.[15] Although, I've been unceremoniously pushed out of the way by many a manther who clearly regarded me as his first obstacle.

I remember one supposed Norwegian, who was very insistent, despite his poor command of English and Shiv's lack of interest. Then his mate, in a broad scouse accent, called him away - turns out they were both from Birkenhead and he'd never even visited Norway, let alone been born there.

---

15   *My favourite **chat up line** to date is: "If I sleep with you tonight, it doesn't mean I'll ski with you in the morning!"*

Apparently it's quite common to invent a holiday persona and indeed an interesting career for oneself when on tour with the lads or indeed laddettes (the female equivalent). It's important that this is predetermined and shared with your mates so, if you're challenged, they can corroborate your story. But then men have always tried to impress women by lying.

Often, the married of both sexes are the worst, let loose from their spouses, safe in the knowledge that 'what goes on tour, stays on tour' is the golden rule of any lads' or ladettes' trip. Most don't cross the line between flirtation and infidelity due to the lack of single bedrooms and the fact that too much alcohol is the best prophylactic!

The primary cougar stalking ground is the Buddha Bar, the scene of many an abduction and the setting for many of my own holiday memories. I never imagined, then, I'd become such a frequent, and now reluctant, worshipper in this temple. It changed its name to The Tibetan Café a few years ago but veterans like me still refer to it as 'The Buddha', thanks to the numerous statues of the Buddha it still contains.

Like most après bars, you will hear *Sweet Home Alabama* (by Lynyrd Skynyrd) at least once a night in the Buddha. Known as the 'skier's anthem' it seems to have endured. Rock classics get played a lot in ski resorts. On the continent, music doesn't seem to move on as fast as it does in the UK[16] – which suits the cougars and the manthers and indeed me.

All good things must come to an end and during Season 4, I started to avoid going into the Buddha. It's a great place for one or two big nights on an annual ski trip, but not being a manther, well not anymore, I've grown tired of the cougar attacks. It's too much

16   *I have a theory that it is not possible to go a day in the Alps without hearing*
   ***Sweet Home Alabama**, at least one Bob Marley and one Jimmy Hendrix song*
   - next time you're skiing, test it out!

effort making small talk with drunken women when you've been doing it with chalet guests all day. It's also a struggle to hear above the loud music especially when, like me, you're going a bit deaf.

If I ignore my own après guidelines and find myself sober in the Buddha when it's really packed, it feels like I've been trapped in Sodom or possibly Gomorrah. I then start looking for salvation or at least a way out. However, sometimes it's impossible to leave, the only exit being blocked by drunken bodies. I'm really getting far too old for bars where you can't hear yourself speak or get a seat!

7. THE SKI NAZIS

My ski-parents were often referred to as 'The Ski Nazis' by my skiing siblings - I wasn't the only debutant they'd unwittingly adopted. I hasten to add, this nickname summed up their skiing ideology rather than their belief in National Socialism. Their enthusiasm for skiing, even in appalling conditions, was admirable. They believed it was a crime to waste even a minute of potential skiing time and they had a way of making you feel guilty if you did.

David was the worst. He regarded it as failure if he wasn't on the first lift up the mountain every morning or if he came down before the last one had closed. On many occasions I would find myself standing outside a lift station with him, waiting for it to open, wondering if ski fascism was really for me. But despite my whinging, it was great to be the first down a run in the morning, especially on a powder day.[17]

Well, second down at least. David usually led whoever had foolishly agreed to ski with him the previous evening and taken the Hemingway Oath. We knew, despite his reassurances of an 'easy day', that he would lead us to the top of at least one icy black run at some stage, with no options but to ski it. This, I discovered, was mainly due to him needing glasses to read a piste map, neither of which he ever carried. But we trusted him to get us down. If he led us to the top of an especially difficult run, the Wall for instance, he would revert from leader to back-marker by way of an apology.

A back-marker, usually one of the better skiers in a group, deliberately hangs back in order to help any fallers find, gather

---

17 *A **powder day** describes the day after it has snowed all night and the mountains are covered in fresh powder snow.*

and remount their skis. The problem with being the back-marker is that, if you fall and lose a ski, you'll have to find it on your own. Climbing uphill in deep powder takes a Herculean effort and even a true friend will be reluctant to hike back up to help. More seriously, if it's you rather than your ski that gets buried, it will take a considerable amount of time for your companions to reach you, before they can start digging. Speedy rescue always comes from above!

In David's case, back-marking also included shouting advice and encouragement from behind to anyone who had 'gone ostrich' on him. Despite his idea of what was helpful advice often differing to the recipient's, it was always reassuring to see David above you, ready to swoop down and help.

The downside of following David was that he often took little off-piste forays, which, if you weren't paying attention and blindly followed, could quickly turn into brutal aerobic workouts, or more accurately described, climb-outs, if he got the route wrong.[18] But what doesn't kill you makes you a stronger skier and, thanks to these little forays, I learnt ways of dealing with tricky off-piste.

David would prefer to eat sandwiches on a chairlift rather than stop for lunch. For him, lunchtime was the best time to ski because all the 'part-time' skiers would be in the restaurants and he'd have the slopes to himself. He wasn't too keen on midmorning hot chocolate stops either, an important part of the female skiing day. Needless to say, he had a zero-tolerance approach to ski-faffers.

---

18 *Critical, when skiing off-piste, is the avoidance of terrain traps. Common terrain traps include riverbeds or bowl-shaped valleys, out of which there is no skiable (down hill) route out, making them impossible to escape without climbing (**climb-outs**) or, more usually, crawling.*

Ski-faffing, mostly a female affliction, describes the wasting of time preparing for, rather than actually, skiing - be it in the morning when leaving the chalet or setting off after a drinks stop on the mountain. Faffing can involve the application of sunscreen or lippy, the cleaning or swapping of goggles and sunglasses or simply taking forever to mount a pair of skis. Fiddling with gloves and their liners seems to be popular too.

Taking off layers then putting them back on again five minutes later, is standard practice for experienced ski-faffers. Better-equipped faffers will also fiddle with boot heating devices, hand warmers, phones and helmet cameras. Extreme ski-faffers will run through their entire routine at the top and bottom of every lift.

Ski-faffing is by no means exclusively associated with female skiers, it's just that women have a lot more items to faff with: lipstick, scarves, headbands, buffs etc. and they often have some difficulty locating them. This is because ski jackets have many pockets. Blokes are used to dealing with multi-pocket scenarios having worn blazers at school and suits to work. Men systematically allocate pockets for specific items. Women are more familiar with the everything-in-one-bag approach but rucksacks are a pain to get on and off and you can't ski with a handbag, although believe me, some of my guests have tried.

David would severely chastise anyone caught ski-faffing, especially his wife. Val wasn't quite so dedicated to Ski Nazism, she preferred to have a sit-down lunch at least - in a restaurant, that is, not on a chairlift.

When they started skiing, many decades ago, Val's goal was to leave the first tracks (fresh-tracks) down a mountain, side-by-side with David's, then to lookup and take a photo of them. They achieved this goal despite only skiing one or two week a year.

They have since set and achieved many other goals - that's the problem with skiing; after every triumph, there's always a bigger challenge waiting for you.

The Ski Nazis work ethic and enthusiasm for a skiing challenge was infectious. I did take some professional lessons, but often their skiing tips were more helpful. Without their encouragement I wouldn't have gone skiing a second time or set a few goals of my own – primarily to ski as well as them. Without their mentoring and sometimes goading I wouldn't have collected so many signature runs myself and certainly never have ventured off-piste. I wouldn't have fallen in love with the Alps either – so the Chalet Project is really all their fault!

There were a few problems with having Ski Nazis as stepparents. After so many years of indoctrination, I too had developed fascist skiing tendencies. I used to get visibly frustrated with faffers when I was leading. Ordering a coffee after lunch or requesting a loo stop ten minutes after we'd left the restaurant would make steam come out of my ears too.

I was also very intolerant of slowcoaches, especially snowboarders who have to go through a mandatory faff, clipping in and out of their board before and after every chairlift. You really didn't want to be T. E. Charlie in any group I was leading. But I soon realised it was wrong for me to shout at paying guests and so I developed an alternate skiing philosophy called 'Girlfriend Skiing' to counter my ski fascism (you'll hear more about that later).

Now the Ski Nazis have retired they can spend much more time skiing and continue to improve. However, now I ski for fourteen weeks a year, my improvement has arguably been faster. I joke with David that someday I'll overtake him and the 'Student will become the Master'.

He's a frequent visitor to Chalet Neige and is often taken for a member of staff. If we're out with other guests, I lead and he back-marks and it's still reassuring for me to see him bringing up the rear. Now, with less pressure on his skiing time, David has mellowed and he sometimes catches the second lift up the mountain and is not always on the last one back. He's occasionally seen in a restaurant at lunchtime too, especially if we're skiing with pretty guests.

When he does get tired of skiing with the less able, he now joins up with The Ski Club of Great Britain (the Club), which is full of more ideologically compatible skiers. In which case he gets up early and heads to Avoriaz where the Club meets. If I've got no other guests to look after, he still makes me feel guilty and I go with him, despite our increasing years, nothing much has changed.

The Ski Nazis are enthusiastic members of the Club. After much persuasion they got me to join and a whole new world of skiing challenges and skiing friendships were to follow.

8. Morzine Mary

It was St Patrick's Night, a big night in Morzine. Not because Morzine has a large Irish community, although it's a popular destination for skiers from the Emerald Isle, but because it's an excuse for an especially big piss up, even by Morzine standards.

I found myself in the Dixie Bar. Unlike most ski resorts, or indeed most towns in the world, Morzine doesn't have an actual themed Irish pub. The Dixie is the closest you'll get. It is a more generic French sports bar, but it has a slightly dingy cave-like room in the back, where its Irish house band, the Dixie Mics, play. (Do you see what they did there?) And it *does* sell Guinness.

It's a favourite haunt for the expat community and winter migratory inhabitants of the town. That night the Mics were fiddling even more furiously than usual, belting out Dubliners' and U2 classics and anyone with the slightest claim to an Irish heritage was in fine voice singing the chorus lines. Becky, an authentic Irish beauty, was frantically serving the black stuff behind the bar - she even gave me a smile.

Everyone seemed to be there. Mike the one legged ski instructor (I kid you not), Paul the transfer driver, Richard the Brummie builder, Sarah the air hostess, Liz the South African, Roland the hairdresser, Michel the ski shop owner, Gaddhafi the bohemian land owner - along with a myriad of other familiar faces. And of course Morzine Mary was there too. A veteran of some thirteen consecutive ski seasons in Morzine, it was thanks to her that I knew most of the people in the bar.

The odd French accent could be heard but it was predominately an English crowd (pretending to be Irish). I sometimes regret the fact that I haven't got to know more French locals during my time in Morzine, but there are so few of them, in what is often referred to as 'Morzineshire'. Thanks to Shiv and Mary, another

Scouser, I have however met most of the population of Liverpool, which was not part of the escape plan but has been an equally entertaining cultural immersion.

If Morzine is the gateway to Liverpool, then Mary was my gateway to Morzine. We first met while skiing with the Club. She is a petite woman and skis like I imagine a gazelle would. When I first met her, we were both wearing helmets and goggles. A common problem with meeting people on the slopes in similar garb, is that it is difficult to recognise them when they are not in their ski gear.

After chasing this gazelle down the slopes all morning, we stopped for lunch and everyone took off their goggles and helmets. A long flop of glamorous hair fell out of Mary's and a much more mature face than I was expecting appeared, given she'd just skied me off the mountain. I hope she was equally surprised that a bald middle-aged man appeared from beneath my helmet. Since then, we've become great friends, spending a lot of time on and off the slopes together. It's always a pleasure to ski with Mary or more accurately to chase her down the slopes.

We frequently après together and I suspect most people started to think we were an item, and that I was her new, not so young toy-boy. An assumption I was happy to go along with because VIP entrance to many bars and complimentary drinks came along with the role. On occasions, when her female mates from Liverpool were in town, I was made an honorary member of the Morzine International Ladies Federation (MILFS) as they called themselves. I did once try and explain to them the more common meaning of the acronym MILF, but I suspect they already knew. They referred to me as 'Chalet Chris'.

A riot would almost certainly pursue them whenever they entered the Buddha, as would a lot of unwelcome (for me at least) male attention, although their presence did prevent attacks from more predatory cougars. Once the party got going (10pm), Mary would routinely be thrown around the bar like a ragdoll by drunken revellers often still in their sweaty ski gear.

The ripeness of the atmosphere was further enhanced by the smell of stale alcohol, the dry ice and the inadequacies of the single door to the toilets. Seldom did the MILFS leave with their assailants turned victims, who were invariably middle-aged, married men. The flirting was the crack, not the hope of a one-night stand.

On the odd occasion when the chalet was empty I'd invite the MILFS round for a dinner party and an evening of great humour, outrageous flirting and dad-dancing would be had. Mary would often reciprocate throwing similar parties in her chalet, cooking 'scouse' and plying everyone with wine. She would often retell stories of previous big nights from her heyday, but it was hard to imagine more debauched nights than I have more recently witnessed. Like myself, it's no longer possible for Mary to ski hard and party hard and theoretically skiing must now take precedence, although sometimes we forget.

That Paddies night in the Dixie was, by comparison, a more civilised affair with only a few tourists dancing in ski boots and most people had washed. Those assembled had a more long-term commitment to hedonism than the average holidaymakers. They had moved to Morzine pursuing an alternative way of life, or at least had some more permanent connection with the town. For once I remembered how bad I'd felt skiing that morning and bailed early, although it was hard to tear myself away from the infectious music and the general bonhomie. Before I could leave, more faces appeared, wanting me to stay. One new fresh young face, a lad from Liverpool (where else?), was introduced to Mary. His eyes lit up – 'Are you Morzine Mary?' he enquired. She grinned – 'I thought you were a myth' he exclaimed!

I sometimes look at Mary and think, will I still want this winter lifestyle in ten years' time? Would four seasons turn into fourteen? Or would I get tired of the skiing and the partying? During every season, at some stage, I proclaim it will be my last – but hedonism is a hard drug to give up. Thirteen consecutive seasons has taken its toll on Mary's body, her knees, legs, and feet require constant summer repairs. I suspect my own lower limbs, if not my liver, will be the first to suggest retirement. However Morzine Mary, not a myth but a legend, is proof you can ignore your body, for 'just one more season' at a time.

9. The Vallée Blanche

The mountains around Chamonix have a reputation for being difficult whether you're climbing up them or sliding down them. In 'Cham' everything is higher, bigger and steeper than anywhere else in the Alps, and that includes the restaurant bills and hotel prices. The town itself is a large, sprawling place, somewhat lacking in alpine charm. It sits at the bottom of Mt Blanc, Western Europe's highest mountain. Only a couple of valleys to the south of Morzine, Chamonix is less than an hour's drive away and I often go there with friends or guests who are after a special day out.

Many decades ago, French skiing legend and famous son of Morzine, Anselme Baud, also visited Chamonix frequently, not to cruise its pistes but to ski where no others had skied before. Anselme, most famously, was the first man to ski down the north face of the Aiguille du Midi, a rocky outcrop glued to the side of Mt Blanc. Along with his skiing partner, Patrick Vallençant, he claimed many other first descents in the Chamonix valley and pioneered a new form of alpinism now known as *Le Ski Extreme* (extreme-skiing). Patrick's famous motto, 'You fall, you die', perfectly summed up the risks they took. Sadly, that is exactly what Patrick did in 1989, although in a climbing accident not a skiing one.

Chamonix became the home of extreme-skiing not just because of its huge mountains, but also because they were accessible. Other countries, such as the USA, have epic mountains too, but they've effectively outlawed extreme-skiers. Skiing 'out of bounds' was banned by US resort operators to prevent them being sued by bereaved relatives.

Unfortunately, the UK, like the US, is now infested with personal injury lawyers and there are worrying signs that they've crossed the channel to France as well, making personal indemnity insurance for instructors, guides and hire shops a must. In Anselme's time, nobody looked for others to blame for their own stupidity. The French didn't mind if people wanted to risk their own lives seeking adventure in the mountains. In fact they positively encouraged it by building a cable car to the top of the highest one they had – Mt Blanc.

The Aiguille du Midi cable car goes up to 3842 metres and is still the highest and scariest cable car in the world. Unlike most cable cars in other ski resorts, there are no marked runs or prepared safe skiing areas at the top. It's an unmarked, unmaintained, unpatrolled mountain area. The cable car simply gives people access to a beautiful but dangerous, icy wilderness. Nowadays the French do insist you take a qualified guide along with you. The problem with skiing on unfamiliar glaciers is the high likelihood of falling into a crevasse. It's best to follow someone with more local knowledge across a glacier and let him fall in first. Similar advice applies to crossing a minefield.

Anselme was born in Morzine (in 1948), from where Mt Blanc can often be seen, towering in the south above all the other peaks. I often point it out to guests and embellish a drama I once had myself on the famous mountain.

Most men think they're better skiers than they actually are; I'm no different. Many flock to Chamonix to test themselves against Europe's greatest peaks; I like to do the same at least once a season. One year, I decided it would be a *good* idea to go up the Aiguille du

Midi and ski down Mt Blanc. It was the season just prior to the start of the Chalet Project and I had *good* ideas in abundance.

This was actually a particularly *bad* idea because, being male, I was not the accomplished skier I thought I was – or, indeed, think I am now. I was less fit too, overweight and a smoker. I'd had very little off-piste, let alone backcountry skiing experience at that point, and I persuaded my friend Peter, who had even less experience than me, to come along.

I didn't intend to follow Anselme's route down the north face though – I was foolish not crazy – but to ski down the less radical, southerly slope known as the Vallée Blanche (White Valley) the most famous of all signature runs. Strictly speaking it's not a run at all, being off-piste and there are several ways down. The easiest is called '*la route classique*' (the classic route), which we intended to do. We'd planned to leave the Vallée Blanche near the top, ski round the Gros Rognon (Big Rock) and down the Glacier du Géant (Giant Glacier) onto the Mer du Glace (Sea of Ice). As you may have noticed, early French alpinists were not very imaginative when it came to naming geographical features.

In order to access the Vallée from the cable car, skiers need to cross one of the world's scariest bridges to a tunnel. The tunnel leads to a door that gives access to the Arête. The Arête is a ridge of snow, three metres wide, that might best be described as 'character building': there being a 3.8 kilometre drop down to Chamonix on one side and a two hundred metre drop to the glacier on the other side. During peak season they do install a safety rope at least, which gives some comfort.

Initially, I couldn't find a guide willing to take us after being too honest about our experience levels. One of them suggested we try skiing a black run of similar difficulty from the top Les Grands Montets, a mere 3300-metre peak that neighbours Mt Blanc.[19] It

---

19 ***Les Grands Montets*** *is the largest ski area in the Chamonix Valley and has a reputation for having the highest, longest and steepest pistes in Europe.*

was quite an adventure but we got down in reasonable comfort, benefitting from good weather and perfect snow conditions. We took the news of our recent success to the ESF booking office who convinced a young guide, called Baptiste, to take us down the Vallée Blanche. He was a local boy, born in Chamonix, so who better to trust?

The weather then turned nasty and a snowstorm raged for three days closing most of the lifts in the Chamonix Valley and Baptiste sensibly kept postponing the trip. Finally, with only one day of our holiday left, the weather broke. He rang me up that night to say it was on for the following morning. A twelve-hour window in the weather had been forecast and he'd booked us on the first car up the Aiguille du Midi at 8am. He advised us to have an early night.

Even though this was the news I'd wanted to hear, my sphincter loosened as I heard his words. At the time I was still nursing a phobia of cable cars and my fear of heights has never really left me - I know, skiing isn't really an ideal pastime for me! But, in the morning I would be spending twenty minutes on the world's scariest cable car, crossing the world's scariest bridge and descending the Alps most vertiginous arête - I was about to find out if aversion therapy really works.

My apprehension was primarily being fuelled by the excessive amount of online research I'd done prior to the trip. I'd seen dozens of images of the cable car, the bridge and the arête in extreme conditions and read too many articles about crevasse rescue, pulmonary oedema (altitude sickness) and avalanche deaths for my own good – Peter was in blissful ignorance. As Baptiste advised, we went to bed early and relatively sober that night but I didn't get much sleep. The next morning, while waiting for our slot on the cable car, Baptiste checked our safety equipment and I wondered if it was too late to back out.

I always find the safety talks and equipment demonstrations given by guides, just before departing on backcountry trips, unnerving. It's why I never pay attention to safety briefings on airplanes. Making people focus on crashing just before take-off seems like really bad karma. He yanked at the climbing harness I'd just put on, crushing my genitals, which did get my attention. I told myself that statistically, only one in five thousand people who ski the Vallée Blanche, die, one of the many such facts I'd read online. Soon all of me was being crushed as we were herded into the famous cable car.

The French ram people into cable cars like cattle. Cable cars usually have a turnstile that allows a set number of people into the loading area to wait for each car in turn. The French always seem to set that number ten too high for my comfort. Being a nation unfamiliar with the concept of queuing, there's always a bit of a ruck for the best position in a car when its doors open. On a powder day it can get a bit vicious. In Chamonix you'll get shouted at if you don't take your rucksack off and put it between your legs to make space for the last ten sardines. Once a Liftie in Chamonix put his foot on my back and shoved me further into a cable car so he could close the door.[20] The door shut before I could pivot round and kick him back, although I think he got the idea I wasn't too impressed through the glass. I used a collection of expletives that would have transcended any linguistic barrier to communicating my displeasure.

---

20 Lift attendants (**Lifties**) have possibly the world's most difficult job. While being mindlessly bored they are responsible for passenger safety. They have to stay focused, their finger hovering over the emergency stop button, while being distracted by the world's best scenery. Many achieve this while smoking marijuana and listening to Bob Marley.

On this occasion in Chamonix, I was rammed up against an Indian gentleman, unusual because, skiing isn't that popular in the subcontinent even though they have some seriously big mountains there. Having said that, there is a Bombay Ski Club in Morzine - a curry house. He was very polite considering we were close enough to procreate. I assumed his dilated pupils where a sign of anxiety rather than his love for me. When I'm having a panic attack on lifts I talk a lot, trying to distract myself. My new friend obviously had the same strategy, asking lots of question about where I was from and where I'd skied. The conversation was a welcome distraction for us both.

We reached the halfway station and waited for the second cable car to take us to the top. It was then I noticed that Baptiste had telemark bindings on his skis, which was a little worrying.[21] People who like telemarking are usually odd. More importantly, they like to be odd, because choosing this outmoded form of skiing sets them apart from 'normal' skiers. I could draw one of two conclusions from my observation: either the trip was going to be so mundane that Baptiste had brought his comedy skis to amuse himself, or we had a nutter for a guide. In all other respect he seemed like a normal guide so I concluded it must be the former.

At the top, I said goodbye to my Indian friend and wished him luck then everyone put on their helmets and goggles and became unrecognisable. Baptiste put on a woolly hat that was clearly a family heirloom, leading me to review my previous conclusion. Relieved that the cable car part of the trip was over, I was keen to get a look at the bridge and arête, to see just how wide it actually was.

---

21 **Telemarking** *is arguably the oldest form of skiing, where the heels are not attached to the skis. Named after the Telemark region of Norway, where it originated. I like to mispronounce it 'telemarketing' because it looks as much fun as cold-calling people all day would be.*

The bridge was a bit of a let down considering how much sleep I'd lost over it. You could see down through its floorboard slats into the abyss below, but it had reassuringly high sidewalls. While crossing it, I noticed I was having trouble breathing in the thin air. This didn't seem to affect Baptiste who lit a rollie, one of many he'd smoke that day. Once we'd got to the other side we waited in the tunnel for our turn to descend the arête. As I leant against the granite sides, I wondered what large mechanical rabbit had been used to burrow the tunnel and how had they hauled it up to this altitude.

We moved to the door at the end of the tunnel and a chilly wind greeted us. Baptiste attached a rope to our harnesses and put his crampons on. He was smaller than me and although he looked sturdy enough, I doubted he could arrest the fall of a fourteen-stone man (me), even wearing crampons. I suspected that, if I fell off one side, his only option would be to push Peter off the other, to counterbalance me.

Finally, the waiting was over and it was our turn. Baptiste gave my nuts one last tug for luck and we went outside. To my relief the path down the arête had been very well prepared, with wide, solid steps cut down its length. I looked over the safety rope at the uninterrupted near-vertical drop down to Chamonix town centre. Its large hotels looked like specs of dust. I wondered how on earth Anselme managed to ski down it without a parachute.

When we got to the bottom of the arête my relief was palpable, all the scary bits were over, I could now enjoy the ski down - or so I thought. The sun briefly came out to congratulate us and I decided to take a photo of Peter and Baptiste. I took my glove off to operate the camera, carelessly dropped it then watched in horror, as the wind swept it towards the edge of the arête.

Luckily, the guide of the group behind us speared it with his pole. He lowered his buff, revealing a wrinkled, leathery face that looked like it should have belonged to a mountain goat. He chastised me; the more polite gist of his communication was that the photograph might have cost me some fingers to frostbite.

We skied down the Vallée to the glacier, which was surprisingly hard work in the oxygen-depleted air. This didn't bother Baptiste who lit another rollie while he waited for us to catch up. I relaxed and started to admire the lunar landscape. The snow was quite deep but conditions were not dissimilar to those we'd encountered on the Grant Montet earlier that week.

Unfortunately, I took an early fall which allowed the Ski Demons to chirp up. After arguing with them for ten minutes while trying to get upright in the deep powder, I resorted to kicking my skis off and remounting them, a big no-no off-piste.[22] Baptiste chastised me for being so foolish, but I'd taken a gamble to get the demons off my back and got away with it. Fatigued by the recent flailing around in the snow, my turns became more laboured. Instead of following Baptiste's tracks, a prerequisite for crevasse avoidance, I skied wider turns than his. He shouted at me again. He was starting to remind me of Ingrid, my first ski instructor.

Peter was being shouted at too, but at least he was a fit young man who could fall over all day and not get tired, or so I thought. We started to mutter between us as Baptiste's bonhomie vanished and he urged us to ski faster. But, we had all day, what was the rush? I postulated that there might be a big ice hockey match on the TV that afternoon and he'd forgotten to recorder it.

The truth was that the weather was closing in fast and Baptiste had not anticipated us being so slow. It was now doubtful that the

---

22 *If you **take your skis off**, you may lose one (under the snow or down the hill) leaving you in need of rescue – in deep snow you can't go anywhere without skis. Secondly, skis are very difficult to remount if you're not on a flat firm surface. If you're on a steep slope covered in deep powder, often a small platform has to be made in the snow to facilitate a successful remount.*

weather window would be big enough to see us safely down. The wind had got up to gale force and was whipping up a blizzard.

We reached the long traverse under the Gros Rognon and, after about 800 metres or so, my downhill leg, which was taking most of the load, felt like jelly. If it gave way it was not clear what I would fall into because the convex slope below disappeared out of view. Every time I paused for a rest, Baptiste shouted at me. He pointed up at the snowfield above. *'Très dangereux,'* he said – and promptly sped off and was soon almost out of sight.

I felt a bit miffed and thought he should have stayed with us. Now, knowing much more about avalanche safety, I realise it was best we didn't all get caught in the same avalanche leaving someone on the surface – him – to dig us out. As I fell further behind Baptiste, Goat Face, the guide who had saved my glove earlier, and his group caught up with me. He stayed behind me, giving me constant encouragement. Luckily he had a few slow coaches in his group too. At one stage, I lost sight of Baptiste, the guide I was actually paying to get me home relying instead on this stranger to do the job. I should have taken Chris De Burgh's advice about Ferrymen, I thought - having paid Baptiste in advance.

The traverse ended and we descended onto the Glacier du Géant, at a place called Salle à Manger (Dining Room), but we weren't stopping for lunch. The avalanche danger was obviously over because Baptiste was waiting for me to catch up. Actually he'd stopped to converse with Goat Face behind me and to light a fag – an impressive feat given the damp conditions.

By this time visibility was poor. But I could see several swathes of electric blue ice in front of us. The guides discussed the best path through the crevasse field and I could just hear their animated conversation above the now howling wind. Peter and I exchanged pleasantries with the other group in a very British, stiff-upper-lip sort of way, ignoring the life-threatening environment we were in. Suddenly, the girl I was talking to vanished in front of my very eyes!

Unbeknown to her or me, she'd been standing on a snow bridge[23] that had collapsed into a crevasse below. I peered over the edge craning my neck, more worried about following her than about what I might see. Only a couple of metres below, I could see a disorganised collection of skis, poles and limbs, piled up on a shelf, half way down the crevasse. One of the limbs calmly waved up at me – she was okay but in a precarious position, the crevasse looked like it continued much further down into the ice.

As we stood dumbstruck, not sure what to do next, the guides rushed over. Baptiste, kicked off his skis and lay down, looking over the edge of the now exposed trench. That was what I should have done, I thought. Goat Face chucked Baptiste one end of a rope while bracing himself with the other. Baptiste lowered the rope to the girl, whom I discovered later, was about sixteen years old and, mercifully, unhurt. She tied it to her harness. Before she was pulled out, she was told to rescue her skis because without them she wasn't leaving the mountain. She stood on the ledge and passed them up to me where I too had adopted the prone position. As she was hauled out, she laughed rather apologetically and seemed embarrassed about all the fuss. She thanked the guides emphatically for the rescue despite the fact they'd failed their primary task – that of preventing her from needing one.

I was taken aback by her amusement about the incident. Youth has so much more courage than age. I suspect, as we get older and more bad things happen to us, we expect the worst

---

23 *A **snow bridge** is an arc across a crevasse or stream, formed by drifting snow. Snow builds up on top of it until it becomes indistinguishable from that on the terra firma around it.*

or expect our bodies to let us down. Now I'm old, relatively speaking, I can see the anatomy of disaster everywhere I look. Oblivious to potential dangers, youth is only scared by imminent danger, not the danger it cannot see.

Once the rescue was complete, we huddled together like a penguin colony while the guides returned to the problem of which was the best way forward. By my reckoning, we still had another five kilometres of glacial minefield to cross and the girl's narrow escape had done nothing to give me confidence in either of the guides.

We pressed on with Goat Face leading and Baptiste as back-marker. I doubled my efforts to follow Goat Face's tracks having now seen the consequence of deviating from proven ground. It was a balancing act, given the poor visibility, keeping him in sight but not getting too close in case he also did a vanishing act. I settled on five metres.

We picked our way through a field of ice boulders, which involved a lot of poling and sidestepping, but it was a sign that we were getting to the end of the glacier. I noticed that Baptiste's telemark skis were the perfect vehicles for this terrain. Maybe he wasn't so daft in bringing his comedy skis after all, I thought. Finally, an hour later, we dropped off the Géant though a gap in the ice debris below it. With the opaque glacial wall glistening in a turquoise shade of blue behind us, we set off across the billiard-table-flat Sea of Ice. We skied, or rather skated, the length of it then sat on some boulders the receding glacier had left behind.

From there it was all *terra firma* and, reportedly, a simple ski to a small bubble lift that would take us to the modest peek of Montenvers (1913 metres), where we could catch a small train down into Chamonix. I celebrated my imminent survival by drinking an energy drink and eating a chocolate bar. Unfortunately, I dropped the wrapper and had to use most of the energy gained from the snack, trying to recapture it. Baptiste looked on in disgust. He clearly hated people who littered even more than people who took their skis off mid-descent. Then I noticed that the Montenvers lift wasn't running; apparently it had been closed due to high winds. I asked Baptiste what the alternatives were, he pointed at a 600-metre escarpment in front of us and what looked like a line of ants clambering up it. My heart sank. 'You've got to be joking,' I exclaimed. Baptiste gave a Gallic shrug. The same one I planned to give him if he came looking for a tip later, I thought.

After a sleepless night and four hours of what had been extreme-skiing for me, I was outfaced by Baptiste's aerobic proposition. I looked up at the ascending ants and the Ski Demons chirped up again. 'That would be an ambitious climb for you in walking boots, never mind in ski boots,' they gleefully informed me, 'Not to mention carrying skis,' they added.

We skied over to the foot of the escarpment, from where it looked like a vertical cliff. The ants had been using a set of foot holes worn in the snow by the dozens of equally unfortunate souls trapped by the closure of the Montenvers lift. We started the climb and before long I started to fall behind. Other climbers came up behind me so I let them past while I hung on to a rock, hyperventilating. I offered each one a chirpy comment to assure them I was okay, despite looking like a packhorse that no amount of whipping would get back on its feet again.

I finally crawled onto the top about forty minutes after my fitter companions had finished their assent. Peter later told me he'd thought about descending without his skis, to help me carry mine up. I told him that, 'Contrary to popular belief, it's not always the thought that counts.' A little hut was selling hot drinks at the top, a welcome sign that civilisation was near. All we had to do now was jump on the train down into Chamonix. However, like most of the lifts, this too had been closed due to high winds. Baptiste informed us we'd have to ski back down through the forest using a farm path.

Being in trees was reassuring. Although not strictly accurate, I felt safe from avalanches in the forest. My feeling of wellbeing didn't last however, because we soon came across a landslide that had obliterated a section of the path. The icy rubble had washed over it and uprooted the trees below, exposing a deep ravine and only leaving a one-foot wide, twenty-metre long ledge of skiable snow. Time for Baptiste to get out his rope again I thought, but I guess he didn't want his fate to be literally tied to mine so, without stopping, he skied across the ledge. He beckoned me to follow, helpfully suggesting that I didn't look down. I held my breath as I committed to the traverse. This was my Patrick Vallençant moment, I thought to myself – you fall, you die. I'm pretty sure my heart stopped for the ten seconds it took to reach safety on the other side. Peter had a better head for heights and followed in short order, seemingly unfazed.

The rest of the journey was uneventful. The path took us to a blue run, which we used to cruise to the outskirts of Chamonix. None of the skiers on the piste took any notice of us, seemingly unaware that we'd made the greatest escape since Shackleton walked his way out of the Antarctic. At the bottom we kicked off our skis and thanked Baptiste politely if insincerely. I gave him a €20 tip simply because I didn't have enough energy left for the Gallic shrug I'd been planning.

My generosity was matched by my mood. Peter and I stumbled into the nearest bar shattered and started drinking cold beer in the quantities we'd been discussing since summiting Montenvers. The evening rather predictably 'went large' on us and at four in the morning we fell out of a rather dodgy club (Alpine Angels), almost missing our transfer bus to the airport.

While sobering up on the plane, I looked out of the window to see Mt. Blanc glistening in the morning sunshine. I smiled and drew a deep breath. My lungs filled with air and a warm feeling of pride filled my chest. I then knew why Anselme, and in fact many lesser skiers, always want to ski increasingly difficult slopes. The feeling of accomplishment after a first descent, even if it's only a first for you personally, is truly addictive. I returned from Chamonix that year wanting more – and later that season, while skiing in Morzine, the Chalet Project was born.

10. Summer of Discontent

Season 2 had ended badly in Reims but worse was to follow. The Après Aliens had followed me home and this time they abducted me for most of the following summer.

I woke up on the 6th June 2012 in a small white box-room, once again, with no idea where I was. I lay in the unfamiliar bed looking at the walls trying to find a point of reference, something that would identify my location. Even by recent standards, this was taking an alarming amount of time.

It looked like some sort of hotel room but then I spotted a picture on the wall - of me sailing my dinghy, a long since forgotten passion. I last recalled seeing it hanging in the downstairs toilet at home. Bleary eyed I got up and tried to open the bedroom door but there was no handle. After some initial confusion, I discovered that it slid along the wall on a rail. It soon became obvious why: there was no space to swing a dead cat in this place, never mind a door. I slid the door open and a tiny living room presented itself. I walked in, opened the curtain to my left and looked out. Three walls of windows looking back at me, forming the other sides of a square glass atrium - I was in some sort of tower block. I then noticed a set of skis lent against the wall behind me; I recognised them. The truly terrifying bout of Alzheimer's was over – they were my skis (they had my name written on them). Still shaking, but glad the confusion was over, the events of the last two months came flooding back.

I was in the Cube, a block of flats in the centre of Birmingham, not far from my home. I'd bought a tiny one-bed flat there a few years back, as an investment - never thinking I'd ever live there, but now apparently I did! After returning from Morzine with a broken Land Rover and a broken face, I'd fought a dogged rear-guard action to save my marriage and stay in my home. I'd spent a month in my own spare room then reluctantly moved out and into the Cube.

The Loft, where I'd lived for nearly two decades with my wife, was a large open-plan apartment in an old warehouse. It looked over a canal basin and was a short walk for both of us to work - until I sold out and moved offices to Sutton Coldfield, where most of my troubles seemed to begin. Along with our like-minded neighbours we had pioneered city-living in central Birmingham and had converted a large industrial space into a modern luxury apartment. Building and furnishing it to the height of urban chic had taken vast resources, both in time and money, but we'd built a very special home.

City-living is fun when you live in a fabulous apartment, work nearby and have lots of disposable income. But I discovered that summer it's not so much fun when you're unemployed, running out of money and living in a tiny box. I knew mountains could be lonely places but that summer I discovered cities are far worse when you're on your own.

I'd been brought up in the country, a Yorkshireman by birth and I loved all things outdoors. Like many people of rural origin, I'd been attracted to the bright lights of the city and the careers offered in them. My wife, a Brummie, had always been a townie and I'd moved to the city centre with her. Now, it no longer made sense for a mountain-loving country boy to be living in the centre of a sprawling conurbation. I'd always thought I'd retire back to the sticks - ending my days alone in Birmingham City Centre wasn't in my game plan.

I tried to make the Cube feel like home, hanging up my photos of the Alps, but they were no substitute for the real thing. Nor was the polluted air that trickled in through the single window during that particularly hot summer. With no way of creating a draught and no balcony to stand on, you couldn't escape the sweatbox. I lay there at night wondering what circle of Dante's hell I'd ended up in.

I knew that I'd been a poor husband. I had however provided the majority of the cash for our life-style, up to that point at least, but the Chalet Project, a foolhardy business venture that promised little profit, was clearly the straw that broke the camel's back.

Many of the items in the 'poor husband' dossier that my wife kept were marked as 'drink related'. Although whether drink was cause or symptom was not recorded. Drinking had certainly been responsible for getting me into many regrettable, if now amusing, situations. It had definitely led me to spending too much time in dubious company and partaking in a lot of inappropriate dancing.

City-living presents many opportunities to imbibe after work with no driving to worry about. Like most small businessmen, 'networking', usually in bars, was the best way to find new customers. There were no kids to pick up from school and, most nights no wife to rush back for either - she was an industrial networker herself.

The previous year, my wife had been on a summer long campaign to affect a separation, unhappy with my winter absence and general behaviour. She seemed to bring the subject up every time we did make it home for a meal together. She would cook a pleasant meal then calmly discuss various options for us to separate while we consumed it. Being told you're no longer loved, while trying to eat, not only caused terrible indigestion but made me drink heavily at home too. Towards the end of that summer, in order to escape my Sword of Damocles,[24] I agreed to move out of the Loft on my return from Morzine the following spring.

I'd only paid lip service to this agreement in order to appease her, hoping the Hemingway Oath wouldn't apply, hoping she'd change her mind or that some hormonal imbalance would somehow be corrected over the winter. That Christmas was endured hoping it wouldn't be my last in the Loft – it was. Winter (Season 2) sped past and I'd loitered in the Alps long after my last guests had left. I was putting off the inevitable – going home to face the music. When I finally did return, sadly the music hadn't changed.

Many friends had admired my decision to 'live the dream' but few realised what I'd risked and ultimately lost, in doing so. Despite voicing disgruntlement with their own lives (and in some cases spouses), few would want to swap places with me now I was effectively living in a hotel room on my own.

The Cube flats lend themselves to voyeurism because many of the windows faced inwards. I became fascination with the lives of other Cube dwellers, mostly rich foreign students, young professionals and other successful people on their way up, not on their way down like me. Most apartments were used as *pied-à-terres* rather than real homes.

There was a Chinese girl who lived opposite who did a lot of Yoga in her underwear who I'll certainly miss. Other than that, the Cube's window offered a depressing vista for someone used to looking out on the Alps so I spent little time there. Most evenings were spent in my favourite wine bar or staying with friends and family. In the three months I 'lived' in the Cube, I don't think I spent

---

24 *Damocles was force to enjoy all the luxuries of a king, including fine food, but he was made to eat it with a sharp **sword** suspended over his head, by a single horsehair.*

a single evening there. It was simply a place to keep my clothes, to crash when drunk, and somewhere to leave early in the morning.

The worse thing about living in the Cube was that when I left the gym, the only place familiar to me, I had to turn left towards the Cube rather than right towards the Loft. I made the mistake of turning the wrong way on many occasions. I was occasionally invited back to the Loft to fix something and, specifically, to help prepare for a long-planned party to celebrate the start of the London Olympics. It's a bizarre experience to be a party guest in your own home. At least I don't have to stay and help clear up, I thought, when I left with some of the other guests.

When I moved out, I hardly took any possessions with me; subconsciously, I wanted to leave the Loft intact. Most of our furniture, although mutually procured, felt like my wife's anyway, as she had chosen it. I took the few knick-knacks I could truly call mine and my favourite bottle opener; I was going to need it. I surveyed the meagre possessions I'd installed in the Cube. Not much to show for a lifetime of worshiping at the altar of consumerism, I thought.

One thing I couldn't take from the Loft was my treasured marine fish tank because it was built into the wall. So, reluctantly, I broke up the reef I'd spent the last ten years cultivating before taking a hammer to the tank itself. It was like being forced to shoot your own dog. I took the corals and the other inhabitants to the pet shop. Other customers looked on in bemusement as I tearfully said goodbye to my prized clownfish. We'd been through a lot together. I felt like I was grieving, but not for the loss of my clownfish. I'd experienced bereavement before but, even though nobody had actually died, this felt worse.

I was subsequently enlightened by a chairlift conversation with a friend, Liz. You get to hear a lot of life stories and home-grown philosophy on chairlifts, especially if they break down (the lifts, not the passengers, that is). She'd lost three husbands, which she admits, was rather careless. Two of them died, but one of them left her and he was the one that took longest to get over. 'At least the others didn't want to leave' she said. Divorce, she concluded, is indeed worse than bereavement.

I've noticed that most of the men I ski with have at least one failed marriage behind them. I haven't conducted a scientific study - there could be a statistical anomaly around Morzine or indeed amongst men who ski with me, but I estimate the percentage at around 85%, which is well above the divorce average in the UK (currently 50%). I've also noticed that most who have remarried, met their second wives while skiing. This evidence suggests that skiers make poor first husbands but are pretty easy to pick up second-hand in a resort.

Husbands, who are prevented from skiing because their wives hate the cold, will go on their own and may wander. Women who are bullied into skiing and shouted at when they go-ostrich on a black run, will end up hating their husbands and probably leave them for a golfer instead.

I conclude that keen skiers should always marry other keen skiers if the marriage is to last. More importantly, if your dream is to live in the mountains then it has to be one shared with your spouse.

Even harder than leaving the Loft that summer, was telling my mother that I'd done so. I kept putting it off. In fact, the whole summer was punctuated by awkward moments when I bumped into people and had to tell them about the split – awkward for them and emotional for me. Often they'd seen my wife recently and she'd neglected to mention my departure, presumably to avoid those moments. But you would have thought it was worth mentioning, at least to closer friends.

The week before the Edgbaston Test match and my parents annual visit to Birmingham, I plucked up some courage and visited them to break the news in person. If I'd left it any later they would have turned up at the Loft the following week and wondered why I didn't live there anymore. A demon inside me thought it might be entertaining to let them and have my wife do the explaining.

Managing my mother's grief and rage was harder than managing my own. I felt like I'd let her down. Even worse she wouldn't let me have a second glass of wine with dinner that night, when I needed my old friend the most. I got a lot of irritating advice from other people about the evils of drink that summer. 'Thanks for pointing out the obvious' – I used to say 'But you're right, now is the perfect time to go cold-turkey as everything else is going *so* well', but the sarcasm was lost on most - every time I picked up a glass it felt like people were watching me.

The situation I found myself in was frighteningly similar to that of my father some forty years earlier. He'd been a semi-functioning alcoholic too. He'd ended up a middle-aged divorcee living in a bedsit too. He died a bitter man. Worryingly, it looked like history was repeating itself and my future looked equally bleak. Every time I saw a group of homeless people, I wondered how long it would be before I ended up sitting on a park bench, drinking cider with them. I'd set out to be a ski bum but there was a real danger I was going to end up being just a bum. At one point, moving to a park bench looked decidedly imminent. Just when I thought things couldn't get any worse, I discovered my bank account had been cleaned out by fraudsters. It took an agonising week before I convinced HSBC that I hadn't transferred every penny I owned to an offshore account then withdrawn the cash - mercifully they did refund me.

However, there was still one part of my life that made sense that summer - my winters in Morzine. I clung on to that thought like a life raft. If I could just survive the summer, I could return to Chalet Neige and regroup.

My strategy to surviving the summer was simple; avoid being alone in the Cube. So I made sure I was around people all day and had a social engagement every night. My friends were very supportive and seemed to be taking it in turns to get drunk with me or at least make sure I ate. Many suggested I throw myself back into work. So, with a heavy heart and a recommendation from a friend, I landed some consultancy work and reluctantly re-entered the vacuous world of marketing. Once again, I found myself using PowerPoint and talking bollocks about Social Media. I hated every minute of it, but at least I had some money coming in and every day brought winter closer.

The problem was I didn't have any other marketable skills. I'd lost all my technical skills having been a director not a doer, for so long and there are few summer-only jobs for senior management. The truth is once you've been the boss for a long time you become almost unemployable and if you've been self-employed it's very difficult to convince anyone, including yourself, you'll be happy being an employee again.

Ski instructors are their own bosses and can find work in the southern hemisphere during our summer months too. Chile, Argentina, Australia and New Zealand all have ski resorts. So, while briefly in a more positive frame of mind, I decided to start training as an instructor. The nearest practical summer ski resort for me was actually in the Northern hemisphere – Tamworth.

So that summer I took my first instructor's course at the Snow Dome there - which I failed!

There were lots of mitigating circumstances and I tried to laugh it off. It was quite funny - I was a failure at the thing I'd wrecked my life to do. More seriously, being told I wasn't a 'good skier' (whatever that means), was all I needed to hear that summer. I christened it the 'Summer of Discontent' because absolutely nothing seemed to go my way that year - apart from one thing.

A lot of divorced women stay at the chalet every year, not all of them cougars I hasten to add, and flirting with them makes for good repeat business. The first season I'd relied on a fit chalet boy to do most of the work however Season 2 I did solo and took on all the arduous tasks myself.

One repeat guest, a doctor called Debbie (divorced/non-cougar), I really liked. I knew she'd enjoyed her first stay during Season 1, as she was very keen to write in my visitors' book. Only problem was I didn't have one. So she went out and bought one and left me a kind message on the first page, along with her email address.

She returned with her kids the following season seemingly to review the book's contents and by then it had been filled with nice comments and had become my prized possession – I had few others. No doubt I'll be reading the comments out loud one day in my old people's home. She worked in Birmingham, so I contacted her that summer to see if she wanted to meet up for what, unwittingly, turned into a first date. She did cancel on me twice but, despite my lack of recent practise at first dates, it went well. After convincing her I wasn't on the rebound, while not being entirely convinced myself, romance blossomed.

Thanks to Debbie and my friends, I survived that summer, avoided the park bench and eventually made it back to Morzine when, finally, the Summer of Discontent turned into glorious winter for this Son of York (apologies to the Bard). But before it did, the summer had one last twist in its tail.

11. Je Suis un Moniteur de Ski

I've always thought the question 'What do you do for a living?' rather an impertinent one, especially when asked by strangers. The enquirer either wants to measure your worth or more likely your wealth. I find it especially rude when the question is asked on holiday because, if you answer truthfully, it invariably leads to further questions about your job – a job most of us are on holiday to forget about!

On principle, I never ask chalet guests the question, although some will volunteer the information anyway, presumably because they love their job, which in itself can be a bit sickening. But I'm happy to be talking about their work, rather than about mine; I'd cringe telling people I was a 'digital marketing consultant'. Not just because I wasn't especially proud of the fact, but also because it was very difficult to explain to the layman what that meant other than – 'I used to annoy people with spam emails.'

I'm often temped to lie in such a way as to kill the conversation dead. 'I run a car clamping company' or 'I'm an arms dealer' or even 'I do remedial circumcisions at bar mitzvahs!'

When asked the dreaded question back in England I'd usually answer 'I'm a ski bum', but that didn't really sum up the magnitudes of my endeavours in the Alps, although it did satisfy the enquirer's curiosity about my wealth and worth. So I'd decided that 'ski instructor' was a better answer and, despite my initial fluffed attempt I continued to toil at the Snow Dome trying to make it true.

Tamworth Snow Dome is a rather grand title for a 170-metre indoor ski slope that was built in the Nineties. But it has real snow (sort of) and BASI[25] run their Alpine Instructor Level-1 courses

---

25 *The British Association of Snow Sport Instructors (**BASI**) has four ascending levels of qualification.*

there. I had expected to breeze through my Level-1. Having spent three seasons skiing down real mountains what challenges could an indoor slope possibly present to me? My hubris spectacularly backfired when I failed the course.

Many factors contributed to my first fluffed attempt: I'd taken the course in the middle of the Summer of Discontent for starters – my mind really wasn't on the job. Secondly, I didn't understand the language the trainer, Tim, was speaking. He was using all sorts of weird terminology that apparently related to skiing. He did hand out a copy of 'The BASI Bible' (their Alpine Manual) at the start of the course, which I used to crack the BASI code some months later. Tim had suggested my fellow students and I, most of whom were much younger and less academic than me, read through the manual during the evenings, but I wasn't really in a studying mood that summer.

I seemed to be doing well on the course, until it came to demonstrating the three different stages of the snowplough, which I failed to do, at least not to Tim's satisfaction. His inability to communicate what was wrong with my snowploughs frustrated both of us. Although I'm willing to admit I was suffering from an attention deficit disorder, having not slept properly for three months, I couldn't see the subtle variations of leg movement in his demonstrations, let alone mimic them.

Despite being inflicted with Duck Feet I did actually have an effective snowplough, [26] I could stop and turn with it but, apparently, it wasn't a 'BASI snowplough'. I soon came to understand that there's the right way, the wrong way and the BASI way of doing things.

---

26   *'Duck Feet'* is a condition where a person's toes point outwards as they walk, or 'doing a Charlie Chaplin' as it's known, makes snowploughing, which is a pigeon-toed stance, very painful.

There's a very good reason why BASI want all its instructors to ski like identical robots. If you have a lesson from a BASI instructor, you'll get consistency. From my own experience, I knew foreign instructors' teaching techniques could be as random as a chicken's reason for crossing the road. Their advice often conflicted. Common questions like 'how far apart should I have my skis?' 'How much should I bend my knees?' 'Where should I position my poles?' would all solicit different answers depending on which instructor you asked.[27] BASI instructors all sing from the same hymn sheet. If the Alpine Manual is their bible then the 'Central Theme' is their psalm. It's a rather complicated, but effective, methodology for turning a non-skier into a parallel skier (not snowploughing), which involves learning several types of snowplough. New instructors will inevitably spend most of their time taking beginners through the Central Theme, so admittedly, it was important for me to be able to demonstrate all stages of it – perfectly.

There wasn't an exam at the end of my course. The result (pass/fail) was based on the trainer's continuous assessment of your performance over the entire week. I found being under the microscope for seven days, very intense. Every time I did something well, I'd look up to see if Tim was watching – he usually wasn't. Every time I made a mistake, he seemed to be staring right at me. With very little positive feedback coming my way, I felt defeated by the end of day three.

By the last day, I knew I was going to get the thumbs down from Tim. He did pass me on all points but the Central Theme.

---

27 *The correct **answer** to all these questions is 'It depends' - on the terrain and how you want to ski it.*

I asked him 'If I promise never to try and teach anyone to ski, would you give me a pass?' For the first time that week he cracked a smile and almost laughed, but I wasn't joking.

The week left me with an initial loathing of the Snow Dome. I remembered Ingrid, my Austrian tormentor, struggling to teach me to snowplough. It seemed preposterous that, two decades later, after skiing down some of the most difficult runs in the Alps, I still hadn't mastered it!

I *did* meet with triumph a year later when I returned to the Dome and exorcised the ghosts of Tamworth, by passing my Level-1 on a second attempt – this time with a different trainer. By then I'd read the entire Alpine Manual and learnt all the verses from its Central Theme. I'd also spent many hours practicing in the Dome prior to the retake. In fact I spent so much time practicing the plough, I started to walk with pigeon toes, a trauma my knees have yet to recover from. But most of all I went through the reassessment without a hangover and with plenty of sleep. Everything in life is easier a second time round, I find, because you know what to expect.

Now the Snow Dome has become a place of summer fun. I meet and practise with other instructors there every Thursday night. It turns out there are quite a lot of ski bums that migrate to the Midlands for the summer.

My friends found my desire to be a ski instructor rather odd. I professed to hate teaching and most of them had me down as a child hater too, which wasn't strictly true - it was usually just *their* children I disliked. Some also pointed out that I wasn't actually that good at skiing either, which was true.

Like me, most beginners assume ski instructors have a wonderful life. After all, they get paid to do what we love - ski. It doesn't help that most are charismatic individuals who appear to love what they do for a living and, in most cases they're young, athletic and good-looking - luckily for me the last three aren't BASI requirements.

During Season 4, while doing my 'shadowing' (work experience) and effectively became a ski-borne nanny for two weeks, I learnt the truth. In reality, an instructor's life wasn't a glamorous or indeed a lucrative one. I discovered that their working day was long, often dull and involved surprisingly little actual skiing. I concluded that the main attraction of the job was the location of its office.

But, I'd already had an office in the Alps, so why did I still want to qualify as an instructor? Especially since it was an expensive and laborious task, not to mention a difficult one, for a person who had only just recently mastered the snowplough. Putting my ability aside, gaining enough qualifications to legally teach in France would be nigh on impossible for any fifty-year-old.[28]

However, I had another reason for undertaking instructor training that had nothing to do with wanting to teach. I'd realised that if I wanted to get any better at skiing steeps and deeps myself, I'd have to go back to basics. Fitness aside, I'd gone as far as I could with my home-grown technique. I needed to strip my skiing down to the basics and rebuild a better platform to move on from the skiing plateau I'd been stuck on for years. I had met a lot of skiers who had taken the BASI courses simply to improve their own skiing and it had worked for them.

Well that was one excuse. More likely, I just wanted people to know that I *was* a 'good skier' (whatever that means) and to have an instructors badge to prove it!

One interesting guest, Raphe, an archetypal ski dude, had done just that. He was now a professional skier and had his sponsor's name plastered all over his skis to prove it. Being a ski dude is one up from being a ski bum and is a much more radical vocation. It requires a skiing ability infinitely better than that of mere mortals. It's not actually possible to talk to a ski dude about skiing for lack of common reference points. We *ski* on skis; they do other things on them. Those that compete in a sport called 'big mountain skiing' use them to descend un-skiable slopes. Those who compete in an aerobatic sport called 'freeskiing' use them for take-off and landing equipment. Neither bears any similarity to the *normal* skiing we humans do.

Raphe made money by jumping off cliffs, making skiing movies for humans to watch while getting drunk in après bars. His girlfriend was working in Morzine and I put him up for a couple of nights. He had the regulation tan, goatee and ponytail along with the widest set of planks (skis) I'd even seen. Raphe was a qualified instructor but he needed no badges to prove he was a 'good skier' (whatever that means), you could tell just by looking at him. He mentioned over dinner one night that he'd initially failed his Level-1 because he couldn't master the snowplough, much to everyone's amusement. I laughed too, not knowing I shared his fate.

Before BASI would give me my all-important instructor's badge, I had to do thirty-five hours of shadowing. The British Alpine Ski School (BASS), the best English-speaking ski school in Morzine, generously let me shadow their instructors. When they allocated me to the kindergarten class, I quickly discovered that this wasn't such a one-sided deal. A second pair of hands and broad shoulders seemed almost essential to run this class and mine were free of charge.

Tom, the young instructor running the class, had the patience of a saint. I soon discovered that he'd drawn the short straw that week. The class involved no actual skiing - just running around in ski boots picking the toddlers up, pointing their skis in the right direction, watching them fall over again, then repeating the process a back-breaking number of times. None of the kids had a long enough attention span to listen and therefore they didn't follow any of Tom's instructions. I even suspected that, for some, English wasn't their first language. It was fascinating to see how, by a process of trial and error, they mastered the snowplough in a few hours - something that had taken me over twenty years to do!

Mercifully, they gave me a class of eight year olds to shadow in the afternoons. They were vaguely capable of following instructions and their instructor, John, spent the week trying to stop them from using the plough and to ski parallel. It amused me that I'd spend the mornings watching one instructor trying to make kids snowplough and the afternoons watching another try and stop them. My afternoon class consisted of four boys called Merlin, Valentine, Hugo and Benedict, which reminded me what an upper-middleclass sport skiing was. They could all ski enough to be dangerous and, although they fell over less often, they were significantly heavier to pick up. Benedict had recently grown huge, daddy longlegs like limbs but hadn't yet worked out how to control them. Having to help him untangle them after his frequent falls soon became a considerable burden.

At one stage during my shadowing, I was asked to take a little boy to the toilet. This was a parenting task that, even at the age of fifty, I'd successfully managed to avoid until then. If my wife could see me, 'the child hater', now - she would split her sides laughing, I thought. Strangely, I discovered that I was actually quite 'good with kids,' as one instructor put it. They seemed to like me and, more surprisingly, I discovered that I quite liked skiing with them – safe in the knowledge that I could hand them back to their parents afterwards. They, like me, love messing about in snow.

BASI also insisted I complete a child safety course before they would issue me with my badge. This forced me to learn about the many stages of a normal child's development and how to spot abnormalities in their behaviour that might indicate abuse. By the time I'd qualified as a Level-1 instructor, I probably knew more about parenting than most of my friends who had their own kids. I then confounded many of them by passing a CRB check, making it officially safe for them to leave their children with me - although my ex and mother-in-law would still strongly disagree.

So, after many hours of toiling in both the UK & France, the British Association of Snow Sport Instructors reluctantly let me into their ranks. Shortly after getting my instructors badge I had to fill in a form that asked me what my occupation was. Not having anything else to put that was particularly accurate, I wrote 'ski instructor' in the box, with a smile on my face.

Now, when asked by strangers 'what do I do for a living?' I say 'I'm a ski instructor' with a great deal of pride, which is now technically true. They don't need to know I have never earned a penny teaching skiing, nor am I likely to in France anytime soon.

12. Come Dine With Me (in the Alps)

I'll admit that before I started the Chalet Project I wasn't very domesticated. Actually, by blokes' standards I don't think I was actually that bad - although my ex might not agree. I suffered from two serious medical conditions. Firstly, I had 'Domestic Blindness'; this condition mostly afflicts men and prevents them from noticing dirt and dust. A classic symptom is not being able to find anything in the fridge. To a lesser extent, I suffered from 'Domestic Deafness', which commonly affects teenagers of both sexes. The symptoms include ignoring repeated requests to perform a domestic task and irritability when unable to hear the TV above the sound of other people hoovering.

Despite these disabilities, I was fully familiar with the location, the purpose and the operation of most of the domestic appliances in our home. However, for most of the twenty-five years I'd been with my wife we'd employed a cleaner, so there really was no need for me to actually use them. I knew how to clean, wash, iron and make a bed, having been brought up by a working mother, but, mercifully, I do not suffer from the 'Obsessive Cleaning Disorder' (OCD) that seems to have afflicted most of the women I've lived with since. But, thanks to the project, I found myself in the professional cleaning business and, since many of my guests were women, I had to get a little OCD myself.

Prior to the project, I was however completely clueless about cooking. Most of my life I'd out-sourced the acquisition and preparation of food to females or ate takeaways if one wasn't available. I knew that the oven was the cupboard with the glass door under the grill that, I occasionally *did* use (mostly for cooking bacon), but I never opened it. It was next to the microwave where most of my 'cooking' took place. I wasn't ashamed of this fact. All the women in my life had been accomplished cooks, and indeed enjoyed cooking, so there'd seemed little point in me stealing their enjoyment. My talent lay in washing up - or so I thought.

The project's initial business plan limited my catering exposure to breakfast, although I did want it to be a hearty English affair. However, towards the end of Season 2, it became clear that I needed to offer guests an evening meal too, particularly if they arrived late or on Wednesdays (Morzine's chalet night-off) when it was hard to get a table in a restaurant. It would also help me take the project into profit. So, at the age of forty-seven having barely boiled an egg, I also found myself in the professional catering business!

Luckily, having made the decision to cook for guests myself, I discovered my inner chef. Cooking for paying guests was stressful at first but, by the end of Season 4, I'd learnt to cook a small number of carefully chosen dishes really well. I designed the chalet's evening menu to be low stress. It was full of items that could be prepared in advance (stews and curries), dishes that appeal to skiers wanting a hearty meal after a day on the mountains. Most importantly, the dishes had to be 'drunk proof', *i.e.* very difficult to burn or overcook.

During the long summers, I discovered that domestic cooking was actually enjoyable. Using friends and family as guinea pigs, I tested new menu items. Better still, after dinner, I could slob on the sofa with my top trouser button undone while someone else slaved over the sink. A role reversal I'd been dreaming of for most of my adult life.

Before the project, I'd found grocery shopping very stressful, because my Domestic Blindness prevented me from finding the right items on supermarkets shelves even if they were in plain sight. The chef (my ex-wife) would send me out on a mission to fetch some forgotten exotic ingredient for a dinner party. The chances of a successful mission where low and the consequences of failure high. I'd often return with the wrong type of cream or brand of rice and have to deal with the face-of-incredulity my wife did so well.

Now, even though French supermarkets present an extra linguistic challenge, I enjoy the experience. I like procuring ingredients and making recipe adjustments depending on what I can and can't find. I too now have strong opinions on the origins and varieties of produce and know the difference between *crème fraiche* and *fromage frais* and that basmati rice goes with Thai and long-grain rice with an Indian curry.

Before the project, I hated dinner parties. I thought the food and the table got in the way of more interesting forms of social intercourse such as chatting, dancing and drinking. There was always the potential for getting stuck at the wrong end of the table with someone's boring spouse – or, in their case, me.

If we were throwing a dinner party there was the tedious task of cleaning the apartment to OCD levels, even if the cleaner had been the previous day. Thanks to the project, I now refer to this as a 'Deep Clean', normally done at the end of the season – or maybe if the Queen was about to visit your house.

I would be given a list of ancillary tasks: getting out the expensive glasses, folding napkins, polishing silverware, and rearranging furniture – emergency interior decorating often featured. By the time the guests arrived I was usually exhausted, ratty and more than ready for a drink. I would be given table-waiting duties, which I mostly forgot about, preferring to focus on getting everyone drunk as fast as possible - it seems I was born to be an après-ski guide!

Needless to say I out drank most of our guests, although our group of hedonistic child-free friends could give me a run for my money. The few that did have young children either left early or fell asleep on the cheeseboard. Don't get me wrong, I enjoyed entertaining friends - once dinner was over and I was off duty. But I preferred parties where everyone has to stand up and mingle. My concept of a good party hadn't matured much since my student days. Back then, sit-down dinner parties were for old people like my parents.

Back then, the main conversation at dinner parties seemed to be about the food. I realise it's polite to compliment the hostess on her creations but this invariably lead to others describing their own past culinary successes and I had none to offer. Similar conversations, between my wife and her mother dominated the frequent meals with my in-laws - interspersed with tales about my mother-in-law's grandchildren, the ranks of which I had failed to swell.

Now that I'm a passable cook myself, I would willingly participate in such conversations - but unfortunately I'm no longer invited to Sunday dinner anymore – which, unexpectedly, I now miss.

Now, having spent so much time in France, I realise what a philistine I had been; food is one of the most important parts of life, especially if you're French, and *is* worth talking about. Maybe I've just matured. Perhaps food becomes more interesting when skiers get older because eating is one of the few activities that doesn't hurt their knees. By the end of Season 4, despite having spent a lifetime professing to hate dinner parties, I was effectively throwing them in the chalet several nights a week. I was enjoying being the cook and the praise that often resulted - the only down side being that I usually had to wash up too.

Perhaps, if my wife had seen the project as a way holding lots of dinner parties while getting her guests to pay, she might have spent more time with me in the Alps. She did manage to teach me a few simple dishes that I occasionally cooked during Season 1, but her Gordon Ramsay approach to training kitchen staff and my unwillingness to be subordinate didn't help. I sometimes wonder, if I'd done more cooking than drinking at home, might we still be together?

By Season 4, word of my new culinary prowess had obviously spread because dining in at Chalet Neige became very popular. Either that, or I'd got my market research right. Dinner for €20, including unlimited wine, was clearly an attractive proposition. The price was set to match expectations (low) and to be cheaper than dining out.

Like most chalets my evening meals are strictly *'menu du jour'* – everyone eats the same. I will create a vegetarian permutation for anyone who is so afflicted, but few vegetarians go skiing because most don't have the requisite strength. I think the French turn most of them away at the border, so few make it to my door.

I try to avoid being responsible for feeding people who have complex relationships with food, especially if they're likely to slip into anaphylactic shock or exhibit other forms of attention-seeking behaviour. I now always ask if there are any special dietary requirements before taking a booking that included catering. I'm not really looking for details, just a yes or no. If the answer is lengthy or elaborate, I'll suggest they self-cater. And after witnessing a particularly vicious domestic argument over how to dress a salad properly, I never cook for the French.

I avoid cooking for children too. I start twitching if they pick out the vegetables or leave stuff they've piled onto their plate themselves. My parents, who experienced rationing during the war, taught me that having any kind of food was a privilege and I should show my gratitude by eating everything put on my plate. They always presented me with two options at dinnertime:

1. Eat what was put in front of me.
2. Starve.

If I tried to leave anything on my plate, I was reminded of the starving children in Africa. When I once told my mum to send the Africans my leftovers, she answered me with a swift clip around my ear. Unfortunately hitting kids, especially other peoples, is now frowned on so, despite a strong urge to start some kids' remedial education, I refrain. Often the fussy-eating kids are on the plump side too due to poor diet and they could do with taking the 'starve' option more often but, since their parents are paying me to feed them, I feel I have to try. I've also learnt that fussy eating is a learnt behaviour and most of the inflicted kids will have at least one fussy-eating parent, which is double trouble for me – so best avoided.

One memorable child would only eat spaghetti bolognese or cheese sandwiches. Nothing else would pass his lips. His parents told me they'd tried starving him but, after three days, the child won the battle of wills. I always hate seeing defeated parents so I suggested they let me try another approach. As I couldn't hit him, I tried explaining evolution. I told him that early humans had thrived because of the diversity of foods they were prepared to eat. I told him that species with narrow food sources, just '*spag-bol*' for instance, soon become extinct. Unfortunately he found Darwinism hard to grasp, being only six.

Oscar, my adopted Labrador, understands evolution. Also known as the 'Food Seeking Missile', he eats most things he comes across. The only decision he has to make is whether something is edible or not, and he doesn't often err on the side of caution either. He doesn't mind if his eggs are runny or overcooked. In fact he's not all that bothered if they're still in their shells. It must be said he doesn't have the other two key ingredients needed for evolutionary success – opposable thumbs and intelligence. Not many Labradors can ski either, so I have to pamper to their fussy-eating masters, the humans.

I once took a booking for a fully catered week without asking if there were any dietary requirements. I didn't get round to asking the all-important question until a few days before the guests were due to arrive. The response was shocking; two didn't eat fish and one was a vegetarian - my heart always sinks when I hear the 'V' word. I toyed with the idea of making the others eat veggie all week as punishment for choosing to holiday with a herbivore.

On arrival, I then discovered that one of them was a Muslim (so no pork), another was pregnant (ruling out soft cheese and shellfish), and one suffered from IBS so anything spicy was off the menu too. As I scratched my head, wondering if I could get away with serving them beans on toast all week, I also found out that two of them ran a gastro pub and another was an online food critic!

Somehow I weathered the culinary equivalent of a perfect storm and even got some good feedback on Tripadvisor. I suspect the pub managers, being in the catering business themselves, felt my pain and were suitably magnanimous. I made a lot of money that week but I didn't get any time to go skiing. I vowed never to fully cater again - I wasn't in the Alps to be a cook.

Over the seasons I evolved my menu to make serving dinner easier, and allow me time to go skiing the same day too. I always serve a cold starter, which can be assembled in minutes, and mains that can be cooked in advance and left to simmer, or reheated and served in a big help-yourself pot.

Because dinner at the chalet feels like a private dinner party, I often get offers to help wash up. Unlike a real dinner party, where I believe it's polite for the host to decline, I usually accept.

I also encourage guests to cook for themselves, as many fussy eaters or families like to do.

Self-catered weeks can be awkward because I can become confined to the garage, although many families take pity on me and invite me up for dinner, which I usually accept. I find myself feeling like a child who has been invited round to his friend's for tea, wondering what passes for food in his house. Thanks to the project, I've met dozens of interesting families and eaten wonderful, if sometimes challenging, meals. But luckily my taste buds are highly evolved – I will eat just about anything.

I had one family from Bradford who booked the chalet on a self-catered basis. I had intended to enjoy a week out of the kitchen, after surviving the culinary perfect storm, but was intrigued by the smells coming from it. They brought their own Indian spices, including their own especially hot chillies, which I was informed were grown by the inmates of a Guatemala insane asylum (they were joking – I think).

They were an interesting family of Malaysian decent, four siblings who had brought their spouses and kids along. One spouse was from Chester, one was a Parisian and the third was a Norwegian. I'm usually the architect of an eclectic dinner table mix but this one came fully formed.

The siblings took it in turns to cook some wonderful curries and generously invited me to join them. The Frenchman declared that he was sick of rice and decided he would cook a classic French meal for us one night. This involved opening tins of *confit de canard* and roasting potatoes in the surplus goose fat – slightly cheating but equally delicious. After being given all this wonderful food, I felt honour-bound to cook for them one night. I chose a classic English dish - seafood paella! Well, curry had already been done. The paella went down well. There were dozens of kids and there wasn't a fussy eater amongst them.

The Bradfordians left me a stash of their suicide chillies that I inadvertently put in the curry I made for my next guests, a Dutch family. It was so hot that even I couldn't eat it without breaking into a sweat. The stalwart Dutch took on my English Curry Challenge with enthusiasm and asking me what the dish was called while mopping their own brows. I said it was called '*Chicken Tarka*'. They hadn't heard of it. I explained that it was like Chicken Tikka only much '*otter!*'

Unfortunately, even though their English was good, they didn't get the joke – 'Tarka the Otter' was obviously not a popular book in Holland. I tried again. I told them not to worry about any side effects in the morning. I'd taken the precaution of putting lots of toilet roll in the fridge – which got the laugh I was after. Toilet humour always spans cultural differences, I find.

The chalet can sometimes be full of people who don't know each other and often they can all be strangers to me too – it can sometimes feel like I'm in the Big Brother house. So, on their first night, I encourage guests to dine with me, and each other, in order to break the ice. If there are any cooks around the table, I badger them to throw a dinner party themselves during their stay, which they usually agree to after a few drinks – then I make them take the Hemingway Oath.

I tell them that they can 'eat for free' all week if they cook for the chalet on just one night and that I will provide the ingredients and supply the social lubricant, wine. It's amazing how many guests want to take a turn, if only to save money. Some guests cook because they hate slow service and the cramped restaurants that proliferate in France. I know how they feel; it starts to frustrate me towards the end of a season too. And then there are those who fancy being a chalet chef – if only for one night. By the end of Season 3, with so many people cooking instead of me, I realised that I might have created something quite unique. I didn't hand out scorecards, but I'd accidentally created 'Come Dine With Me in the Alps'.

I knew my transformation into a cook was complete when I found myself buying a wok. My wife spent a fortune on cooking equipment; now I too was coveting pots and pans. We used to receive cooking-related joint presents that I unwrapped with disdain. In contrast, at my fiftieth, I opened an envelope with a cookery-course voucher inside and I was highly delighted. Although the present was from friends who had stayed in the chalet, so I wasn't quite sure whether it was a compliment or a hint?

Playing at being a Chalet chef has given me insight into the life of a professional chef: unsociable hours, poor wages, constant deadlines, poor working conditions, not to mention dealing with difficult clients. I think I'd rather work in Marketing. I accidentally entered the world of catering in order to fund my skiing, but discovered cooking has its own rewards – the satisfaction gained from completing a complex logistical challenge (getting dinner on the table) and the compliments from replete diners, even if they're just being polite. But the most gratification I get is when I collect a set of clean plates (from evolved mammals) because the proof of the pudding has always been in the eating.

13. Is Skiing a Sport?

It does seem a bit pointless. Spending a fortune getting to the top of a mountain so, at great personal risk, we can slide down it. We end up exactly where we started (at the bottom of the lift) and then we repeat the process for a week!

But then all sport is pointless – right? Depending on the sport, there maybe some health benefit to playing it. Humans used to get their exercise from chasing food; instead they now chase each other to keep in shape. There are educational benefits too – playing sport can teach us how to collaborate or focus on an objective. That's why we encourage our kids to play sport, but why does an adult, who has presumably learnt how to do those things, want to risk injury for no obvious gain?

Given that most people usually return from a skiing holiday fatter, dehydrated, sunburnt and often in plaster, we can rule out any net health benefits. If you attend ski school, the main educational benefit is getting better at doing something pointless. So, other than being pointless, what does skiing have in common with other sports? Is skiing actually a sport at all?

Of course there are versions of skiing (downhill, slalom, biathlon etc.) that involve the wearing of lycra and sometimes the carrying of a gun, which are clearly sports, but they bear little resemblance to what most of us do on our skiing holiday - 'recreational skiing' as I'm going to call it. Not only do skiing athletes wear different clothes, but they also use very different skis to us. They ski on different terrain, usually pre-prepared ice, which we go to great lengths to avoid. They never ski in bad visibility or have to take emergency action to avoid a snowboarder sat in the middle of the pistes. They never stop half way down it for lunch, or go binge drinking afterwards, either.

I've heard many a drunken opinion on what constitutes a sport. There are those who think an activity must be done in shorts, not long trousers, to be deemed a 'sport' because it implies some physical exertion will be undertaken. But then cricket, a very physically demanding activity, would get thrown out along with the bathwater (golf, snooker and darts). We skiers would also go down the plughole because, apart from the Scottish, we seldom ski bare-legged. The pub definition I like the most is known as the 'Shoe Test'. Does the activity require specialist foot wear? If the answer is *yes*, then it's a sport. If *no*, then it isn't. This gets rid of pub-based activities but keeps football, rugby, cricket and most importantly skiing. Skiers have the ultimate in specialist footwear after all. Unfortunately it does let ten-pin bowling in – so it's not the perfect litmus.

Rather than look for clothing based definitions we should head to the Oxford English Dictionary which defines 'sport' as: 'an activity involving physical exertion and skill in which an individual or team competes against another or others.' Skiing does involve exertion and requires skill, but, unless you're wearing Lycra, or carrying a gun, you're not competing against anyone else. So recreational skiing fails this test.

There are those who try and turn recreational skiing into a competitive sport – mostly men. Some, I'm convinced, think it's a contact sport too, given their disregard for the safety of others on the piste. They try to be the first down every run or record the highest speed of the day on SkiTracks.[29] Other competitions

---

29 **SkiTracks** *is an app that allows skiers to record, amongst other things, their top speed of the day. It's often indirectly the cause of many a serious accident and in my opinion should be banned.*

run in the background; who falls over the least and who can ski the steepest slope. But they mistake ability for bottle. Any fool can point their skis down the slope and play chicken with their life. But most of us are not consciously entering a competition when we go skiing. If we are in a competition, it is with the mountain, and mountains can never truly be beaten.

There are also fitness freaks that see recreational skiing as an endurance test. Ski Touring is popular amongst these types, the metric of success being the distance travelled or the height gained in a day. They cover vast distances and often stay overnight in remote mountain huts - which I like the sound of. However they spend most of the day 'skinning-up' slopes, which I don't.[30] Spending four hours skinning for ten minutes of skiing seems a very poor reward for a lot of effort (it could just be that they're too mean to buy a lift pass?) I like to have a geographical objective when skiing too - usually a nice restaurant in Switzerland - but I feel it's better to go with gravity rather than against it. I get a free lift pass with my job, so it would be a shame not to use it.

Others see recreational skiing as an exercise in orienteering and love navigating their way around the slopes in military fashion. It's always good to have at least one person like this along (if they remember to bring their reading glasses). For them, skiing is just a giant game of snakes and ladders - the pistes being the snakes and the lifts the ladders - making recreational skiing more of a board game than a sport.

Then there are the collectors. Like twitchers or train spotters, they tick off ski resorts and their signature run, but that makes skiing more of a hobby for them, than a sport.

There are also the thrill seekers, the adrenaline junkies, who get a buzz from going deeper and steeper. They seek radical

---

30 **Skinning-up** is the practise of ambulating up a slope after attaching special skins to the bottom of your skis that make them grip the snow.

experiences and sometimes jump out of perfectly serviceable helicopters. For them, recreational skiing is a sequence of escalating challenges – not a sport.

Perhaps the best way to define skiing is to look at the history of the Alps before it became a playground for the rich. Skiing wasn't invented to be a sport, a competition, a hobby or a challenge but a means of winter transportation. The indigenous farming population made essential journeys on skies - their skiing wasn't pointless. They regarded skis as simple transportation devices.

Like them, for many of us, skiing is just the best way to get to our favourite mountain restaurants and back; an effective way of moving between lunch and après locations that unfortunately means wearing long trousers and specialised shoes.

Most importantly, skis also allow us to access an ancient wilderness normally too difficult for bipeds to move around in. Ski resorts are a type of Jurassic Park; the mountains being the dinosaurs. Stay behind the marker poles and the zookeepers (the pisteurs) promise that an avalanche won't eat you. For those prepared to risk it and go beyond the poles, skiing allows them to explore places *Homo sapiens* were not designed to go.

I'll admit that I fall into most of the above categories. I enjoy all aspect of skiing, if not all at the same time. My mental approach to skiing depends on the mood I'm in, the company I'm with and the weather. Skiing is many things to many people but for most of us skiing is much more than just a sport.

14. Breakfast of Skiing Champions

Being a Yorkshireman, I hold the continental breakfast in great contempt and rue the day it crossed the Channel and became commonplace in UK hotels. Even if it's free, to me a continental breakfast is never complimentary.

Access to a meagre buffet of rubber cheese, anaemic ham, a fruit yogurt or two and a croissant doesn't constitute a 'proper breakfast' for me. If you're lucky, you may also be given a facility to boil your own egg in some aquatic version of a toaster, but using these communal devices is ill advised. In my experience, it can lead to confusion over which egg belongs to whom and the damaging of international relations.

Theoretically, a buffet breakfast should at least mean no interaction with elusive waiting staff or the speaking of French. However, the one thing I need first in the morning, a cup of tea, is usually the one thing that has to be ordered. But there is little point ordering tea south of Folkestone because, when it eventually turns up, it will consist of a lukewarm *glass* of water with a tea bag, propped up against it, still high and dry in its wrapper. Honestly, it's enough to turn an Englishman to coffee!

Granted this is not exclusively a French problem. Frankly it's difficult to get a proper cup of tea anywhere outside of Yorkshire. But the problem, in France at least, stems from not being able to purchase teabags without strings attached. I'm not referring to some small print in their contract-of-sale that mandates they are served next to, not *in,* water but the actual *string* and the label they attach to the other end of it. Attaching a string to a teabag, for the purposes of dunking in a cup of tepid water, shows a failure to comprehend the fundamentals of tea making. The string prevents proper stirring in a pot – the correct place for a teabag to meet water. Even if the inferior builder's method has to be used, where the brew is made in a mug, the water should always be boiling.

Leaving tea aside, I really don't know what makes a Frenchman get out of bed because it can't be his traditional breakfast. Don't get me wrong, nobody likes the smell of fresh croissants more than me, but no-one should be asked to take on the Wall with only a *pain au chocolat* and an espresso for fuel.

When I started the Chalet Project, I wanted to send chalet guests skiing with a proper breakfast inside them. I therefore offer my guests a *'petit déjeuner Anglais complet'* – a Full English Breakfast. To achieve true authenticity I import most of the ingredients from the UK.

For my first two seasons, breakfast was such an elaborate affair that I needed a helper to service it. The last of who, despite being a Muslim, helped me (a Jewish boy) serve up several pigs' worth of pork products to my guests. If only my Rabbi and his Imam could see us now, I used to think. I scaled down breakfast for Season 2 after realising that not all skiers shared my cholesterol death wish. Now I offer a simple 'hot option' every morning, usually involving eggs accompanied by some form of dead pig.

For those actually wanting to combat cholesterol, I always have porridge on offer. I personally won't leave the chalet without a bowl of the stuff inside me, otherwise I won't make it to lunch. Skiing burns calories fast and this slow-release carbohydrate is the perfect skiing fuel. In order to encourage younger skiers to do the same, I've tried to put a marketing spin on the stuff, calling it 'The Breakfast of Skiing Champions', but it turns out porridge is even harder to promote than pre-washed lettuce.

It seems even its inventors, the Scots, are divided on the porridge issue. When one guest professing to be Scottish said he couldn't stand the stuff, I questioned the fact. He replied *'Yer ah Sassernach, but ye dunnae go Morris dancin – dae ye?'* - a fair point. Instead of porridge he had the full *English* everyday but insisted on calling it a full *British* so he didn't have to admit preferring something English to something Scottish for breakfast.

For those wanting to go native, I also provide freshly baked baguettes, croissants and *pain au chocolat*. I fetch the baguettes from the *boulangerie* every morning, a French breakfast ritual I do approve of, and not just because I love freshly baked bread. It also allows me to assess the weather conditions for skiing, while the crisp air helps clear my head. En route, I survey the peaks around me, which always serves to remind me why I've got up so early and agreed to cook ten people breakfast – so I can spend my winters in the Alps. On my return, I'll often find Breakfast Zombies (sleepwalking guests) wondering round the kitchen trying to find carbohydrate and liquid along with implements to consume them with - all of which I laboriously put on the table before I left.

Breakfast Zombies suffer from acute domestic blindness; they continually ask me where stuff is, to which I reply, 'It's on the table', which has become my early morning mantra. Their blindness also means they often sit at recently vacated places at the table rather than seating themselves at a fully equipped clean ones, leading to more requests for breakfast artefacts.

Once seated, I offer guests whatever the hot option is that day and the men will usually say 'Yes' and devour whatever I put in front of them. Some guests, mostly women, will start listing items they do and don't want to see on their plate. Some go further and specify quantities and give cooking instructions – which I ignore.

Fussy eaters tend to focus on how they like their eggs cooked. Considering most eggs come from a chicken's arse, people can be very fussy about how they're prepared. I then have to explain that bespoke egg delivery isn't in my manifesto and that today, by popular demand, the eggs are scrambled. 'My kids won't eat scrambled eggs' one father once replied. I explained that his kids could do with them what they liked but unscrambling them would be difficult.

My heart always sinks when I discover I've got a my-kids-wont-eat parent staying. I've come to dread the phrase. I feel like saying 'I prepare food for discerning adults. If your kids won't eat my eggs because of the smoked salmon I've mixed in or because the chives I've sprinkled on top are technically vegetables, it's your fault not mine. You need to educate your kids or, better still, starve them.' But I never do. It's hard to know how some of these delicate constitutions ever get enough sustenance to go skiing, or indeed get so fat. I point out that I may not be providing a bespoke egg service but guests can have whatever quantity of my eggs they like. Although I do tell them that, in France, most people think that one egg is 'un oeuf'!

After breakfast, some guests like to make a token gesture and carry their dirty plate into the kitchen and place it *near* the dishwasher, not actually *in* it of course. As every teenager will tell you, dishwashers are like Pandora's Box. If you open them you may find an unimaginable horror - a load of clean dishes, then be faced with the unbelievably arduous task of emptying it before you can insert your dirty dish. If I catch them looking in the dishwasher clutching a dish I tell them 'Best just leave it on the kitchen top, son, no need to be a hero'.

I spend most of the early part of the week defending the kitchen area from Breakfast Zombies and generally breaking new guests in. I've been tempted to rope off the kitchen and generally plaster officious notices everywhere in the chalet:

'Please don't leave clothes all over the chalet.'
'Please don't unplug the coffee machine to charge your phone.'
'Please don't leave your bedroom heater on and window open.'
'Please don't lock the front door and go to bed with the key.'
'This switch can be used to turn the lights off as well as on!'

However, I've so far resisted the temptation because I don't want to be the sort of person I'm turning into - one with a growing list of petty hates.

The first morning is the hardest with new guests, because neither party knows what to expect. I explain how things work at Chalet Neige and answer a myriad of predictable questions about Morzine, its ski area and about me. I call the latter the 'Groundhog Questions':

'Where are you from?' (Hull/Birmingham)
'How old are you?' (Fifty)
'Got any kids?'(No – thank god)
'When did you buy the chalet?' (I don't own it, I rent it)
'What did you do before this?' (*Cringe* - online marketing)
'Can you speak French?' ('*Un peu*')
'What do you do in the summer?' (circumcisions!)

The above will usually be asked while I'm frantically trying to cook. I know they're just being polite and making conversation, but I feel like preparing a fact sheet about myself and putting it in their rooms. (From now on, of course, I can just sell them a book!) Meanwhile I'm trying to remember their names.

I struggle to remember the names of new guests, especially when I'm introduced to ten of them at a time − which is often the case. Then I finally get them right just before they all leave. I know it's rude to ask someone their name more than twice, so I have developed strategies to find them out rather than ask a third time. If they have kids I ask them 'What's your mummy and daddy called?' when the parent are out of earshot. Or eavesdrop conversations hoping a proper noun will crop up. Failing that, I revert to colloquialisms such as: my friend, mate, fella, pet, squire, guvnor, and if they're Cornish and female − my-special-lover always works.

On the whole, most guests are pleasant and very well behaved. I find most people are at their best on holiday - assuming their holiday is going well. The chalet feels like someone's home (mine) so most are respectful, considerate and courteous, like I would be if I were invited to stay in their home. Of course, I like to think there isn't much to complain about either, because it's my job to make sure their holiday is indeed going well.

When I had a 'proper' job I hated clients who were morning people and invited me to breakfast meetings. I used to need breakfast before I could be civil, never mind talk business. Ironically, my new winter job involves a type of breakfast meeting with clients seven days a week. Although, unlike my old job, I don't mind because I'm usually going skiing after the meeting is over.

However, some people just aren't morning people at all, even on holiday, and can be easily upset if things are not as they like. Complaints have included: the service being too fast (or too slow), offensive items they didn't order contaminating their plate, coffee being too strong (or too weak), and milk not being the right amount of skimmed-ness. One woman complained that I asked too many questions. Presumably I should have guessed what she wanted for breakfast. My favourite complaint of all time was – 'My toilet door squeaks, can you oil it?'

Many guests seem to need background noise in the morning disguised as news. Some insist on inflicting commercial breakfast TV on me, if they can work out how to turn the telly on, I'm tempted to tell them it's broken or to hide the remote control. My wife insisted on having Sky News on each morning, although this was more to do with her fancying Eamonn Holmes, I suspect, than being interested in world affairs. Others, still drunk, feel the need to treat the chalet to their favourite dance track during breakfast. I point out the error of their ways by pulling the plug on the HiFi.

Being the adopted son of Ski Nazis, I'm always on a mission in the morning to get guests up the mountain as fast as possible, especially if it's a powder day and I want to go skiing myself. One of my favourite regulars, Ali, a mother of six, has a similar morning mission at home; to get her kids fed and out the house to school on time. She jokes that she's effectively running a chalet back in Liverpool, only her guests are long-term residents and unlikely to ever settle their bills.

Once breakfast is done, I set about liberating Landie from any snow that has hopefully fallen over night and load the guests' skis onto the roof rack. I then sit on the bonnet and wait for the guests to appear in their ski gear – which can, for some, take an extraordinary amount of time. Going skiing is a complicated business, I grant you, there's a lot of gear to assemble and forgetting an item can ruin your day. But some people just don't want to be rushed. Hopefully there will be a Ski Nazi in the group who will chastise ski-faffers and hurry them up, if not, I try to bite my tongue – honestly, it's like some of my guests think they're on holiday!

Once the last guest is finally up the mountain, I can relax or go skiing myself. If I don't go skiing, I feel guilty because the Ski Nazis would regard this as a crime. I try and remember why

I've become a cook and taxi driver; it's so I can ski every day – something many seasonaires forget. If you don't go skiing when you can, what was the point of becoming a domestic slave?

Once sat on the first chairlift of the day, I relax, my morning work all done. I've once again got all the *kids* dressed, fed, watered and up the mountain – including myself. I mentally review the frantic morning, which has got me to that point and usually conclude it was worth it. I'm what psychologists might call 'self-actualized'. At that moment, everything is right in my world. I'm content, fulfilled and free of any immediate worries – other than where to take those following me for lunch.

I reflect on the beauty of my new work place while the chair ascends through the tranquil pine forest and I fill my lungs with the crisp mountain air. At that point life couldn't be better, breakfast once again done. Unless I agreed to cook dinner, there's no more hassle to face until the following morning when I wake up and my alpine version of Groundhog Day begins once again.

15. The Ski Club of Great Britain

I don't like skiing on my own. Apart from the safety risk involved, I find my own company boring – not least because I've heard most of my own jokes before. It's not that I hate my own company; I just prefer that of others, especially if they have an interesting life story, a few good jokes to tell themselves or are particularly good-looking. I can often ski with chalet guests, indeed many want me to lead them round the mountains for a day. But when they ski too badly for me to tolerate for more than a day or they don't meet the aforementioned social criteria, I used to find myself stuck.

It can also get tiresome always being the leader too, especially with intermediate skiers. Making all the route decisions, assessing the difficulty of each run and the risks of someone going-ostrich is burdensome. Making sure everyone, even T. E. Charlie, is having a good time can sometimes detract from my own enjoyment. That's always the big problem when you turn a hobby into a job.

So, on days when I don't want to ski with my guests or they don't want to ski with me; or when I simply want to be a follower not a leader, I head to Avoriaz and ski with the Ski Club of Great Britain.

The Club stations 'Leaders' in many popular resorts. It's important not to call them 'guides' because that upsets people, particularly the French,[31] since they're not qualified international

---

31 Like *'Instructor'*, the French are very protective of the job title *'Guide'* and require anyone acting, in their opinion, as a guide to have a full set of international qualifications.

mountain guides. Leaders are essentially volunteers who, in exchange for having a bunch of random Brits follow them around, get their skiing expenses paid by the Club. They essentially get a highly subsidised skiing holiday – some several times a year.

The Club is ideal for people who don't have anyone to ski with. Sometimes this can be because they're on holiday with people of lesser ability. They can ski with the Club while their friends are at ski school or their non-Nazi spouse is having a day off. Then there are those who are holidaying on their own – which can be worrying if you've intending to spend the day with them. My excuse for being Billy no-mates is usually that I have a chalet full of beginners.

I've made many friends at the Club: some that regularly visit the Portes du Soleil, some who are resident all season. Being a member of the Club means I never have to drink alone either, because it's almost impossible for me to walk into a bar without bumping into a Club crony. It also allows me to meet lots of keen skiers who might turn into potential chalet guests.

Several of the regular Avoriaz Leaders have become good friends. With their encouragement and a degree of self-delusion, I convinced myself I had the necessary skiing and social skills to become a Leader like them. Armed with their references, I lined up an interview at the Club's Wimbledon headquarters where I managed to complete the deception. Ironically, I was almost late for the interview having got lost on the Underground. I chose not to mention this when I finally arrived. Admitting I wasn't able to successfully interpret the tube diagram would probably have cast serious doubt on my ability to interpret a piste map!

I'm not sure why I wanted to be a Leader. With the Chalet Project, I'd already found a way of getting others to subsidise my skiing. Admittedly the idea of going skiing, without having to cook a load of eggs first, was appealing but I was already a ski leader of sorts. I effectively had my own ski club - the regulars at Chalet Neige who often follow me around the mountains.

However, the project did prevent me from skiing in other resorts. I loved the Portes du Soleil but missed skiing in Austria and had barely started to explore the Rockies before the project tied me to Morzine. Being a Ski Club Leader would give me another skiing option, should I decide to retire from the chalet business, to go further afield.

There was one very practical reason for becoming a Leader too - I needed more training. Although I often took on the responsibility of leading people around the mountains, I'd had no formal training on how to do so safely. Even if I never did any leading for the Club, the mountain craft I would acquire on the course would be invaluable for my private skiing exploits.

Subconsciously, I probably wanted to be a Leader simply so I could wear their distinctive blue Leaders' jacket, the closest I was going to get to a red ESF one − it had the same kudos if not the same pulling power. In the final analysis the main reason, subconscious or otherwise, for wanting to wear the blue jacket was to gain validation. I wanted confirmation that I was indeed a 'good skier' (whatever that means) - just like my quest to be an instructor, despite not wanting to teach.

Unless teaching or chaperoning, it's always best to ski with people of a similar ability. You don't want to be T. E. Charlie, or indeed be held up by one. The Club has created a system for measuring its members skiing ability. Club grades can be a controversial subject. Many members get very disgruntled at being graded too low and some even demand a right of appeal. It falls to the Leaders to interpret the parameters set out by the Club to grade members as either bronze, silver, purple or gold standard. Simple enough, you would have thought - until you add a plus or minus subgrade, a score out of ten for fitness and a separate grade for on- and off-piste ability.

When I filled in the application form I was in complete ignorance of the Club's grading system and simple ticked the gold boxes (their highest grade) for both my on- and off-piste skiing ability. My ignorance was initially mistaken for arrogance but I managed to talk my way out of the gold/gold self-assessment and suggested the Club contact another Leader I'd skied with more recently. She confirmed that, in her opinion, I was a purple/purple skier, the minimum grade required to be a Leader. I didn't really know what that meant either apart from that, in her opinion, I was a 'good enough' skier to lead. Finally, a few weeks later, I got the nod and I was booked onto the 2012 Ski Club of Great Britain Leaders' Course.

Back in my naive world, assessing someone's on-piste ability wasn't that complicated. In fact skiers graded themselves. Most would declare themselves a green, blue, red, or black-run skier.[32] I was capable of getting down any black run, in any conditions and they were the most difficult, so I ticked the 'gold' box on the application form. In my old world, off-piste skiing was basically about losing altitude without doing any actual falling or, indeed, any actual dying. The off-piste isn't colour-coded so skiers can't simply grade themselves by the difficulty of the slopes they can consistently achieve without either falling or dying.

---

32   *There is no international standard, but most resorts grade the difficulty of their pistes by colour.* **Green** *being almost flat, increasing in steepness and difficulty, through* **blue** *and* **red** *to* **black,** *the steepest.*

There's no system I'm aware of that can meaningfully grade off-piste slopes. Steepness and narrowness play a part, as does the type, condition and depth of the snow. Then there's the fear factor. If the slope is near a precipice, or called something like 'The Couloir of Almost Certain Death' for instance, it can be psychologically more difficult to ski. All of which makes it fairly hard to put variables into a spreadsheet and come out with a colour for the difficulty.

Also, the difference between falling and skiing is tricky to determine. The fastest way to lose altitude is to ski down what is referred to as the 'fall line', the direction you would take if you were, well – falling.[33] The better skier you are the more time you spend on the fall line. Therefore, in my analysis, skiing off-piste was controlled falling and I was 'gold standard' at that.

The two week long Leaders' Course is held in Tignes every December. I'd skied there once before, while staying in neighbouring Val d'Isère, and hadn't been very impressed. Both are part of the Espace Killy ski area, which is small compared to the Portes du Soleil but very popular with Brits. In its favour, Tignes is perched at over three kilometres above sea level and usually has fresh snow in early December. But if not, it has access to a glacier, which can be skied on all year round. So it's a logical place to hold a pre-season course. I'd heard that the course should more accurately be called the 'Leaders' Boot Camp' and that my fitness would be seriously tested. So, late that October, while still being bludgeoned by the Summer of Discontent, I started a fitness campaign and took up a pastime I'd always ridiculed - running.

---

33 *In alpine skiing, the **fall line** refers to the direction a ball would roll if it were free to move on the slope under gravity alone, if it wasn't wearing skis!.*

I've hated running since I was child. I'd played team sports that required running but running for running's sake was always an anathema to me. At first I was pitiful to watch, I could barely go a mile without stopping. A week into the campaign, I was completely demoralised when an old lady overtook me – she was running for her bus – it looked like her shopping was quite heavy too! I did manage to get up to two miles each morning and I did lose some weight, mostly by drinking one less bottle of wine each night. I was quietly confident. I'd skied with many Leaders over the last two seasons and had few problems keeping up with them, admittedly only ever for a day at a time. Some had indeed recommended me to the Club, so surely my skiing was good enough to pass? The reality was that my body was in no shape for the high altitude skiing marathon that was to follow.

As December approached, I was looking forward to the course and I was delighted to be returning to the Alps a month earlier than usual. I was also looking forward to skiing somewhere other than the Portes du Soleil for a change. However, the Summer of Discontent wasn't ready to let me go.

16. Languid at Luton Airport

This is a true story, although sometimes I can scarcely believe it, but I know there can be many versions of the truth depending on one's perspective. We can search for evidence to prove our version is the most accurate, but not all truths can be made empirical. Our 'truth' can change through revelation or reflection. What is indisputable is how what we think is the truth makes us feel at the time.

A week before the Ski Club Leaders' course, someone decided that I deserved 'the truth'. I was inaccurately informed that someone else had moved into the Loft – another man!

With hindsight and after a couple of hundred miles of skiing, I don't know why I didn't dismiss this as gossip. But cynics (which, I'd forgotten, included me) will tell you that when couples split, there's *always* someone else involved.

Six months down the line, it looked to some like the 'someone else' was actually Debbie. One mutual friend, who thought that my infidelity was to blame, completely blanked me at a party, confirming my fears. I couldn't fault her logic: I must have been at fault, otherwise why would I have moved out?

The sober truth was that I couldn't have afforded to live in the Loft on my own because my new vocation wasn't exactly lucrative. I was spending three months of the year in Morzine anyway and it made sense for me to be the one to move out. It had been hard leaving a place I'd invested so much time, money and emotion constructing. I knew every floorboard, every tile and every nail because I'd put many of them in place myself.

Now, I had to deal with a false truth: that a cuckoo, as I childishly named him, was living in my nest. The prospect that someone else might now be enjoying my life's work, sitting on my settee and watching my TV was more than galling. I only hoped that my DIY mistakes, of which there were many, would distract him as much as they had me.

There was one indisputable truth: even if the gossip had been founded, I now had another romantic partner and my wife had every right to seek happiness too.

I spent the next few days with the Après Aliens, who deposited me at Luton in the world's most depressing airport. At 4am I found myself sat in the departure lounge waiting for a flight to France – the world's most depressed man.

17. No Friends on a Powder Day

For me, being able to ski off-piste was always the ultimate goal, and not just because it's more difficult. Some people are happy to cruise around the pistes on their annual skiing holiday, never taking that next step, never venturing beyond the marker poles. But not far behind those poles are the magic forests, the hidden valleys and fields-of-dreams, where you can meet nature at its most breathtaking.[34]

The pistes are, after all, just prepared skiing motorways, highly controlled and sometimes crowded. Like a golf course, the on-piste world is an artificial environment, albeit very pleasant. When I go hiking in the UK, I head for the wild places; I don't want to go for a walk around a golf course and I certainly don't want the burden of batting a small white ball around with me. No, I head to the Pennines to commune with nature. Once you travel far enough off-piste, deep into the backcountry, all evidence of man disappears and you'll find yourself in a truly wild place. You may even see evidence of wildlife or even the animals themselves that stay well away from the noisy, human-infested, pistes. So, if you want to be *two* with nature (you should always take a friend) head to the backcountry unless, of course, it's a powder day then different rules apply.

Ski dudes refer to it as 'pow', or 'pow-pow' if they have a particularly limited lexicon. But, no matter which way round you wear your baseball cap, fresh powder snow is the Holy Grail for

---

34 *Although not written on any map, many of the popular off-piste routes are given common names by the local ski community.* **The Field Of Dreams** *in Avoriaz is one.*

most skiers. 'Powder Hounds', as they're known, will go to great lengths, and sometimes take great risks, to find fresh pow. Those with local knowledge can keep finding untouched stashes of the stuff several days after a fall by trekking further and further into the backcountry. But if conditions are right, and it has snowed overnight, we can all wake up to a powder day and the whole mountain is once again up for grabs.

The average recreational skier will be lucky to get a dozen powder days in their entire skiing life, but they will remember every one of them. Even for a seasonaire, such days are few and far between and rarely fall on their day off, so they are not to be squandered. You never really know if it's going to be a true powder day until you look out the window in the morning. Even if fresh snow was forecast, waking up to a powder day is like finding Santa has visited; you're delighted he turned up even though you'd rather expected he would.

When I was a child, if snow had started to fall before I went to bed, I'd leap up in the morning, throw back the curtains and see if it was deep enough to prevent me from going to school. Nothing much has changed, except there is a scramble to leave the house and not remain in it.

Most powder hounds will try to be the first person up the mountain. Their goal, to make fresh-tracks, is achieved by being one of the first down a slope. If they do make the very first tracks on a slope they usually hold their poles in the air and shout 'claimed it' at the bottom. Areas easy to access from the piste will usually be 'tracked out' by lunchtime and most of the mountain will have been 'claimed' by the end of the day.

You can always feel an extra buzz in the après bar at the end of a powder day. Everyone is shattered, their red faces are animated, exaggerated tales of spectacular wipeouts and near-death experiences are told around the tables – everyone has had a great day on the mountain.

Getting an accurate snow forecast is essential for a powder hound. If a large dump of the fluffy stuff is forecast, then a relatively early night might even be in order. But professional weather forecasts can often be wrong so I always use local knowledge to prevent having too many disappointments. Ski hire shops are a great repository of information on weather and, more importantly, where to find the best powder. Shop owner and raconteur par excellence, Monsieur Gravier is my weather and powder guru and is seldom wrong when predicting the likelihood of fresh snow. He once told me, '*When mon blonk has iz hat on, zer will be snow zee next day in Morzine.*' He meant that if you see clouds forming around the top of Mt. Blanc, it would snow within twelve hours in Morzine. I don't know what meteorological theories apply and I've heard more learned men explain Mt. Blanc's microclimate, but to this day, the saying has never let me down.

A true powder hound can take on an Eskimo when it comes to describing snow conditions and, unless you're one or the other, it's best not to sit near them at breakfast.

The snow crystal is a very complex character and it can take on many different guises. This is partly why avalanches are so hard to predict. The light, dry and smooth stuff, useless for making snowballs, is considered the best for skiing and referred to as 'champagne powder' by hounds. Despite the American resort of Steamboat Colorado trademarking the term, it continues to fall in the Alps too. Generally the less dense the snow, the better it is for skiing. Hard packed ice, or 'Scottish Powder' as it's affectionately known, being the least enjoyable. Alaskan Powder is famous for sticking to steep slopes - unfortunately you usually have to jump out of helicopters to access it.

No matter where you ski, you never really know what the powder is going to be like until you launch yourself into it. Often in March, it can snow all night, getting everyone very excited, but in the morning we can find ourselves ploughing through heavy, wet snow or 'Californian Concrete' as the Yanks call it. Such false powder days are exhausting and a great disappointment.

Interestingly, there are more terms to describe bad snow than good snow: 'hard pack', 'slushy', 'crusty', 'cruddy', 'wet', 'patchy', 'heavy', 'rutted', 'lumpy', 'sticky', 'breakable crust' and 'artificial' (snow from snow cannons) – and that's just in English. But be careful not to over use them or you might be branded a 'Snow Whinger'.

Snow Whingers are skiers who constantly complain about the snow conditions, usually as an excuse for not skiing. Either they've been brought up in Alaska and are spoilt or they are just not good skiers (whatever that means). Some conditions are clearly harder to ski in than others but a good skier will have developed techniques to deal with most types of snow. Some conditions are more enjoyable, fresh powder for instance, but all must be mastered because many different types can be encountered in a single day or even on the same run. I may be a masochist, but I regard dealing and adapting to even bad snow conditions as part of the fun. If every day was a powder day we would get bored – eventually!

Having said all that, snow whinging can be skilfully used to justify a late start, an early lunch or an extended après session by those not wanting to ruin their drinking holiday with unnecessary skiing. I've seen a few masters use it to great effect.

To successfully ski powder snow requires significant alterations to your on-piste skiing technique – well, it did for mine at least.

Getting good in 'pow' takes a lot of practice and often finding enough 'pow' to practise in is a challenge in itself.

Learning to ski powder is like learning to ride a runaway horse. Initially you have no control over direction or speed and hang on for grim death until you eventually fall off. Luckily the falling usually doesn't hurt because you land in soft powder – but getting back up is time consuming and exhausting. If a ski comes off in the fall, it can be hard to find and is often some distance from where its owner ends up. Once found, putting skis back on in deep powder is tricky; a bit like getting dressed underwater – I imagine!

Needless to say, like learning to ski on-piste, learning to ski 'pow' is a process best done while young, fit and fearless. It's been made easier by the invention of wider, specialised 'powder skis'[35]. Until I got a pair of them, my attempts to venture beyond the piste marker poles usually ended in frustration and an aerobic workout.

Before the Leaders' course, most of my off-piste experiences had been on relatively hard-packed snow. Despite living in the Alps for two seasons, I hadn't had many powder days. It wasn't that I suffered from meteorological bad luck, but I was normally busy looking after guests when the snow fell. Many were not powder hounds and when they looked out of the window they just saw 'bad weather' and showed no urgency to get up the mountain. I was often tempted to leave a note on the breakfast table saying, 'Powder day, gone skiing, your breakfast is in the fridge,' but I decided that would be bad for business. After all, if they didn't know the significance of a powder day or the unspoken rules associated with one, they might get disgruntled and ask for a refund.

---

35 *Like water skis, once up to speed, **powder skis** float on top of deep snow. The wider the ski, the better it works. Consequently, the width of your skis has now replaced their length as a statement of manhood, even if you never ski powder!*

For the similarly uninformed here are my ten powder day commandments:

Commandment 1. 'Thou shalt have no friends on a powder day.'

This might seem a little antisocial, but it means you shouldn't compromise your day for others. On a practical level it means going out with likeminded skiers of equal ability, who are not necessarily your best friends. Admittedly, if you're a true powder hound they will be the one and the same. It means pretending to be French in lift queues and pushing to the front. It means using the first available seat on a chair, rather than waiting to share one with your friends.

Commandment 2: 'Thou shalt not ski with more than four people.'

Don't take 1 literally. Skiing alone off-piste is particularly unsafe on a powder day. If you get injured or buried, you'll want someone to notice. There's also a more philosophical question to ask about skiing solo: can you have a good time on your own? For me, a shared experience is always a better one. If you ski alone, there's also nobody to take videos of your skiing or corroborate your stories of epic descents in the après bar later. However, to ski with too many people can be problematic. The smaller the group, the easier it is to agree an itinerary, the fewer people to get lost or need help after a wipeout. Four is a perfect number, as long as they obey the same Ten Commandments.

Commandment 3: 'Thou shalt not be late for the first lift.'

Waiting for a tardy companion is frustrating at the best of times. I hate people who are late, even if it's only by ten minutes. I'm usually early by ten minutes, so I've been waiting for twenty. Time is of the essence on a powder day if the primary objective, to get fresh-tracks, is to be achieved. In March, the powder can turn to slush in an hour, so blink and you might miss it. As a general rule, never ski with people who don't wear watches.

Commandment 4: 'Thou shalt carry lunch.'

There really is no time for a sit-down lunch on a powder day. Besides which, you won't get fresh-tracks heading towards a restaurant unless it's closed or not a very good one. So a selection of snacks, that are easy to eat on a chairlift, need to be carried. Camel packs are very useful for rehydration on the move too. Adding a splash of vodka while filling them up can prevent them freezing - even if you do end up smelling like a Russian. It's also very important that you eat porridge for breakfast.

Commandment 5: 'Thou shalt not faff.'

If your kit or clothing needs adjusting, it must be done on the lifts. Untried and untested kit, including skis and boots, should not be taken on a powder day – it's not the time to experiment with new gear.

Commandment 6: 'Thou shalt not whinge.'

Nobody wants their powder day ruined by a whinger. No one really cares if your boots are hurting or your legs are tired. If you're tired, ski home down the next available piste. If you're cold, think warm thoughts. If you brought the wrong skis or the wrong legs for that matter, suffer in silence; the others can't do anything about your problems. And definitely no snow-whinging.

Commandment 7: 'He who finds it shalt drop in first.'

When you find a virgin field of fresh snow, etiquette dictates that the guide, or whoever has led the group to the Promised Land, makes the first tracks. This can be useful if you've not skied a particular pitch (powder field) before because you can watch and see what line they take. Assuming the pitch is wide enough to fight over, you can still make fresh-tracks next to theirs. The last person down may not get fresh-tracks but usually finds the best line by observing those that went before. A tip for the weaker powder skiers here is: don't be the last to descend either - remember, speedy rescues always come from above!

Commandment 8. 'Thou shalt not cross thy neighbours tracks.'

If you're lucky enough to be with the first group to descend a slope of fresh 'pow - pow' try not to cross the tracks laid down by your comrades. They may want to admire and possibly photograph their tracks from the bottom or, indeed, compare them to yours.

Commandment 9. 'Thou shalt not ski with thy girlfriend on a powder day.'

If your girlfriend isn't a powder hound (or just a hound) best point her in the direction of the hotel spa on a powder day. 'Girlfriend Skiing', as I call it, can be a pleasant experience if approached with the right attitude - one I will outline later. However it should never be done within twenty-four hours of fresh snowfall. If she's a 'keeper', your poorly disguised resentment at losing a powder day may come back to haunt you in future marriage guidance sessions.

Commandment 10. 'Thou shalt not cause death – especially your own!'

Most fatal avalanches occur twenty-four hours after a new dump of snow, so powder days can be very dangerous.[36] Learn all you can about avoiding avalanches and carry the right rescue equipment. Never lead unless you know the area well and have successfully skied the intended pitch before with a qualified guide. Never ski too close or more importantly *above* other skiers. And never ski under a rope – someone put it there for a reason. Most importantly, don't be goaded into a descent you're not happy with. If it doesn't look or feel right to you, don't drop in.

Needless to say the Ski Nazis never waste a powder day. They used to abide by the above Ten Commandments every skiing day, whether there was fresh powder or slush. My wife did once persuade David into a Michelin starred restaurant in Chamonix for lunch on one memorable powder day, a six-course affair that dragged on until late afternoon. Twenty years on, he still refers to that atrocity with bitterness.

Back in Morzine, once the local mountains have all been shredded, I find myself habitually staring at Mt. Blanc, willing there to be clouds circling its distinctive peak. I wonder how long it will be before the next fresh dump will arrive, filling in all the tracks, healing the mountain of its many scars and giving us all a new canvas to work on.

---

36 *I'm not sure we should trust this **statistic**. Is the snowpack at its most unstable during that initial period or is it just that the number of skiers, who head off-piste to play in it, is higher and so more die?*

18. Fear on the Fall-line

As my plane landed at Geneva I had cause to celebrate. I'd survived the Summer of Discontent, the worst summer of my life, and I'd made it back to the Alps. However, I was too exhausted to raise more than an internal smile. I wasn't heading to Morzine, but to Tignes, for the 2012 Ski Club of Great Britain Leaders' Course. Still processing the false information that a cuckoo was now living in my nest, I tried to focus on the task in hand: for the next two weeks I had to prove to the Club that I was a 'good skier' – whatever that meant.

As the thirty or so, wannabe Leaders assembled outside Arrivals, it started to feel a bit like the scene from Top Gun where the 'best of the best arrive in Fighter Town.' As one ski dude after another, many much younger than me, boarded the transfer coach, it became clear that I was out of my league. I consoled myself by remembering that the Club wasn't just looking for brilliant skiers but for all-rounders with good management and people skills too. Surely I must have those attributes after so many years in business, I thought.

After the 4am start, I soon grew tired of making chit-chat on the four-hour coach journey to Tignes. The previous week's tally of sleepless and alcohol-soaked nights had taken its toll. We arrived at the hotel and I was allocated a room with three other candidates, mercifully of a similar age. The room could accurately be described as 'intimate' - the beds were less than a metre apart. I was desperate for some privacy but it soon became apparent that little or no privacy would be available for the next two weeks. I knew from chalet life that being with strangers all the time can be exhausting - at least there I have my garage to hide in.

Closest to my bed was Bill, a retired policeman from the Met. On the mezzanine above was Mark, a fellow ski bum, fresh from completing his BASI Level-2 in Zermatt. Next to Mark was

Shaun, a fifty-five-year-old Irishman, back for a second attempt to pass the course - he'd failed to impress the judges two years earlier and was living proof that, even though we'd all been vetted, it *was* possible to fail.

We sat down to dinner that night and I had to engage in more small-talk. Rather alarmingly, no social lubricant, wine, was served with dinner. If you wanted you could order some, but nobody did. Presumably everyone, like me, was pretending to be an athlete still in training. It felt a bit strange; I thought the French considered it a crime to eat without wine. In fact, I thought it was mandatory to get drunk on the first night of a skiing holiday. But this was no holiday. The course would turn out to be the longest period I would ever spent in the Alps without getting drunk!

Despite being exhausted, I couldn't sleep that night and not just because of the lack of wine. It was the first of fourteen very long nights that I spent staring into the darkness, listening to the three baritones snore, exhausted, but unable to sleep.

The social awkwardness of being with strangers would soon be replaced with a common bond against the shared adversity - the appalling weather, the challenging snow conditions, the constant threat of avalanche and physical deterioration. Despite the diversity in age and background, we all had one thing in common, a love of skiing - although mine was soon to be tested.

One unexpected challenge I faced on the course was that of humouring the 'Leadership' sessions and the team building activities they contained. These classroom sessions, although a welcome respite from the brutal conditions outside, made me cringe. During my first career, I'd been forced to go on many management courses and had become very cynical about the pseudoscience they were usually laden with.

I'd been over exposed to such pop psychology, back at the agency, organised by my slightly manic if well-meaning boss. She'd read too many books written by self-appointed management gurus with titles such as *Motivating Teams to Achieve Excellence*. Required reading for the Leaders' course included *Leadership and Self-Deception* - an equally painful read. She often inflicted team-building exercises on the introverted group of programmers that worked for me. They hated the sessions even more than I did. Although it was fun watching these slightly awkward geeks endure forced human interaction. Their idea of team-building was playing World of War Craft together not falling into each other's arms to prove trust. Mine was getting them pissed down the pub on the company credit card, which I generally did afterwards to compensate them for being tortured.

At least Dave, who ran the Leadership sessions, turned out to be a humorous and self-deprecating fellow. He was an ex-royal marine and a Leader himself, both achievements commanded respect. One exercise devised to prove that 90% of communication was non-verbal involved sitting in a circle wearing blindfolds discussing a fictitious problem, which, in my case, facilitated a much-needed nap. In between the classroom sessions, presumably to prevent such napping, we were made to run around outside in the snow completing tasks designed to 'build our energy'.

Along with everyone else, once I was over the embarrassment of physical interaction with strangers, I thought the exercises were quite good fun, if pointless. One, where we sat on each other's knees supporting each other in one big circle, made me chuckle while I imagined a load of squaddies being made to perform this rather gay activity. Still, I'd had worse management experiences.

My boss back at the agency once made all the staff stand in a circle and state three things they admired about the person stood to their left, an excruciating hour from which my programmers emerged emotionally scarred and in need of several drinks.

What was truly exhausting for me was maintaining an outward enthusiasm during these sessions. I knew the Club were looking for Leaders with a high level of interpersonal skills and I didn't want to fail the course on that account. But it was hard not being morose, given the personal stuff that was sloshing around in my head. The slide projector was plugged into a blue power extension lead, which kept distracting me. It was identical to the one my fish tank had used and kept reminding me of its painful demolition.

But no score or feedback was ever given to us for Leadership Quality, so I guess we all must have passed. I suspect unless a candidate exhibited pathological or clear psychopathic tendencies, the leadership tutorials weren't going to affect their final grades. However not knowing for sure, meant the whole course was spent wondering if my every move was being noted and analysed – it was like living in a Petri dish for two weeks.

The first day got the course off to an auspicious start. The candidates had been divided randomly into three groups and my group was to have its first skiing session that afternoon. We were going to be taken up the mountains by skiing legend Phil Smith. Once a BASI trainer (an instructor's instructor), he was now a maverick who taught 'all-mountain' skiing, as he called it.

I wasn't looking forward to it. A ridiculous amount of snow had fallen in the last forty-eight hours and the official avalanche risk was set to 4.[37] Drifting snow had forced the pisteurs to close most of the runs and high winds had made them close all but one chairlift, the Tichot - which was worrying. By leaving one lift working, the resort was technically still open and so no ski pass refunds would need to be given. I assured myself that, despite the commercial pressures, they would not compromise our safety. Hopefully, if the lift was open then the area it served would be safe, rather than just the least unsafe in the resort.

After a morning of painful leadership training, my group headed into the equally brutal conditions with Phil. Safe or not, we ascended on the Tichot chairlift. According to my watch, the temperature was -15°C and I estimated that the wind was gusting at 35mph. Visibility could have been justifiably described as 'poor'. I'd skied in some pretty appalling conditions before but I'd never deliberately set out in them. If caught out in the Portes du Soleil, which I knew like the back of my hand, I could practically ski home blindfolded from anywhere, but these mountains were unfamiliar. Besides which, I'd not been up any mountain in any kind of weather for over nine months, making the hostile environment even more intimidating.

At the top, we stepped off the chairlift into the blizzard. Despite having done some aerobic training prior to the trip, I was struggling to breathe before we even set off. I put this down to mild altitude sickness.[38] I normally ski below 2,000 metres in the Portes du

---

37 *The **avalanche risk scale** goes from 1 to 5. 4 is defined as: 'Natural avalanches likely, human triggered avalanches very likely, with very large avalanches in specific areas', and 5 roughly translated says: 'Don't go up the mountain if you want to live'.*

38 ***Altitude Sickness*** *commonly occurs above 2,400m due to low air pressure. It presents as a collection of nonspecific symptoms resembling a case of flu, carbon monoxide poisoning or a hangover!*

Soleil and the pistes of Tignes are at 3,000 metres plus. Then the voices in my head started. My Ski Demons had awoken, seen their host weak from lack of sleep and started to feast on its remains. They told me 'I was literally out of my depth' and managed to convince me 'I was going to die.'

Despite the conditions, Phil delivered his radical doctrine with an enthusiasm and passion that was infectious. He seemed to contradict every other BASI instructor I'd ever had, including those giving other parts of the course. He wasn't telling us what to do with our arms, legs or what posture to stand in - but how to make our skis work with the snow:

'Don't ask me how far your skis should be apart. What does it feel like to *you*?'
'Don't turn your skis, just push the snow left then right.'
'Express yourself, live in the now, be at one with the snow.'

In his lecture that night he discussed the fundamental nature of alpine skiing and why it was an 'open' not a 'closed' sport. He explained why millions of skiers around the world get stuck on learning plateaus, unable to progress, no matter how many ski lessons they had. He amused us all by demonstrating what people would look like if BASI had taught them to walk. He then re-enacted something from Monty Python's 'Ministry of Silly Walks' sketch. By the end of the lecture he had at least one new disciple – me.

That first afternoon on the slopes I found myself simply trying to keep up, rather than follow Phil's suggested exercises. I was struggling to get my skis to work. It felt like I had two oil tankers attached to my feet, given the considerable effort and distance it was taking me to make them turn. I'd left my old faithful powder skis at home, thinking I'd hire more up-to-date 'planks' for the week. I'd hired the oil tankers from a shop opposite the hotel and had given little thought to their choosing.

Initially I put their unresponsiveness down to what I called 'Bambi Hour',[39] it being my first ski of the season, but unfortunately there didn't seem to be any other Bambis in the group. I soon became T. E. Charlie and, it being a position of diminishing returns, not one I'd escape for the rest of the day.

That evening, over another wine-less dinner, I rationalised my jumbled thoughts. The prospect of being T. E. Charlie for two weeks was a daunting one, but I concluded that most of the others skiers I'd effectively been competing with that day, had got some skiing in, immediately prior to the course, and I was just getting warmed up. I kicked myself - why had I not thought to arrive a few days in advance to get Bambi Hour over while nobody was watching.

Over the following days, having not been to boarding school, the lack of private space would take its toll. Everyone has a limit to the number of consecutive hours they can be pleasant and polite for, and my limit is about six. The weather was too appalling to leave the hotel for a solitary stroll unless you had snowshoes, which I didn't. The only private space available for thinking was the toilet!

Like most budget French hotels, the WC in my room was tiny, no larger than a phone box. Only a contortionist could

39 *I invented the term '**Bambi Hour**' to describe what happens the first time you try to ski after a long period of abstinence. Your legs seem uncontrollable and you ski like a beginner. Usually, after about an hour, your leg muscle-memory kicks in and you start skiing properly again.*

have taken care of business in it without bashing some part of his anatomy against a wall. A head injury was the most likely because the toilet itself was under the stairs restricting headroom in this vital area. Once on the throne, the pine door was no more than an inch from my nose. During the course, I would develop a strong bond with that door. Each morning, while staring at its knotted grains, I would give myself a pep talk; I just had to 'get through one day at a time,' I told myself, which is always easy advice to follow because that's how time works!

The course schedule was relentless and included lectures every evening before dinner. Most of the lectures were interesting enough to keep me awake. I knew we had a rest day on Saturday (day seven) and was mentally striking each day off in my head, if not actually scoring them on the toilet door. I thought that, if I could make it to day seven, I might be able to regroup.

On the second day my group headed up the mountain with Andy Jerram, another BASI trainer, a regular Club coach and all-round nice guy. He'd given us a lecture on ski technology the night before where, in order to break the ice, he'd declared that one of his hobbies was nudism! That morning Andy turned up fully clothed, which was sensible, given that it was 8°C below zero without the wind-chill factor. It soon became clear why the Club had used him for so many years to train its Leaders. He gave clear comprehensive instructions and helpful if somewhat quirky advice.

Like me, Andy is based in Morzine for most of the winter (small world). Coincidentally, he spends his summers in the Midlands too (the world gets smaller). During the course, I discovered he ran regular training sessions for instructors at the

Snow Dome (the world gets minute), which I now attend. More recently, he suggested that I imagine myself as a 'Page Three girl strangling two chickens' to improve my posture[40] – which turned out to be surprisingly helpful advice. Now, whenever I see someone ski past with a look of concentration on their face, I wonder what mental image they might be holding.

That second morning, compared to the previous one, went relatively well. The weather abated briefly so we could actually see where we were going and hear what Andy had to say. I deployed all my reserve energy in a concerted effort not to be T. E. Charlie again and succeeded in escaping the role for most of the day.

That evening one candidate turned up for dinner on crutches, she'd snapped her Anterior Cruciate Ligament (ACL) - a common skiing injury. I felt a little envious that she had a legitimate excuse to give up and go home. Maybe, I could break a leg tomorrow and it would all be over for me too? During dinner, I shared a table with a group of candidates who were especially interested in 'kit'. The endless discussions about skis, boots and bindings soon became boring. More interestingly, now that everyone had seen each other ski, rumours about the pass criteria were rife. Shaun, my roommate, who was back for his second attempt, had his final reassessment the next day and was living proof that it was possible to fail. After dinner, I sat and chatted to him in the bar, feeling empathy with a man drinking coke in his last-chance-saloon. I already suspected I would be facing a similar fate.

---

40 *Translation: 'keep your chest and bum sticking out (like a **Page Thee girl**), holding your poles out in front of you, gripping their handles like you would a chicken's neck'.*

By day three, my Tignes routine had developed: get up early and have a chat with the toilet door; go down for an underwhelming continental breakfast; humour a Leadership session; be T. E. Charlie for five hours; come back exhausted; listen to a lecture; have a wineless dinner and go to bed early. Then lie awake all night, replaying events of the summer, while listening to a policeman snore!

On day four I found myself heading up the now familiar Tichot chairlift, still the only one open, with Gareth Roberts, the surprisingly young chairman of BASI and an excellent ski coach. As I sat on the chair shivering, holding my gloved hand across my mouth to prevent my lips from getting frostbite, I wondered what on earth I was doing. Any sane mammal, except maybe a polar bear, would find the fastest way out of such an inhospitable environment. I was a mammal and my mammalian instincts were screaming at me that this was a bad idea – the ski demons were in agreement. We wouldn't be doing this if we didn't have to prove we could and, in Gareth's case I suspect, if he wasn't being paid. No Leader I knew would take members skiing in these conditions, I thought, even if they had any takers.

Once at the top, we left the small psychological comfort of the lift behind us and headed off-piste into the deepest powder I'd ever experienced - and feelings of panic welled up inside me. The Ski Demons were screaming in my head, 'You're going to embarrass yourself and then die.' I was an experienced off-piste skier, I'd survived some pretty gnarly descents in my time, Gareth was a professional who would not be taking skiers of unknown ability to him, down anything remotely unsafe. Yet I was terrified.

I pushed my pole in to measure the snow depth. The whole pole vanished. Terra firma was a long way below – the Ski Demons might have a point, I thought. If I fell over it would be an epic struggle to get back up. If a ski came off in the fall it would take hours of exhausting probing to find. One or maybe two wipe outs in these conditions would have me succumb to exhaustion or more likely a heart attack, given how the old ticker was already racing. I doubted I had the ability or the stamina to survive the descent.

In reality, it was only a short traverse over to the Stade de Slalom, a red run and, if visibility had been better, I would have seen that the safety of the car park was only 1600 metres away. But it felt like I was skiing into a white abyss never to return. Then, as I fell back a long way behind the others, Britain's most famous mountain guide, Nigel Sheppard, appeared next to me!

A veteran international mountain guide, 'Shep', is the Club's Alpine Safety Officer. He was also the Course Director putting him in overall charge of the two-week assessment and giving him the final say on most matters, including who passed and failed the course. Shep has written many books on climbing, mountaineering techniques, mountain safety and taken some fantastic photographs.

Unbeknown to me, Shep had been following my group. His presence reassured me, if you're going to get lost, this was the best man to get lost with. We caught up with the others who had finished the traverse and were waiting to drop into the Stade. Being T. E. Charlie, the group set off again, before I'd caught my breath. I followed but, try as I might, I couldn't make my oil tankers turn quickly in the deep snow. Each turn took a monumental effort. Shep noticed and commented that I didn't seem to be able to make more than three turns without stopping, which was true.

When I finally got to the bottom of the run, I was shattered. Everyone else looked pretty tired too which was consoling and as I started to celebrate being alive, Gareth announced that he intended to go back up and do it again - my heart sank. The following week, in better conditions, on better skis and in better mental shape, I went up and down the same run several times with relative ease, but that day the Ski Demons had won. Without thinking it through, I articulated my despair by blurting out the words 'I am spent, I'll be a liability to you if I go back up.' Shep pulled a rather stern face and suggested I returned to the hotel and that he would have a 'chat' with me when he got back.

That evening, when Shep summoned me, it was like being called into the headmaster's office. He asked if I'd done any fitness training prior to the course. I explained that I had (which was true) and that I didn't know what was causing me to underperform, other than a suspected chest infection (which wasn't), or possibly altitude sickness (which might have been). I made a wheezy cough to reinforce the point. He said he would allow me to continue if I didn't drop out of another session. He did have some good news though, for the next phase of the course we were being put in groups of similar ability, although 'Frankly,' he said, 'There's nobody skiing as slowly as you.'

After an evening of soul searching, I decided to quit the course and go back to the UK. But just as I'd resigned myself to failure I received a text message from David (my ski-father) asking how I was getting on. I just couldn't face telling him I'd quit so I decided to give it one more day. Then came the news that avalanches had blocked the road to Geneva, so I couldn't have left anyway.

The next morning I discovered Shep had allocated me to a group called the 'North Face'. All the groups had been given clothing brand names. I don't think they were actually sponsoring us and I'm not sure that North Face would have wanted to sponsor my group, given it was clearly the group for the slow coaches. It consisted of two female candidates, Belinda and Amanda, the latter was recovering from knee surgery, and my roommate PC Bill. He found it hard to disguise his dismay at being put in the same group as me because he'd realised that any group I was in would be the bottom one.

We were going out with Phil again and little did anyone know that the real assessment of our skiing ability was about to start. It transpired that the first week of the course (they had called it the 'Performance Clinic') was just for training purposes and no one had been paying much attention to our skiing until now. In fact, one of the main judges (Roland) had yet to arrive in Tignes.

The slower pace of the North Face group was a welcome relief although I still couldn't get my skiing mojo together and I was still T. E. Charlie most of the morning. Phil, with his supreme ability to analyse a skier's technique, noted my surprising inability to sideslip, an elementary skiing manoeuver.

The one thing I've always been good at is sideslipping. In my formative skiing years, thanks to blindly following David, I'd had a lot of practice mostly on icy blacks. My sideslip had got me out of many a tight situation in the past. I could, if required, sideslip down an entire run and, in the early days, I often did. So, something was badly wrong.

Phil looked at my skis, asked me where I'd hired them from and, on receiving the information, decided to try them for himself. We swapped skis and he couldn't sideslip in them either! 'No wonder you're exhausted' he declared, 'your skis are concave.'[41] Having recently attended Andy's 'I'm a nudist' lecture on ski performance, I knew what that meant - my skis had been poorly serviced.

Phil sent me off to hire some better skis from a different shop, which I did with delight. I'd finally found the reason why I was skiing so badly. I know a bad workman blames his tools but I was going to grab this excuse with both hands (or should that be both feet?) Why I'd thought it was a good idea to take the course on anything other than my own familiar planks, I don't know?

---

41 *If the machine used to* **service a ski** *is working incorrectly it leaves a depression down the centre of the ski, making it difficult to slide laterally. I'm now very careful about who I let service my skis.*

I took the skis back and hired a new set, elsewhere, as Phil suggested. I re-joined the group and started to ski reasonably well. As if to celebrate with me the sun made a brief appearance and, as the eye of the storm passed over Tignes, temperatures and visibility temporarily improved. I knew skiing could be an emotional rollercoaster. I often have really bad days on the mountain, only to find the next one magical. I'd almost resigned from the course the night before and now I was actually skiing well and (almost) having some fun!

We found ourselves ascending on the main lift out of the Le Lac, it was operating for the first time that week, a sure sign that conditions were improving. While the bubble car hauled itself up the wire, we surveyed the mountains around us through its windows, attentively listening to Phil's pearls of wisdom. He suddenly froze and stopped talking. Then, after a brief pause, he started repeating the words: 'Oh my God, Oh my God, Oh my God.' We followed his gaze.

On the slope below us, we could see a group of people frantically probing a massive field of avalanche debris. What seemed like half the mountain had fallen onto the black run beneath the bubble and, judging by the frantic activity, clearly someone had been buried in it. There was only one thing for us to do - we had to go and help.

19. GIRLFRIEND SKIING

I refer to it as 'Girlfriend Skiing', or GF skiing for short, but any romantic connection between the participants is optional. Those who sometimes ski with their less able partner, whatever their gender, will know what I mean. In my case, it usually does involve a female, be they a chalet guest, someone else's girlfriend, or indeed my own.

I first heard the term *girlfriend skiing* when buying ski boots in Snow & Rock. The ski dude serving me pointed out the switch on the back of a pair of boots. 'In walk mode,' he explained, 'the boot allows some ankle movement to aid walking.' He continued, 'For comfort, I leave my boots in walk mode when I'm *girlfriend skiing*, then put them in ski mode when going-large with my mates down the park.' Now, I only ever enter a snow park through navigational error and if anything ever *'goes large'* on me, it's usually involuntary, but I knew exactly what he meant.

GF skiing means setting off for the day knowing that the deepest powder you're likely to meet will be the chocolate on top of a cappuccino and the steepest encounter you'll have to deal with will be the lunch bill. It involves a late start, usually due to some excessive ski-faffing, cruising some blues, a midmorning drink and loo stop (usually not synchronised), a two-hour lunch, then a gentle ski back to the resort for an early après session.

If you've signed up for a full week of GF skiing because you're recently in love, it may even involve not skiing and taking a day off mid-holiday to rest, especially if something unpleasant is happening outside that day, like it's snowing for instance.

When GF skiing it's important to accept, from the beginning of the day, that all Ski Nazi tendencies must be subdued. You must wake up and say 'Today I'm girlfriend skiing' and flick your boots into walk mode and accept your pleasant fate. Make sure you take an extra layer to wear because there will be a lot of standing around getting cold whilst waiting for the snowplough queen to descend. When you get up the mountain (eventually), you mustn't get tempted by any untracked field of powder you might spot or juicy-looking black runs, otherwise you'll turn girlfriend skiing into 'Wife Skiing' and you really don't want to do that.

Wife Skiing happens when a husband persuades his nervous wife to ski with him under the false pretence that his ambitions for the day are modest. Invariably he ends up shouting at her when she goes-ostrich at the top of a difficult run. Secretly, he's a Ski Nazi and wants to do the polar opposite of GF skiing during his precious week on the slopes. Wife skiing can often lead to divorce - although on-piste domestics are usually just small apertures into a deeper crevasse of marital disharmony that opens on family skiing holidays.

I know I'm a fine one to be giving matrimonial advice, but it is very important that husbands *never* attempt to teach their wives to ski. The same rule applies to driving, sailing and cooking by the way. So, if your spouse isn't that keen on skiing, it's best to take her girlfriend skiing for a week somewhere quaint and then book a boys' trip to somewhere hardcore like Chamonix or St Anton, to work out your frustrations.

I often go GF skiing with other people's wives and girlfriends. It's sort of an ancillary service I provide. The blokes go 'lad skiing' and I take their more fragrant halves for a potter round the mountains and a nice lunch. Hard work, I know, but someone's got to do it. Frankly I'd rather ski with the girls than the boys, especially if they're attractive (the girlfriends that is). I get plenty of 'proper' skiing with the Club, so it's nice to have a day off to enjoy the scenery before, after and during my lunch.

Before you think me a complete letch, I must explain that I often go GF skiing with men too - along with the unfit, the infirm and, if really pushed, with children. I'll basically GF ski with anyone who needs me, or just needs someone, to look after them on the mountain. The goal is to take all the anxiety and hassle away from them. I even offer to carry the girlfriend's skis to the lift - although that can be a mistake if they have strong feminist views.

I don't regard GF skiing as a waste of skiing time but look upon it as research. I use GF skiing to study the psychology of people's skiing demons. I'm fascinated by the situations that cause people to freak on the mountain and their rationale for being afraid. I'm generally interested in all phobias, not just skiing ones, having had so many of my own. Or course, I think my fears are more rational than other people's. When off-piste it's possible to wander into situations where dying is a potential outcome, so I think my fears are rational.

Many girlfriends seem to be equally scared despite never leaving the piste where death is significantly harder to achieve. For some of them everything is too narrow, too busy, too icy or too bumpy and, generally, everything is always too steep. The most common underlying problem is a fear of speed and of being out of control. They lack the most important of skiing attributes – confidence.

I try to convince them that 'speed is their friend' - a hard proposition to sell to someone who's frightened, but it's a mantra I encourage them to use. If they were to go faster, turning their skis would be easier and they would have more control, with the added bonus of getting to the restaurant faster.

Morbid fear of T-bars, schusses and long traverses are common, especially amongst snowboarders. They all stem from traumatic events that happened while they were learning to ski (or board). We all carry emotional scars of our early experiences in life and skiing is no different. I always try and empathise with nervous girlfriends by telling them about the raft of phobias I developed while learning.

I hated cramped cable cars because they played on both my claustrophobia and agoraphobia at the same time. Even now, I still have to focus when aboard them to prevent panic setting in. I'm not too keen on going *down* in chairlifts either.[42]

The Ski Demons know my phobias and, if I let them, they can use them to great effect. I try to drown their voices out by babbling on to my fellow passengers about something irrelevant, even if they aren't interested. Hopefully it distracts them from listening to their skiing demons too.

GF skiing has allowed me to discover many new phobias, some that even the sufferer hadn't discovered until they went skiing with me. I always consider it an honour to be present at the birth of a new phobia.

Before taking anyone GF skiing, it's imperative to establish that you are indeed a significantly better skier than they are – no bloke wants to be out-skied by their girlfriend. If this basic pre-ski check is done, GF skiing can be very good for your ego. There is however an art to showing off without looking like a show-off. Nonchalantly dropping off the side of a run to do a little powder, going over a tiny jump or skiing backwards while conducting a conversation are all good, if done in moderation. Don't be too ambitious, a little showboating is fine but you don't want to blow it by falling over. If you do, examine your bindings closely and intimate that you must have had an 'equipment failure'.

---

42 ***Descending*** *in a chair means facing outwards, looking at a huge drop with only a single thin bar in front of you; going up is fine because you're looking at a rock face or other terrain, which is usually only a few metres in front of you.*

March is the best time to go GF skiing because the weather is usually sunny and lunch can be taken alfresco. The off-piste snow conditions are generally poor in March, so you're not missing out. Morzine in March turns into Cougar town, as you know, so there are lots of potential girlfriends about. Of course, if there is an unexpected dump of snow all bets are off. Remember, committed off-piste skiers don't have friends, never mind girlfriends, on a powder day.

It's important not to overindulge in GF skiing no matter how much you're in love. Too much GF skiing can be counterproductive for two reasons. Firstly, your ski time will become unvalued and your sacrifice unappreciated. Secondly, if you spend too much time cruising blues and eating in restaurants, you'll go soft and get fat, then your girlfriend will probably leave you.

That having been said, I find it important to go GF skiing at least once a week. It reminds me that some people regard 'going skiing' as a holiday and a holiday should be pleasant, relaxing and fun – something a lot of Ski Nazis forget.

20. The Avalanche

I can't imagine a worse way to die than by being buried alive under the snow. Statistically you are likely to live if you are dug out within fifteen minutes.[43] But those fifteen minutes must seem like an eternity spent wondering if the avalanche left anyone on the surface and, more importantly, someone with the wherewithal to effect a rescue. Have they got the right equipment, the right knowledge, a calm head and indeed the fitness to dig you out? You just have to lie in your dark silent tomb and hope they have.

If the unthinkable happens and you find yourself in a powder avalanche, you should do the following. First, try to ski away to the side. Sounds a bit obvious I know, but it needed saying. Once you're no longer 'skiing' but falling (you'll have to decide when that is) throw away your poles (this is why off-piste skiers don't use wrist straps) then pull your goggles over your nose and mouth. This will stop the snow going into your airways and makes a breathing space when you come to rest. Next, start swimming - breaststroke is recommended. Obviously, if you're wearing an airbag, now is the time reap the reward of your investment, so pull the cord and pray you connected the gas bottle correctly. Once entombed, pee yourself so the rescue dogs can find you more easily!

If it ever happened to me, I only hope I have the presence of mind to follow my own advice, although the last part will probably come naturally.

It may seem flippant, but the best way not to die in an avalanche is not to get caught in one. Ever since I first ventured off-piste, I've worried about avalanches and tried to learn how to reduce

---

43 *Statistics tell us that if an avalanche victim is rescued within **fifteen minutes** they have a 92% chance of making a full recovery then the odds reduce rapidly. After thirty minutes it reduces to 30%.*

the risk of being caught in one. One of my reasons for going on the Leaders' Course was to learn more of the 'mountain craft' needed to keep me, and those who follow me, safe. I'd seen the aftermath of many avalanches but never witnessed one, let alone one where someone got buried - until that day in Tignes.

That day, having seen the carnage below, we all jumped off the bubble and followed Phil down to the top of the black run. We passed a *'piste fermé'* (piste closed) sign, which spoke volumes. It meant the pisteurs had spotted a safety risk on the run and wanted to prevent people using it – but clearly the sign had been ignored.

It looked like a difficult ski down; the run was unrecognisable as a piste. I'd only just got my skiing mojo back and I was still shattered from the previous day's exploits. I knew it would be a tough ski, but you can't say you're tired when someone else's life is potentially at stake.

We soon reached the edge of the melee, took off our skis and lined up with those already probing the snow. The snow was so deep my avalanche probe, two metres in length, wasn't long enough to reach the earth. [44] Every time we moved down the slope, we lost our legs up to our thighs – it was extremely hard work. I was worried, with each step we took down the slope, that I wouldn't have enough aerobic reserves to climb back up to my skis. I noticed the weight of snow still on the mountain above us and the chance of a secondary avalanche unduly worried me. More people joined the search and the pisteurs, who had seen the slide from their hut above the run, organised the now-dozens of volunteer rescuers.

---

44   *A **probe** is a light collapsible rod that is used to find bodies under the snow. There's a small chance you might poke the victim's eye out, but frankly, that's the least of their worries.*

Shouting orders in French, they moved us up and down in ranks. The scene started to resemble a Napoleonic battlefield, along with its associated chaos. If there was a General in overall charge, he was not evident.

The number of people buried beneath the snow and their location seemed to be uncertain in the ranks. It turned out that there were three in the party, but only two had been buried. Usually, when someone gets left on the surface, the chances of finding those buried are high, especially if everyone is wearing transceivers.[45] But our search patterns seemed to be wide and prolonged, suggesting that no locating technology was being deployed. One victim was found and dug out unconscious, but he soon came round and was clearly distraught. A first-aider tried to get information out of him about the number and location of his buried companions.

After about forty minutes, there was a commotion further down the slope and a second victim, a girl in her twenties, was found. She was stretchered off the slope by skidoo, while CPR was being applied. (She made it to hospital but tragically didn't survive). The search dogs turned up and they couldn't find anyone else. The dogs are always the last hope in these situations and we knew not to eat, drink, smoke or pee in case we confused them. Two hours had passed and I was desperate to do all four of them despite giving up smoking many years ago. The search was finally called off presumably because, if anyone else was still buried, they were sure to be dead.

Now, I faced the climb back up to our skis. Scrambling on all fours proved the best technique and twenty aerobics minutes later, I was back where I thought I had parted company with them. But I couldn't decide, amongst the dozens of abandoned skis which were mine. I'd only hired them three hours before and couldn't remember

---

45   *A **transceiver** emits a radio beacon that other transceivers, when switched into search mode, can use to locate it and hopefully (if transceiver and skier haven't been separated) its wearer under the snow.*

what they looked like. Embarrassingly, Phil had to identify them for me. He informed us that skiing down from our location wasn't an option because the piste was officially closed. We had to climb up to the blue run a further 500 metres above us.

Slowly, I continued my crawled up the mountain, now burdened with my skis and poles. Fortunately, the foot-holes made by the repeated footsteps of others started to form a staircase in front of me so I reverted to being a biped. Another candidate on the course, a fit young man called Richard, got trapped behind me on the staircase and was clearly getting impatient with my slow progress. I was only 100 metres away from the piste above when I ground to a complete halt. 'I was going to need a skidoo to rescue me,' I exhaled - only partly joking. He picked my skis up and carried them the rest of the way for me, for which I will be eternally grateful. (He had obviously done a lot of GF skiing in his time).

Everyone in the North Face group was waiting at the top for me, not showing any signs of fatigue, ready to get on with the skiing lesson. I felt like I'd just been in my own version of *Touching the Void* having, against all odds, cheated death and climbed out of an icy tomb. 'Someone just died, I almost expired too. I'm going back to the hotel' – I spluttered while hyperventilating.

This was my second unfortunate outburst on the Leaders' course. Saying what you think, regardless of the consequences, is an inherent problem with being a Yorkshireman. Phil pointed out that if I left the group for the hotel, I would fail the course. I insisted that I was suffering from a serious, if self-diagnosed, physiological condition - blood clot, collapsed lung or, at the very least, altitude sickness - and I needed to get off the mountain as quickly as possible. He suggested I had some lunch with them first, before quitting. I agreed and followed him to a restaurant a short way down the blue run, skiing like Bambi again despite my new skis.

Lunch always changes my attitude to skiing, usually because I always have wine with it. No wine this time of course, just another argument with the Ski Demons. What would the toilet door be telling me to do now? I thought. Thankfully, Phil persuaded me to ascend the mountain again. Had he not, I might never have gone skiing again.

He took us down an easy red and I regained some confidence. We bumped into Shep, who noted that I was still with the group. He was clearly surprised to see me. No doubt he'd expected me to quit before the day was out and he was almost right. Better still, Phil told him how the appalling skis I'd hired must have affected my earlier performances that week, and how the Club should blacklist the offending hire shop.

Over a particularly sober dinner that night, those who had been on the scene discussed the avalanche. Poignantly, the lecture that evening had been on how to spot avalanche risks. We all knew we took a risk every time we went off-piste, even before the lectures, and to a greater or lesser extent, we all knew how to minimise it. However, we all now knew the fundamental safety rules the victims that day had broken.

The number one rule is: never go off-piste without a transceiver, a shovel and probe. Number two: know how to use them. Number three: ski with other people who abide by rules one and two. I particularly dislike people that wear a transceiver but don't carry a shovel. It's like them saying, 'I want you to be able to rescue me, but I'm not prepared, literally, to rescue you.' (You can tell those not equipped correctly because they don't have a rucksack on.)

Shockingly the victims that day had been led by professionals, yet had ignored rule one.[46] Their next big mistake was skiing down a closed piste. Theoretically, it's more dangerous to ski on a closed

---

46 The **professionals** involved were prosecuted and given a one year suspended jail sentence and a one year ban.

piste than off-piste. Most of the off-piste will be benign, but a closed run has been identified, by pisteurs, to have a clear safety risk - and they are the experts with local knowledge. You didn't need to be an expert to see the risk either - the slope above the run had 'avalanche' written all over it and the yellow and black, chequered flags (indicating a risks level of 3 or 4) had been flying on the pisteur station above.

Their final, and biggest mistake was being unlucky! Our lives are at risk every time we step outside the front door; life is an inherently risky business. But we can develop strategies for minimising the effects of bad luck: not skiing where a mountain of snow is likely to fall on your head for instance; not skiing in a terrain-trap with no escape route if it does. Not carrying the correct rescue equipment was a particularly poor strategy. They'd been in the wrong place at the wrong time but, more importantly, their strategy for dealing with bad luck had been flawed.

Skiing is an exhilarating but inherently risky business and indeed the exhilaration is enhanced by the risk. The amount of risk we take when skiing off-piste is a function of how poorly our strategy will perform if bad luck occurs. When skiing we all take calculated risks and hope to be lucky!

I collapsed into bed that night, seriously thinking about never going off-piste again. My roommate brought news that the official avalanche risk had been increased to five, effectively closing the resort, no doubt for political reasons. So nobody would be going up the mountain, let alone off-piste in the morning - which was a comforting thought – but I still didn't sleep.

The day after the avalanche, the North Face 'team' had transceiver training scheduled in the children's play area in front of the hotel. We were unlikely to get into too much trouble in a playground, I thought, even though there was two feet of snow on the swings. The avalanche risk had been reduced down to four, but nobody was going up the mountain because all the lifts had been closed due to high winds, even the Tichot.

Kathy was our trainer for the day, a northern lass who had become a Chamonix guide, no mean feat for a foreigner, never mind a woman in a world dominated by French men. Needless to say she appeared to be, and no doubt was, tough as nails. She set about hiding various combinations of transceivers in the playground, which were surprisingly difficult to find. There's a knack to using these devices and I wouldn't want to be finding that out with someone's life at stake. Despite the playground being knee deep in snow, the morning wasn't too demanding.

We had some lunch. Then, disappointingly, the pisteurs managed to get our old friend the Tichot chairlift open so up we went again. Mercifully, we turned left onto the blue run at the top. Kathy started laughing and pointed to an ESF instructor, just off to the side of the piste. He was frantically digging in the deep snow, presumably looking for a lost ski. We all smirked and I felt a little schadenfreude, but it was reassuring to know that even the ESF were struggling in these conditions. Piste etiquette suggested we should go and help him. But Kathy pointed out that he might die of humiliation if forced to accepted help from the Ski Club of Great Britain. The kinder thing was to leave him to his own fate – so we skied past him sniggering.

Further down the run, Kathy suddenly stopped and headed off-piste. My stomach sank at the thought of following her into the whiteout. Everyone hesitated on the edge of the piste. It seemed I wasn't the only one reluctant to enter the white abyss that had just swallowed an ESF instructor. She shouted above the howling wind and gesticulated in an irritated fashion to follow her in. Thankfully, she only went 50 metres from the piste and stopped to give us instructions. We were to return to the piste, ski down to the lift and find our way back to our current location. Then we had to: 'deal with whatever we found on our return' – which was rather intriguing. Only through serendipity did we find our way back. We spotted the ESF instructor, still digging, and followed our tracks from there. We found someone, who certainly looked like Kathy but was behaving very oddly, waving her arms and shouting.

Kathy had obviously been to drama school because she was impersonating a panicking skier, who'd just lost four mates under the snow, very convincingly. The reality of the situation was that she'd buried four transceivers and we had to find them within the critical fifteen minutes. Focused on the task, I stopped listening to the Ski Demons and set about running through the drills we had learnt in the playground. Amazingly, we found all four transceivers in time and without the aerobic exhaustion I was expecting.

That evening everyone seemed to be in good humour. The following day was the long-awaited day off and after dinner we all went out to a local bar. With seldom-seen willpower, I bailed the party at midnight. Bill staggered in at 4am, accidentally turning on all the lights and, like all drunks, made more noise the harder he tried to be quiet. But I wasn't asleep anyway. I was mentally reliving the events of the previous weeks.

I'd had a lot of bad luck: suffering a major abduction prior to departure, encountering difficult conditions, hiring duff skis and witnessing an avalanche death. My strategy for dealing with bad luck - not arriving early to practice and acclimatise, not bringing my own skis and not being fit enough - had proven to be an almost disastrous one.

Despite the bad luck, the poor strategy and the best efforts of the Ski Demons I'd made it through the first week without quitting or indeed dying. More importantly, I still had an outside chance of passing the course.

21. Lad Skiing

By the beginning of Season 4 I'd learnt to expect the unexpected when waking up, but one very memorable January morning I woke to a very strong equine smell. I had mates from home staying in the chalet that week, and the night before had been large, but what on earth had I been eating?

I heard movement and realised I wasn't alone. Had Shiv unexpectedly joined me in the garage? If so, she needed to change her perfume. I opened my eyes to find a horse staring down at me and looking equally perplexed. I resisted the temptation to ask him 'Why the long face?' and leapt to my feet. Thankfully, I was still fully dressed. I shooed my new friend out and closed the garage door behind him.

It was one of the feral ponies that sometimes wander round Morzine at night. They are particularly attracted to the chalet's bins, which they knock over to forage through the disgorged contents. I must have inadvertently left the garage door open and the opportunist nag had sauntered in. But who had left the stale baguettes he was eating on my bed and, if the door had been open all night, why had I not frozen to death? I started to smell something else - a rat.

At breakfast, there was a lot of sniggering, but nobody cracked under my interrogation. My mates admitted they'd tried to hitch a pony-ride home the previous night but said they'd failed to catch one - a mercy for everyone concerned, including the horses. I have yet to identify the culprit and I now make sure that nobody but me has access to the zapper that opens and closes the garage door.

Around thirty Brits die in the Alps every year through 'misadventure'. Surprisingly, avalanches account for only a few of these deaths and even fewer meet their maker at the bottom of cliffs and crevasses. Quite a few ski into immovable objects, usually trees or rocks and often into each other. However, the majority die in what are called 'alcohol related incidents', usually by freezing to death. Most are male and on holiday with mates, and they are usually protagonists of new-laddism.

Officially, new-laddism is a reaction to the postmodern transformation of masculinity that was the 'new man'. Battered by feminism, middle-class men returned to masculine activities associated with the working classes such as drinking, watching sport, being interested in anything with engines and the seeking of casual sex. Actually most men have always liked going out on the lash and reverting to the behaviour of their youth – in the absence of women, men have always behaved badly.

Their womenfolk allow them to go on a 'boys trip', because, *quid pro quo*, they will have equal liberty to behave badly on their annual 'girls trip', another modern phenomenon. Ironically, on both types of trip, a lot of time is spent seeking the company of the other sex despite the stated purpose of the trip being to hang out with same-sex friends or take part in a sport such as golf or skiing. For many, this is clearly just a cover story.

As a chalet host, I prefer not to accommodate all-male groups and I refuse to take stag parties unless the groom is over forty. The chalet is a little upmarket for most groups of young men, so it's not too much of a problem. I prefer to have at least a couple of woman in the chalet at any one time. This is not because female guests are usually better house-trained (which they are) or because I prefer to socialise with women (which I do) but because it keeps the men civilised.

Also, if the all-male group are friends from home, I can easily forget I'm not on holiday myself, and join in with the laddish behaviour. I forget that, after their few mad days of hedonism, they can go back to work and 'rest' while my 'work' is on going.

The most wearing thing about being in the sole company of men is that everything - skiing, drinking, eating, and general grandstanding is turned into a competition. Then there is the battle to determine who is the alpha male. This primeval urge is strange considering there are so few females to compete for, but all herds need a dominant bull – especially when entering an après bar. Then the competition will switch to who can make the crudest remarks – usually about any 'fit' woman they have 'clocked' in the bars. The really funny thing is, if the target of their lewd remarks came over and offered them a night of passion, they'd probably run a mile, as most cougars will testify.

Then there's occasionally someone, usually the best man if it's an actual stag party, who feels that the general debauched behaviour isn't really cutting it and that an illegal act is needed to make the trip truly memorable. He usually wants to steal the kid's train or ride on the roof of the Land Rover. They obviously think that the golden rule 'What goes on tour, stays on tour' is a French statute. Hemingway observed that, 'Everyone behaves badly, given the chance.' Hence actual stag parties are *personae non gratae* at Chalet Neige.

For groups of younger, single men other rules can also apply. It's common for lads to agree that if your roommate pulls, you must offer to sleep on the settee or, if anyone is lucky enough to have a single room, they must swap with the Casanova. I always admire their optimism because in 'Manzine' these rules seldom get applied.

On lad's ski trips, fancy dress is often mandated and some remain in their costumes for the full duration of the trip. The

Dutch, in particular, like dressing up. It's not unusual to see groups of nuns or penguins skiing past you on the mountain in January. Once, I saw the entire cast of HMS Pinafore queuing for the Super Morzine lift!

One stag party that slipped under my radar booked the chalet for a long weekend. They turned up dressed as the Blues Brothers - all except the groom, who was dressed as a French maid. This perplexed me because in the film, a favourite of mine, there are no French maids. I concluded he was wearing the outfit through choice. Seems he knew more than I did about pulling French girls, a scarcity in Morzine at any time of year, judging by the accents floating around the chalet that night.

Strangely enough, lad skiing is not exclusively the preserve of men. Groups of women, usually cougars, can be more laddish than the lads. 'Ladette Skiing', as I call it, is common in Morzine and a wonder to behold. One night, while après-skiing with my favourite group of Liverpudlian girls, we ran into an equally-sized force of Geordie lads in the Dixie Bar. It soon became reminiscent of a scene from Aliens vs. Predators as they fought to see who could be more laddish and drink the most toffee-vodka.

Needless to say, the Geordies ended up back at the chalet and I retreated to the garage, where I often weather out such storms, expecting to find a trashed chalet in the morning. However, when I surfaced there was surprisingly little damage, considering the ruckus I'd listened to all night. There was just one Geordie left, still drunk, staggering around. I showed him the front door and he left to do his 'walk of shame'.

The behavioural standard on a boys' trip is set by the lowest common denominator, often the most immature member of the group, which doesn't always mean the youngest either. Usually he's a rugby playing, ex-public schoolboy, who's still a bachelor for reasons that soon become obvious. He will take on the important job of being the 'Master of Drinking Ceremonies' (MDC) and organise and enforce the rules of the ubiquitous drinking games. He will also be the 'Leader of Singing' and enforcer of other associated tribal rituals.

Drinking games baffle me, not just their rules – which is apparent if you've ever seen me play – but their *raison d'etre*. I don't need any help getting drunk and I especially don't need the process accelerated. I'll get there soon enough at my own pace thanks. The games usually go along similar lines: if you're caught drinking with the wrong hand or you're last to put your thumb on the table, or some other such nonsense, you have to down your drink in one. Those more interested in conversation than the drinking game, but don't want to be a 'spoilsport', get caught most frequently. Their ability to play the game diminishes with each drinking penalty, until they can't be distracted by conversation because they're no longer capable of having one.

Amongst the self-appointed duties of the MDC is that of 'Custodian of the Kitty'. This customary pooling of cash is intended to prevent the heinous crime of round dodging. Joining a kitty might seem like a financially sensible idea and it's seldom optional due to peer pressure, but participants can soon find it a burdensome financial commitment as the MDC's calls for 'cash for the kitty' become ever more frequent. Unless you are the lead alcoholic, the kitty never represents good value either. The kitty never misses a round and never goes to bed early; the kitty stays out all night and comes home empty. Having a kitty also puts the MDC in charge of everyone's alcohol consumption, a dangerous thing because he's usually a 'Stoker'.

By 'Stoker', I'm not referring to people from Stoke on Trent, but to those who enjoy pushing alcohol on others. They like to fan the embers of a quiet drink with shots and unwanted cocktails until it turns into a full-on binge drinking session. Stokers are very dangerous people to be around. I know this because I seem to have collected rather a lot of them as friends. Stokers can simply be borderline or 'functioning' alcoholics, as I believe we call them now. They like to make sure everyone is drunker than they are so they don't stand out. But some Stokers have more sinister objectives: to loosen tongues or to get someone into bed. Some are control freaks that like being sober when everyone else is drunk.

Stokers often claim that 'eating is cheating' or 'just one more before we head to the restaurant'. Soon the drinking becomes asynchronous; those with empty glasses think they might as well have another while they wait for the slow coaches to 'sup-up'. The slow coaches, in their turn, think the same thing fifteen minutes later and get another pint. The process starts to repeat itself and the alcoholic firestorm takes light. Nobody makes it to the restaurant and the Stoker's work is done.

Being an après-guide for a boy's trip is a particularly burdensome task - anyone who has tried to herd eight full-grown drunks into the back of a Land Rover will confirm this. When I load lads into Landie, I always put the drunkest one in the front seat, next to me, where I can keep an eye on him. I look for the 'Trombonist'. If I see the repeated inflating of his cheeks, the placing of a hand over his mouth, or him using an extended arm to brace himself against the dashboard, I know chunks are about to fly. If I see the Trombonist, it's time to stop, lest I have to hose out Landie in the morning – *again*.

One weekend in January, I had a group of well-spoken, polite, and seemingly intelligent young men staying with me. Their leader had assured me, before I let them book, that 'None of them had any imminent intention of entering into matrimonial deadlock.' On their first night inevitably two of then got abducted. Despite scouring every bar in Morzine, I couldn't find them anywhere. I eventually marked them down in the register as 'Missing in Action' and went to bed.

It turned out that neither of them had taken their phone, or knew the name, or indeed the location of the chalet. To avoid freezing to death, they'd broken into a 'similar chalet', as they later described it, spent the night there and left without disturbing the inhabitants. I got a call from Michel at the ski-hire shop early the next morning. '*Chreez, av vous lost some boyz?*' he enquired. Finally, exhibiting some intelligent behaviour, they'd recognised the shop, waited until it opened then asked Michel to call me – they had at least remembered my name. I will always remember *their* names should either of them ever be foolish enough to enter politics.

The following night, when I was emptying the same lads out of the back of Landie, I found they'd kidnapped a rather drunken nanny. She insisted that she was a willing victim and spent the evening in my sauna. All night, a stream of male bodies entered and left the sauna. In the morning, not sure whether her face was red from embarrassment or from 'sleeping' in a sauna, I asked her where she worked and offered her a lift. For some reason she refused to tell me or, subsequently, to say 'Hello' whenever our paths crossed for the rest of the season!

I host an annual 'business trip' for a group of middle-aged men, mostly from Birmingham. Valued clients, despite falling into the 'older and should know better' category, they still serve at the altar of new-laddism. In their case it should really be called old-laddism. Old-laddism is like new-laddism only done with more money. One night, when the Buddha chucked them out, they decided, despite it being 2am, that they hadn't had enough to drink and so they went to The Opera. On being refused entry to the nightclub, their Stoker decided to grab the bouncer by the balls by way of persuasion - which got a rather predictable reaction. They called me for a 'rapid evac' from the ensuing melee. After a swift embarkation, I sped away from the scene in Landie with the irate Frenchman screaming behind me '*Fucking Englaise, you have no respect*' - which sadly just about sums up the modern Englishman abroad.

Perhaps my favourite regular boys' trip (you guessed it) is from Liverpool. Most of them played rugby together although some have retired from the sport. To a man, they are all gifted comedians who should probably have their own stand-up shows. One exhibitionist decided to do his exercise routine on the balcony naked, which made for an interesting backdrop to Debbie, who was sat in front of the balcony window oblivious to the scene behind her. Given the effect arctic conditions have on the male anatomy and that anatomy being on full view, he was the centre of many a resulting joke, but I suspect that's why he did it.

Organiser of the trips, and headline act, is Westy a married man with six kids, his wife (Ali) is a regular at the chalet too. Her girls' trip is often the week before his boys' trip; they literally swap beds, taking it in turns to run 'the orphanage' as he calls their home, back in Liverpool and get drunk in Morzine – it's a very modern marriage. Entertainingly, they both get up to the same sort of behaviour on their respective tours - it's like watching a tag team. Neither gets up to anything they couldn't tell each other, but despite being regularly quizzed, I keep the chalet host's vow of silence – 'What goes on tour …'

Once, when Ali was asked if she wanted sex by an over optimistic young lad, she replied in an outraged and heavy Liverpool accent, 'I'm married with six kids - I've come on holiday to get away from all that!'

Unlike laddettes, lads are more likely to go skiing in the morning, albeit more through bravado than actual enthusiasm. There's a lot less ski-faffing and general time wasting because lads are more interested in rehydration than ablution in the morning. No matter what their gender, there's always some good banter over breakfast, while they chronologically reassemble the events of the previous evening - each protagonist contributing different pieces to the communal jigsaw.

Unlike laddettes, where GF skiing is usually the order of the day, leading a group of lads can be very hazardous, not least because many are still drunk. Despite the best efforts of the alpine air their hangovers won't show up until lunchtime when they'll have the ultimate cure in their hands – another beer. So you'll spend most of your time skiing with the inebriated.

Sober or not, groups of blokes are particularly difficult to keep together once they hit the piste. They say no battle plan survives first contact with the enemy. Well, no skiing plan you make for lads survives first contact with the snow and I'll have lost half my troops by midmorning. I equip many of them with walkie-talkies so at least they can rendezvous for lunch. After lunch and the hair of the dog, everyone's feeling much better and T. E. Charlie gets goaded into steeper and more difficult runs, increasing their chance of death by misadventure.

I'm always surprised that more of the older 'boys' don't have heart attacks. I'm no athlete myself, but when I see fat middle-aged smokers with beads of alcoholic sweat running down their foreheads, gasping for breath, I wonder if something in their chest is about to give. Skiing is the most or only physical exercise some of them get all year. You wouldn't run a marathon without training. You wouldn't go out and have ten pints and a curry the night before either. But that's what most of them are effectively doing on their annual boys' trip.

There's always at least one kamikaze skier amongst their ranks. These suicide skiers have little regard for their own survival. Many seem to be on a mission to prove they can ski faster than me. Many can - but few can stop or turn as fast. As I explained to one kamikaze skier while extracting him from a safety net: it's quite hard to lead people from behind - although much safer for me.

I had one relatively novice skier whom nobody could keep up with, not even me. He took the fall line straight down every run. He was soon nicknamed 'The Crow' because he skied as the bird flies, in a straight line. It turned out he trained as a fighter pilot - which explained a lot, but didn't make him any less dangerous to himself or those unlucky enough to be in his flight path.

Giving verbal directions to blokes is often pointless. Most will instantly forget them. Many get tunnel vision and ski straight past you as you wait for them at an important intersection, ruining any route plans you had for the day. I've taken to wearing a bright yellow jacket with lime green trousers, a unique colour combination that's hard to miss even by the myopic.

Mercifully, thanks to the Chalet Project, I no longer go on boys' trips - they now come to me. I've discovered that, if I play it right, and stick to my Après Guidelines, it can be more fun being an observer than a participant; I'm not bound by the rules of the MDC and there's no pressure from the Stoker. Most importantly, I don't have to contribute to the kitty or dress as a nun - unless I want to.

I'm getting too old for new-laddism and I'm not so keen on old-laddism either. There's something tragic about old blokes rolling around a bar drunk, trying to relive or, worse, tell everyone about their youth. More importantly, I don't mind dying in the Alps through misadventure, I just don't want the coroner's report to say it was in an alcohol related incident - my mother would kill me.

22. The Leaders' Course — Week Two

Once again I found myself in what looked like a scene from *Scott of the Antarctic*. Huddled in a snow trench (2 metres deep) with six other intrepid explorers, a full-on Antarctic storm raging around us. But nobody was going to shout, 'Cut', turn off the wind machine and hand us a cup of tea and a Kit-Kat. This trench was real and located at the top of a mountain, some 3,000 metres above sea level.

I was listening to a talk on snowpack stability, in what was possibly the coldest lecture theatre on earth. I could just about hear the lecturer, a guide called Graham, if I stooped below the surface of the trench. He was pointing out the different layers of snow and taking temperatures at different levels. It was all very interesting stuff. Then he suddenly stopped talking, as if for dramatic effect, and pointed at me. 'That nose looks waxy,' he said!

Being of Jewish decent, my nose has come in for much ridicule, but 'waxy' was a new one to me. 'That's the first sign of frostbite,' he triumphantly declared. 'Time to head back,' he announced. Thank fuck for that, I thought. I'd wanted to ask some questions, primarily 'Why he'd not dug the trench closer to the hotel?' But, for once, I supressed my Yorkshire instinct to speak my mind knowing a question and answer session would prolong the expedition. But, thanks to my nose, the lecture was over and we started the return journey. I wasn't in the Antarctic but still in Tignes, on the second week of the Ski Club of Great Britain Leaders' Course.

Week one had been emotional but my second consecutive week in Tignes had started with cause to celebrate. I was still alive, still on the course and, more surprisingly, still had a slim chance of passing it. I thought I knew what it meant to be down and out in the Cube that summer, but during that first week of winter my despair had plunged to even greater depths – skiing, the thing I loved, had also become a nightmare for me. At least now the end was in sight.

We'd left our skis on the side of the piste only some 500 metres away and had blindly followed Graham on foot to the trench. We'd climbed up a gap, through a cornice and had crossed a col the wind had stripped back to bare rock.[47] The visibility had seriously deteriorated since we had found the trench and now it was hard to tell up from down, never mind in which direction our skis lay. The footprints we'd made on the way in had vanished; they'd been filled in by the blizzard.

Leaning into the wind at forty-five degrees, to stop ourselves falling over, we followed Graham. Having only met him a few days before, it seemed we now had to put our lives in the hands of this stranger, hoping his reputation was well deserved. But he was taking the biggest risk by going first.

He told us to follow in his exact footprints. His instructions were barely audible above the howling gale but were totally unnecessary anyway; none of us were going to be stepping anywhere that hadn't already been proven solid. He suddenly froze in his tracks and made hand gestures for us to stop; he'd found the cornice. He probed along it with his pole and, after a few minutes, his body language changed from tentative to confident – he'd obviously found a solid way down.

---

47   *A **cornice** is an overhanging ledge of snow, formed when snow is blown over terrain breaks such as a ridge or cliff. If approached from above it can be very difficult to tell where solid ground ends and the flimsy balcony of snow begins. A **col** is a saddle-shaped indent that forms the lowest point between two mountain peaks.*

Our passage no longer hindered by uncertainty we slowly progressed back to our skis, but even going downhill I was finding it hard to breathe at such altitude. I could hear the clanking of a draglift above the noise of the wind, which helped to remind me that we were only metres away from safety and not in the middle of the southern ice cap. We finally made it back to the piste, mounted our skis and followed Graham down to a restaurant for lunch, and I had a celebratory Tartiflette.

The afternoon was spent mostly on-piste, looking at the slopes around us, the ones we could see at least, and Graham imparted some of his vast knowledge to us about how to assess their risk of avalanche. For his grand finale he took us up the Tichot chair and we skied down the Stade, which now had two metres of fresh powder on it. I struggled and resumed my role as T. E. Charlie, but I made it down without any drama or, importantly, any outbursts.

That evening at dinner, I found myself on a table of hedonists and we ordered a bottle of wine to share. The instructors and guides, who'd previously always sat on the head table, decided to be sociable and sit amongst us, although I suspect this was because the infamous Roland had arrived and wanted female company over dinner - he was French after all.

Mention the name Roland Steiger to any Ski Club Leader and you'll always get a wry smile back. He has a cult status and enjoys a little infamy amongst those who have passed under his scrutiny. Based in Chamonix, Roland is a guide and instructor par excellence. His role in the training course was to put candidates under pressure — to 'test' them, as he put it. He exudes self-confidence to the point of comical arrogance. Deliberately so, I suspect, this being the attitude needed to take on the big mountains.

As the week went on, Roland's reputation as a crazy skier grew with every group of candidates he took out. Rumour has it that once a young ESF instructor, suspecting Roland of teaching without the correct *paperassière*, approached him and asked if he was a qualified *monitor du ski*. To which Roland replied, *'Oui'* and added that he was a qualified mountain guide too. 'Are you only an instructor?' Roland asked. *'Oui,'* said the youth. 'Well then, come back when you're fit to stand where I shit' was Roland's reply!

The North Face group had a couple of days 'easy skiing' scheduled with two experienced Leaders, Patrick and Paul, before our appointment with Roland.

They clearly worked as a double act. Patrick was young, charming and a very good skier (whatever that means), one of only a few with a gold/gold Ski Club grade. Paul was more of a veteran. A qualified instructor and mountain guide, he projected a rather grumpy cynical persona, the sort that comes with life experience – usually bad. I felt that we had a lot in common in that respect. The older you get the more shit has happened to you and the more you've earned the right to be tetchy. His dog had just died, so he had recent cause, I too had recently experienced loss (my clownfish) and could empathise. He said that he hated being asked 'What he did in the summer?' – I seriously hated that question too.

Paul and Patrick's job was to teach, then assess, our on-snow leading ability. I'd almost forgotten that the Club were not just interested in our skiing ability, but also our ability to organise, manage and safely lead a group of skiers around the slopes and, importantly show them a good time. Theoretically, this is where I would score the most points. I had effectively been a ski-host in Morzine for two full seasons.[48] I had a pretty good track

---

48 *Many chalet companies have a* **ski-host** *(usually an accomplished skier) who is willing to show guests around the pistes and unburden them of navigational worries, to find them the best slopes and a decent restaurant for lunch.*

record for not losing guests on the mountain. None of them have ever died and most seemed to have had a good time. Most importantly nobody had ever gone without a nice lunch - in my book, that made me an excellent ski-host.

First Patrick took us out for a pleasant day's skiing, during which he imparted his knowledge of the do's and don'ts of ski leading. The sun was out and it was almost like being on holiday with your mates. We skied off-piste quite a lot but nothing too serious. It's amazing how much good visibility can improve your skiing.

For our assessment, we were set the task of planning and taking Paul on a typical Ski Club off-piste day. The weather forecast was good but we were all devoid of any local knowledge so we decided to retrace our steps from an earlier outing to Val d'Isère. Unfortunately Paul was a hardcore Ski Nazi, like many of the members, and we were effectively taking him Girlfriend Skiing. After sitting on one particularly long and cold chairlift, his patience snapped: 'What were we playing at?' This was supposed to be an off-piste day. 'Why were we avoiding perfectly good off-piste pitches?' he wanted to know.

We defended ourselves by quoting *the Leader's Manual*, to him, which had become close to all our hearts that week. It stated: 'No Leader is to conduct an off-piste run in terrain that is unknown to them' (it was all unknown to us) or 'terrain where it's not possible to return to a piste within a short period of skiing time for the weakest skier in the group' (that would be me and I didn't travel fast). It also stated that Leaders should not to go off-piste, at all, if the avalanche risk was four or above (which is was).

Paul told us that, for the purposes of the exercise, we should pretend the risk was three not four. I asked him if he could tell the avalanches to pretend it was a three too? (Yorkshiremen never learn to keep their mouth shut). Admittedly we were with a qualified guide, Paul, who did know the area well and would presumably prevent us from leading him over a cliff.

We did up our game, but it's hard to find safe powder when you don't know the resort. In most situations, when someone is acting as a guide, they know more about the terrain than those that follow. But, thanks to the weather, none of us had escaped the Val Claret area to explore. I had studied the piste map the night before and had a vague idea of the run layout but not the unmarked off-piste.

Surprisingly we all passed that day. It was a muddled team effort and it would have been harsh to fail any one individual when the plan was devised by a committee - always a recipe for disaster.

Finally the big day came; the North Face group where to head up the mountain with Roland to be 'tested' off-piste. Although intimidated by his reputation, I knew impressing him was critical if I was to pass the course so I had an extra long chat with the toilet door that morning. Whatever happened, this was going to be a memorable day, I thought.

After completing our transceiver checks we boarded the main lift. While the others exchanged pleasantries with Roland I looked out of the bubble's window, and surveyed the previous scene of death below us. Fresh snow had removed all traces of the frantic human activity that had taken place there only a few days ago. Thankfully, after disembarking, we boarded a chairlift heading in the opposite direction.

Once the chair ride was over Roland gave us a few words of wisdom then pointed to a red run we would ski first in order to *réchauffer* (warm up). He then pointed his skis downhill and simply disappeared!

I've seen some fast skiers in my time, but I've never seen someone do a vanishing act on skis. Even the Crow wouldn't have been able to keep up. I discussed this with my fellow candidates that evening at dinner. No one round the table had seen him put a turn in; we'd see him at the top of a run then we'd see him again at the bottom – usually complaining that he was getting cold standing around waiting for us. Roland encouraged us to go fast too and explained that there were only three outcomes:

'You fall and die.'
'You fall and don't die.'
'You don't fall.'

He explained that, 'He had met God, even though God didn't exist, so which of the three outcomes didn't matter to him' - it didn't make sense to me either. I suspect Roland had been to the same philosophy classes as Eric Cantona.

Clearly, he was never going to fall or, if he did, nobody would know because he would be too far ahead for anyone to see. Luckily, Roland, being French, focused his attention on the girls in our group. He critiqued their skiing first: 'I like your bum, but don't stick it out so much. I want to see your tits more than your bum, stick your tits out more!' I did my best 'Page Three girl strangling two chickens' impression but for some reason he wasn't impressed.

Roland's central theme was that confidence is the key ingredient of a 'good skier'. I knew this already - shame mine had been shattered the previous week. He told us:

'You must ski like you know you're a god - like me.'
'Last year, I was voted zee best ski instructor in zee world.'
'So if you can't ski powder after a day with me, it's your fault not mine!'

He repeatedly advised us to stay '*fuckussed*' (focused) and forget everything but '*zee snow.*' We took on a few easy descents and my confidence was building. All the time I was '*fuckussed*' on my watch, counting each hour that passed without me blotting my copybook with Roland. Each hour was one hour closer to success.

We headed to the tree-filled Fornet valley on the far side of Val d'Isère. It was good to see some trees. They made the environment feel friendlier, more like Morzine and less like Tignes, which is bereft of woods. At the top of the cable car, we came across some netting with a large sign hanging from it. Literally translated, it said 'avalanche - risk of death.' To my horror, Roland lifted the netting and beckoned us to ski under it. We all started twitching. Someone broke ranks and pointed to the sign. '*Bon,*' he smirked, '*I was having zee little joke.*' Thanks a lot, Roland, I thought, as my heart rate recovered. He found another exit from the piste just round the corner. It didn't look any less steep but there was no netting to climb under, so it was apparently safe. A mile of virgin powder disappeared below.

Roland dropped in first making little turns at high speed. I went last, my skis didn't want to turn but I manhandled them, left then right in big arcs, each turn a triumph. I knew my technique was fundamentally flawed but now wasn't the time to experiment with a new one and induce a fall. I suspected that, in my exhausted state, getting back up would probably be beyond me, given the depth of snow. Despite the effort involved, I'd stop after each turn to rest my legs and congratulate myself. If I'd just let one turn flow into another and accepted the increased speed, it would have been so much less effort. I made it down with only one fall, more importantly another hour had passed.

Next we headed up to Val d'Isère's top station, the Du Montet, some 3400 metres above sea level where a glacier allows skiing all year round. We bumped into Phil Smith's group and I rode up in a bubble car with Roland and Phil. They talked about Phil's forthcoming trip to Japan. I felt both alarmed and privileged that I was about to ski a glacier with these two legends and resigned myself to death or glory.

The top was bitterly cold and windy. There was a long traverse over to the bowl Roland and Phil had chosen for our descent route. I soon found myself pulling up the rear, my lungs bleeding trying to pull oxygen out of the thin air. I kept looking up at the cliffs, loaded with snow, above us and kept seeing potential avalanche risks everywhere. On arriving at the lip of the bowl, I discovered it was still full of virgin powder. Normally fresh powder is hard to find in a ski resort two days after it last snowed. Any un-skied areas are either hard to get to or generally considered too dangerous to ski. I concluded that, in this completely untouched valley, the former was the case – and prayed it wasn't the latter.

Everyone set off whooping with joy as they descended into the valley. With my dodgy powder technique, it was easier to turn in broken snow, so I set off last and despite breaking my Powder Day Commandment, I carved everyone's tracks up in an attempt to survive, which I did, but it didn't go unnoticed.

Being French, Roland stopped early for lunch and I congratulated myself on completing half the day and still being alive. He took us to one of his favourite haunts and, for only the second time that trip, I had a pleasant lunch. For a brief hour, sitting in that traditional alpine restaurant, it felt like I was on a skiing holiday, apart from the absence of wine of course. Even better, Roland talked about the need to head back to make sure we didn't miss the last connecting lifts to Tignes and I started internally celebrating my success. Then he changed his mind and declared there was time to redo our first descent again and my heart sank. Fortunately, second time round, I knew I could ski the slope and my fear of it had gone. Unfortunately, so had my legs and I fell several times.

We regrouped at the bottom. It was made clear to everyone by the sweat pouring off my forehead that I was completely spent. Roland looked at his watch and asked if we wanted to do the descent again. Which was met with enthusiasm from everyone but me. The Ski Demons took control of my voice. 'I think I'll expire if I go back up!' they announced. I was annoyed with them for throwing the towel in, because Roland had no intention of returning to the top. He explained that it wasn't a good idea to ski so far off-piste late in the afternoon. Should someone lose a ski (like me, I suspect he was thinking) it could get dark and very serious very quickly. So we headed back to Tignes.

The last run back into Tignes was a black. Usually I would have had no problem with it, but my wobbly legs and the wide powder skis I was using, just didn't want to carve. Roland shot down as usual and for the first time that day, I became aware that he was watching me for a change. It was like he'd just remembered that he needed to assess me too and maybe find something constructive to say. Realising that his opinion of my skiing was probably going to be based on what he saw in the next five minutes, I tried too hard and skied terribly.

We assembled for the usual debrief in the coffee room of the hotel half an hour later, which was more like a summary execution for me. Roland declared that 'Everyone was at zee required standard to be a leader – except you.' He nodded in my direction. In a half-hearted attempt to protest, I declared 'But I've skied down everything they have today!' 'Yes you have,' he admitted, 'But you were at the limit of your ability,' he said 'and they were not,' I couldn't argue with that. They'd looked like 'good skiers' all day – I had not. I knew Roland was right.

I went to bed that evening resigned to my fate, I wasn't going to pass the course, but I was at least pleased I'd given it my best shot given the circumstances.

The next day it was hard to find the motivation to get out of bed. I'd failed to impress the judges with my skiing and therefore would fail the course, but I still had one day of assessment left.

The North Face group was scheduled to go up the mountain with Shep that day. He was going to teach us how to navigate through the backcountry using a map and compass. I suspected this would involve hiking up hills potentially beyond my remaining aerobic capability. I wasn't sure why this was part of the course; if a Leader needed to refer to an OS map he'd already, by any interpretation of the Leader's Manual, gone too far off-piste.

The toilet door convinced me to give it a go. It was the last day and at least the avalanche risk was now three and the sun was out. Besides which I love map reading and wanted to learn more. 'I could always bail out if the going got too tough, I'd got nothing to lose,' the door reassured me. I flushed, stood up, banged my head, and went to breakfast.

Shep's morning classroom session was easy enough. It was indeed interesting and, while studying the map, it occurred to me that his plan might be to visit the couloirs and cols that we'd identified on it - which didn't look awfully hospitable, even on paper. Worryingly, Shep had touring bindings on his skis, which suggested he planned a lot of hiking.

All my suspicions were correct. After a brief period of piste skiing we headed off-piste, traversing round to the first col we'd been studying on the map. A vast field of untracked powder appeared below. I could see the bottom and even I started salivating. It was well within my capabilities; maybe I could still impress someone with my skiing - Shep. One by one we descended while Shep took photos of us skiing. Entertainingly, Shep fell on his descent, blaming 'equipment failure', while inspecting his bindings.

I survived most of the morning including some enjoyable skiing through trees and a technically tricky gully - the type of skiing I did a lot of in Morzine. I started to think I was finally doing a pretty good job of looking like a 'good skier' but unfortunately just before lunch, I took a bad fall right in front of Shep.

Lunch is always a significant waypoint for T. E. Charlies; it's often the only time they get a significant rest. They can also deploy the tactic of ordering something complicated that takes a long time to cook, thus extending lunch and giving them more time to recover. It also shortens the afternoon's ordeal as well.

During lunch, Shep asked me how I'd been doing since our last little chat. He wasn't aware that I'd completed every session since then – frankly, I found it hard to believe too. He then explained that he intended to ski the Chardonnet Bowl that afternoon which would involve a forty-minute climb. He wanted to know if I could manage it. Clearly, he'd not changed his opinion of my fitness despite my morning efforts.

What was the point of further terror and exhaustion? I thought. I asked if I could be frank and he told me to go ahead. I said that I knew I'd failed but wanted to come back next year for another attempt. I asked, if I wimped out of the afternoon's activities would that still be possible? The answer was 'Yes.'

I paused for a moment. It sounded like a tough afternoon and things beginning with 'Chardon' had always left a bad taste in my mouth. The thought of being T. E. Charlie for another afternoon was too much. 'I think I'll head back to the hotel,' I said, admitting defeat.

After lunch, I parted from the North Face group and while skiing back to the hotel I flipped between two different emotions: relief that the ordeal was over and disappointment that so much effort had ended in failure. Despite what I'd told Shep, I mentally debated whether I would *actually* come back for a second attempt. Would I want to live through any part of the last two weeks again? Highly unlikely I thought.

That evening, we all had an exam to take. A multiple choice paper on all the classroom stuff we'd covered during the two weeks – set, presumably, to see if we'd been paying attention and not napping like me. A fail meant failing the course. Despite already knowing that was my fate, I decided to join in and make the point that it was just skiing I was rubbish at, not the mountain craft (which mercifully I passed).

After the exam we had dinner and most headed to the Alpaka, the best bar in the Le Lac area of Tignes. It had been a tough two weeks for everyone, including the guides and instructors. Some of the newly born Leaders where bitching about their grades, others were delighted they had just passed. I was a bit of an oddity and tried to smile through the evening, willing the Après Aliens to turn up but surprisingly they never showed. The next day I woke up, in the correct bed, with a hangover – my first for fourteen days.

Well, not quite over, there was the small matter of the end-of-course race scheduled for that afternoon. A Grand slalom course had been setup by Phil on the Stade for a 'bit of fun' although entering the race was optional. There'd been a lot of camaraderie in the bar the previous night and indeed over the two weeks, but who actually was the fastest skier on this year's course?

Lots had been drawn for starting places the previous evening and I was in position 1 - I would be first down the slalom course - if I turned up. By midday, I thought 'Sod it I'm going to give it a go, hangover or not.' When I turned up, there were a few of the new Leaders missing and one was throwing up on the side of the piste. She put it down to 'food poisoning' – I often use that excuse too.

As I approached the starting gate, I felt nervous with all my peers watching. I decided that the most important thing was not to fall so I took it steady. Others, especially the younger men, took it very seriously, exchanging their powder skis for pure carving race skis. Finally, after two weeks of having our skiing assessed subjectively, there was a chance to be measured by a truly objective judge - a stopwatch – and I came last, but I really didn't mind. I'd given up caring what people thought about my skiing. My desire for validation that I was a 'good skier' (whatever that means) had long since gone. I was just happy to be an average skier and still alive!

The final dinner was a hoot. In contrast to the first night's dinner, the wine flowed and everyone was in a boisterous mood. Most were celebrating their success. Some new lifelong friendships had been made. The dinner culminated in the showing of a compilation video Phil had made of the footage he'd taken during the two weeks, accompanied by his very humorous commentary. For some, it had been the best two weeks of their lives. It was certainly two weeks I'll never forget. I learnt a lot about skiing, a lot about avalanches - and a lot about myself.

The next day I took the transfer bus to Geneva and it broke down – it seemed that Tignes didn't want to let me go. I got to the airport just in time. I was heading back to the UK, to my parent's house in Hull, for Christmas - the first without my wife since we'd met.

23. What does a ski bum do in the Summer?

By the end of Season 3 the Après Aliens had all but left me alone. Seemingly, by way of thanks, they left their best abduction until last. Once again, I found myself waking in an unfamiliar bed and this one was enormous. I'd woken up in many random beds since the Chalet Project had begun, but this was by far the most luxurious. I was tucked up under a thick duvet, my head surrounded by half a dozen fluffy pillows. The bedroom decor was unfamiliar; as was one of the noises coming from downstairs. Being woken up by children stomping around like elephants wasn't uncommon in the chalet, but hearing a dog barking was.

A rather attractive woman sashayed in to the room bearing a gift of tea. I looked at my watch - it was 6:30am, ridiculously early even for a chalet changeover day, I thought. Apparently, I'd offered to do the school run in order to save the children's busy mum some time. I got up and looked out of the window and, instead of seeing the Alps, a gloomy Sutton Coldfield looked back at me!

It was the end of November and the moon was still up. Landie was outside, covered in frost as usual, but she didn't have the backdrop of snow-covered mountains, just some mock Tudor houses lined up along a busy main road. I staggered into the en-suite bathroom - it was unusual for the aliens to provide such luxury. I stood in front of the mirror and a haggard doppelganger looked back. I asked him, 'What are you doing in this middle-class scene and whose identity have you stolen?' There was no reply so I washed my face, walked downstairs and joined the breakfast melee, then I dutifully took the kids to school. While driving I asked myself:

187

'What was I doing back in Sutton, the place I'd escaped three years earlier and why had I turned Landie into a Chelsea Tractor?'

Having been brought up in a rural setting then enjoyed living in a city centre for so many years, I had nothing but contempt for the halfway house that is suburbia. I used to joke that 'In suburbia, no-one can hear you scream.'[49] Well I was back in Sutton and I'd never felt more like screaming.

The house, the dog and the kids, two young teenage boys, belonged to Debbie. Despite our relationship being embryonic, she'd offered me sanctuary from the Cube in her family home, which, poetically, was in Sutton. This was an act of charity that rode against all the best advice she must have received, but it probably saved my life. Despite my prejudice against suburbia, I was extremely grateful to move out of the Cube. I needed people around me; I needed room to swing a dead cat - physically and metaphorically.

Three winters had gone by and I still hadn't found an answer to another troublesome question. I'd found a satisfactory answer to the question, 'What do you do for a living?' - Ski Instructor (unemployed). But it was often followed by 'and what do you do in the summer?' To which I still hadn't found a satisfactory reply.

I didn't have any gainful employment and I had very little money left. During the winter, now that I had no overheads in the UK (such as a home), I could keep my finances on an even keel in Morzine. The wage might be poor but my winter employment came with free board and lodging and, most importantly, a free ski pass. What I needed was a way of staying solvent in the summer too.

---

49 *The famous tagline from the horror movie Alien, is actually 'In space, no-one can **hear you scream**' – because sound cannot travel through a vacuum. Suburbia is often regarded as a cultural vacuum.*

I was offered a job with a local ad agency that still rated my skills, but, frankly, I'd lost touch with the online marketing industry, which wasn't hard to do in such a fast-moving arena. Anyway, keeping up with technology was a young man's job and I no longer fitted that bill. I'd rather get a job as a road sweeper I thought, than get back into that vacuous business. Besides which, if I'd ended up back in 'Marketing' I would have to declare the Chalet Project a failure and I'd not been through the last two years to go back to square one. I was tempted to register with the Sutton Coldfield Job Centre as a ski instructor, but I'd probably have been called a malingerer who was affecting the region's unemployment statistics.

I did get another job offer: Debbie needed a new housekeeper and I was now highly qualified for that role. Thanks to the project, I had extensive work experience in domestic servitude. Like my winter job, this one would have poor wages (none), but would come with board and lodgings, so I decided to take it.

I was concerned that people might think I was taking advantage of Debbie and particularly that her family would think I was some sort of gold digger; after all, I was just a ski bum she'd met on holiday. But it was a real job. A career woman and single mum Debbie desperately needed some domestic backup. She could replace her army of staff - the housekeeper, nanny, dog walker and gardener - all with one ski bum and save herself a fortune each month. If people wanted to accuse me of sleeping with my boss, I'd admit it. I was comfortable with the sexual role reversal. I didn't have to be the breadwinner to affirm my manhood in a relationship. If people called me a 'trophy husband' - so be it! They didn't. 'Slummy daddy' was more likely. I settled on 'house husband' as a job description. It was technically accurate, if a bit misleading. I was still a husband, just not married to the owner of the house.

Despite the role reversal, there were plenty of opportunities to exhibit my manliness. The place was in desperate need of DIY love, no man having ever lived there. I donned my tool belt and set about fixing Debbie's house. I worked my way through a long list of maintenance tasks that would never have made it to the top of a single parent's list, much to her delight. She postulated that I was fixing her house because I couldn't fix my life, but I didn't need a psychoanalytical excuse. I just like fixing broken things.

After running a chalet for ten guests, running a house for six (if you counted the dog and the Grandpa that usually materialised at meal times) would be a doddle. I would have plenty of spare time to pursue other interests: motor biking, hiking and bird watching. I even had time to write a book! I'd seriously under estimated the volume of laundry generated by two teenage boys, but most of the afternoons were mine. I spent most of them writing and walking the dog around Sutton Park.[50] I walked most of its vast acreage that summer formulating chapters, bird spotting and generally sorting my head out. Although the dog was an enthusiastic companion, he wasn't much of a sounding board when it came to literary matters - but he proved a good listener when it came to the affairs of the heart. The dog lost two kilograms that summer and I shed a lot of emotional baggage too.

I'd left Sutton Coldfield looking for a radical career change - but 'house husband' wasn't exactly what I'd had in mind. At least it was a 'proper job' even if it was still in Sutton. Now, when faced with the question, 'What do you do in the summer?' I reply: 'I'm a house husband', and say it with some degree of pride.

---

50 **Sutton Park** *is the largest urban park in Europe, it has 2,400 acres of ancient wood and marshland and several lakes. It's not exactly Yorkshire – but it's significantly closer.*

24. New Year's Eve in the Alps

It felt like I'd been on an amazing odyssey, one that had lasted some thirty years, when I woke up in what appeared to be my childhood bedroom. I'd been drinking reasonably heavily the night before but it was unprecedented, even for the Après Aliens, to deposit abductees deep in their own past. I knew the aliens could accelerate time since I'd lost many hours to them, but I was pretty sure they couldn't reverse it. I sat up and looked across at the dresser mirror. I concluded they might have mastered time travel, but clearly not the ageing process when a familiar middle-aged, bald man looked back at me.

Three decades had passed and I was back where I'd started in South Cave, a village just east of Hull. I thought I'd left that place a lifetime ago, found a wife, built a home, a career, and a business in Birmingham but it seemed the Brummie odyssey was over - they were all lost. I was back in East Yorkshire for Christmas, in the house where I'd spent my teenage years. I was wiser, not much richer and judging by the reflection, I'd put on a considerable amount of weight.

It was an auspicious occasion - the first Christmas without my wife since we'd met. It felt good to be back in the North and it reaffirmed that I always had a sanctuary up there, but I just wanted that Christmas to be over despite the reassuringly familiar surroundings and the company of my parents.

Christmas first became tarnished for me when I uncovered the Santa Claus conspiracy (Santa is really your mum) and it never really recovered. I recall a period where I thought she at least *bought* the presents from Santa because their retail cost seemed to be an issue, but that might just have been a Jewish thing. Once I acquired a significant other, *where* Christmas was spent became controversial too. Negotiations started around July as the matriarchs from both tribes tried to gather their offspring for their traditional family Christmases. My mum usually lost because her tribe only had one member - me. Then, overexposure to in-laws and their misbehaving progeny meant that, by Boxing Day, I'd usually be wishing I were back at work.

Christmas also gets more expensive when you have a spouse, especially if they have fertile siblings, mostly because you have to buy your significant other - well - something significant. You can buy your mum a pair of slippers and she'll be happy - but not your wife. The obvious solution is to provide cash so she can buy her own present. However, you then also need a surprise gift, so there's something to open on the day, but this is equally difficult to procure so you are back where you started - only with a smaller budget.

On a couple of occasions, I bought my wife a skiing holiday for two. Despite being suitably expensive, this was not considered a generous gift because it was always implied she had to take me, so I always got judged on the surprise present. Now instead of a wife, I take a Labrador home every Christmas. He gets on better with my mum and most importantly he's always happy with the same present every year – a pig's ear.

That first Christmas without my wife, all my Christmas wishes had come true. There was no conflict over where I should spend it, there were no screaming kids, I didn't have any problematic presents to buy and I didn't have to take a woman who wanted to be somewhere else. Instead I took an imaginary elephant to my parents and, while it sat in the middle of the living room, the rest of us exchanged slippers and ate turkey.

Season 3 was about to begin and I wasn't looking forward to it. I was depressed, exhausted, demoralised and in desperate need of a holiday. People often think my life is one long holiday, because I work in a ski resort, but it isn't. I also needed to do some GF skiing to remind me that skiing could be fun as well as terrifying after my experiences in Tignes. Luckily my *actual* girlfriend, Debbie, was available and she agreed to drive out to the Alps with me in Landie, a true act of love.

We set off a few days before New Year on her inaugural Bacon Run. I wasn't needed in the chalet until mid-January so I planned to spend ten days in St Jean d'Aulps (St Jon),[51] a small village just north of Morzine. It had been a long time since I'd been on an actual skiing holiday - at least not one of my own.

Unlike Christmas Eve, New Year's Eve had always been the most important night of my social diary. I'd assumed it was for everyone, until I started spending time with grownups. As a student, getting wasted with my childhood best friend on New Year's Eve was obligatory and an annual confirmation of that special friendship. No other evening was as important, and a special venue and mode of getting poleaxed had to be chosen.

Then my best friend became a grownup, got married and had kids and our relationship status changed to 'best mates'. I assume that his wife, for political reasons, now had the 'best friend' title. Unfortunately her idea of what made a great night out was completely different to mine and after a few attempts we stopped spending New Year's Eve together. I've since learnt that special male friendships never truly survive a participant's marriage. The best you can hope for is that the incarcerated party will occasionally be allowed out for good behaviour. If he's really good, he may be allowed on a boys' trip. But that's enough misogyny for now.

---

51   *Part of the Portes du Soleil,* **St Jean d'Aulps** *has its own tiny ski area called Roc d'Enfer, which is perfect girlfriend skiing territory.*

I'd hung onto my immature concept of what made a good New Year's Eve for far too long, even after my own wife had become my best friend. Frankly, by then, the title wasn't that coveted. Finally, after two ski seasons in Morzine, where drunken debauchery was de rigueur and people partied like it was 1999 most nights, even I was looking for something else to do on New Year's Eve other than get drunk.

The 2013 Bacon Run wasn't exactly uneventful (more about that later) but we made it to St Jon a couple of days before New Year's Eve. I popped over to Morzine to deposit the bacon in the chalet freezer, the conclusion of a successful mission. I remember a huge wave of relief coming over me when I pulled onto the chalet drive. Against the odds, I'd made it back to Morzine once again.

An almost unbelievable amount of shit had happened since I'd left. I'd had my face rearranged (in Reims), lost a wife (and a home), faced alcoholic oblivion (in a Cube), discovered I wasn't a 'good skier' (in Tamworth), been saved by a doctor (Debbie), moved to suburbia (where no-one could hear my screams), acquired two annoying flat mates (Debbie's kids), adopted a Labrador (the food seeking missile), been re-possessed by demons and seen death on the slopes of Tignes.

It had been one hell of a ride, but now I was back. A season's supply of bacon was secure in the freezer, my bookings diary was full, and an early dump of snow meant we were in for a bumper ski season. Best of all, I had ten days of GF skiing to look forward to.

The previous New Year's Eve I'd spent in the Dixie Bar. It was just like any other night in there, full of drunken Brits, except that night I'd rather annoyingly had to pay €20 to get in. So this year I booked into a tiny French restaurant, in St Jon. I know, technically, all restaurants in France are French, but the distinction is made to differentiate it from the traditional Haute-Savoie establishments in Morzine. Refreshingly the owner didn't speak English, although it did make booking tricky. It wasn't quite clear what I'd signed us up for – the owner was either planning to serve rabbit or he wanted us to come dressed as one!

I first encountered the French word for rabbit when I asked a waitress what '*Le lapin*' was, having seen it advertised as the *plat du jour*. She replied 'Err, is le Bugs Bunny!' which rather put me off the dish, not wanting to eat a childhood hero.

We walked to the restaurant that evening debating whether dressing up as a rabbit might be a local New Year's Eve tradition, but we had both dressed more sensibly for the cold. Debbie wore her pink salopettes under her black dress, and I had my man-about-yorkshire outfit on. When we stepped into the restaurant our attire seemed to amuse the other diners, who must have thought we were a rather eccentric English couple. The restaurant was full of sophisticated looking French people and, to our relief, none of them were dressed as rabbits. A rather sleazy looking sax player was wafting Gerry Rafferty's Baker Street across the room from a corner.

We were shown to our table, which was right in front of Gerry. This wasn't a problem because each time a course was served he would go and sit down at the bar and eat a plate of it too; he was clearly playing for his supper. After he'd finished it, he'd return to his stool and start at the beginning of his somewhat limited repertoire. He didn't get much of a rest, the courses were tiny and numerous. After three hours we'd completed five courses, drained a similar number of wine bottles and had heard Baker Street more times than I care to remember. Twelve o'clock came and went with little ceremony and we'd yet to see any rabbit. It soon became clear that we needed to leave while we still had the perambulatory power to do so.

Being its only representatives in the establishment we didn't want to let our nation down and cause offence by leaving early. I summoned the waitress and explained that our baby sitter had called and we needed to go home – Wayne was ill. I'm not sure why I gave our fictitious son a name or why I had to lie. The proprietor was upset that we would miss out on the main event, the rabbit, and one or two other courses that were to come before that. He clapped his hands and a sequence of plates came at us in rapid fire and at last Bugsy made an appearance.

We scoffed the tiny morsels quickly, thanked the proprietor, said *'Adieu'* to Gerry and stumbled out of the restaurant, trying not to giggle. By the time we'd made it back to our digs we'd sobered up. Despite spending four hours in a restaurant, we were still hungry so we rooted out some cheese and bread. This is why I hate Michelin starred restaurants.

We could see distant fireworks from our balcony, launched from somewhere near Morzine. They illuminated the jagged snow-covered peaks that surrounded us. It was a beautiful setting. We wished each other a *'Bon année'* (happy new year). It couldn't possibly be any worse than the last one, I thought, as I looked round at the mountains, my love of which had caused all the trouble.

In the morning we went skiing, but not terribly early by Ski Nazi standards. They wouldn't have been impressed with our skiing objectives for the day either – to ski to a nice restaurant for lunch and then ski straight back. As we boarded the first bubble car the waitress, who had served us the previous evening, stepped in behind and recognised us (well more likely she recognised Debbie's salopettes) she smiled and enquired how baby Wayne was doing. Apparently we could have used our mother tongue the night before because she spoke perfect English. '*Votre enfant* (your child)*?*' she added after observing our blank faces, wondering if we spoke it.

'Fine, *bon*,' Debbie spluttered, 'Not well enough to go skiing, obviously, but fine.' The girl's expression changed to that of someone about to report a parent to social services. She enquired into Wayne's age, where we were from, where we were staying, had we been to St Jon before? The usual lift conversation that I have a thousand times a season, unfolded. I smirked as Debbie was forced to expand the lie from the night before yet further. She was willing the lift to move faster up the mountain, waiting for the doors to open and the conversation to be over.

While watching her Oscar winning performance, it occurred to me that next time a tourist started to ask me the Groundhog Questions on a lift, I might invent a fictional life too, safe in the knowledge it was unlikely I'd see them again. I tried it out a few times the following season. It's even more fun if someone you know is on the lift with you in order to appreciate your creativity.

A gourmet chalet chef was one role I played quite a lot. To lie convincingly you need to stick close to the truth and I'd just started cooking in the evening for guests so it was partially true - although I hadn't quite rolled out the *cordon bleu* menu I usually alluded to. It was a role I would try and play for real the following New Year's Eve when, for various reasons, I couldn't find any friends to spend it with and I decided to work. I rather foolishly offered to cook for a rich Swiss family who'd booked the chalet for the week. You need to be rich to stay in a chalet for New Year.

My first experience of catering for paying strangers was very stressful. Despite leaving the UK at 6am, I'd only got to the chalet a few hours before the Swiss and, despite a promise, it had not been cleaned properly by those departing. I spent a crazy two hours cleaning, changing beds and I was still mopping the hall when they arrived. After the meet and greet I set about cooking the Thai green curry they'd ordered for their arrival night, which in my haste I accidentally nuked with extra-hot chillies (imported from Bradford). It was the first, but not the last time, I would make a bunch of foreigners sweat.

They played it safe for New Year's Eve and ordered French onion soup, followed by *navarin of lamb*, then *tarte tatin* for dessert. Presumably thinking not even an Englishman can put chilli in any of those dishes. What they didn't realise was that I hadn't cooked any of those dishes before and I wasn't even sure of the ingredients let alone the outcome. I plied them with Champagne and canapés hoping that they'd get too drunk to be discerning about the food.

It was all a bit of a blur, but one course after another rolled out of my kitchen and was met with rapturous delight. They were not only drunk but clearly hungry. If the food was really so good, it had been because of a sequence of flukes, but they didn't need to know that. After dinner, I bathed in culinary glory while sharing a rather fine cognac with them. I left them to the rest of the bottle and headed down to my local, The Sherpa, feeling like I was Morzine's answer to Jamie Oliver.

Everyone needs a bar where the barman knows their name; the Sherpa is mine. One of the bar staff once beautifully described the Sherpa as 'Just a crappy little bar in the Alps - but it's our crappy little bar.' If I needed to escape from the chalet, or more accurately the guests, I'd often go to the Sherpa. I'd sit at the end of the bar and annoy the staff with my attempts to start conversations. But at least they knew my name. The Sherpa had one notable feature - a Star Wars, themed toilet, sadly now destroyed by new owners.

When you opened the toilet door the theme tune to the George Lucas epic started and a glitter ball illuminated a mural of characters from the trilogy. A full size Princess Leia, in her skimpy leather slave outfit (all men of my age will know the one), was plastered on the back of the door, making it hard to pee if you noticed her looking at you. It was both naff and brilliant at the same time. It was fun to watch the uninitiated enter and come back out with bemused expressions. Although, I was in danger or being known as 'The Weirdo' who sat at the bar on his own, staring at people going to the toilet.

I sat in there one evening (in the bar, not the toilet) and Darth Vader accompanied by six Storm Troopers walked in, presumably a stag party in costumes. Vader went to the loo and returned looking rather disappointed. 'Is that it?' he complained to his Troopers.

Most importantly, the Sherpa has hooks under the bar to hang your ski jacket on, which defines it as a proper ski bar in my book. So many others bars fail this test. The Sherpa is the scene of many an abduction and a place where I've lost countless hats.

That night, at the Sherpa, I bumped into some cronies and I started to play alcoholic catch-up with the bar staff, who were foolishly being supplied with shots by one of the punters. The place was full of chalet staff who, like me, had just come off shift, most were wearing their off duty uniform, a beanie. Despite them all being posh, middle-class kids, their collective persona was that of an underclass blowing off steam after a hard night's work. As I welcomed in the New Year with my youthful comrades I felt happy, and it wasn't just the drink. Even if I'd spent most of it with strangers, an old New Year's Eve tradition of mine had been maintained — it had been a night to remember.

25. The Bacon Run

Given that I'm of Jewish descent, some people think my relationship with bacon is a little odd. Despite being an atheist, I was inclined to agree with them when one morning I awoke on a bed made of the stuff!

For once, this was not the work of the Après Aliens. I'd fabricated the bed myself in the back of Landie and gone to sleep sober upon it. Bacon, it turns out, makes for a surprisingly comfy mattress, if rather unorthodox – in every sense of the word.

I was on the second of my now annual winter migrations from Birmingham to Morzine, now known as 'The Bacon Run' due to the most precious part of the cargo carried – real English bacon. The return journey in spring is called 'The Wine Run' the main cargo (you guessed it) being wine. Unable to find a hotel room I'd pulled into a layby, fashioned a platform out of the catering size bacon packets and crawled into my sleeping bag on top of it.

One cannot truly appreciate how vast France is until one has driven its length in a Land Rover Defender. Its varied terrains and diversity of climates are all experienced on the route. But that is not why I undertake this annual migration in such an uncomfortable mode of transport. No, it's because of the scarcity of 'real' bacon in France, or so I fool myself. The French, despite their culinary prowess, do not understand bacon nor, in fact, pork products in general. Somewhere between gammon and lardon lies the perfect slice of breakfast bacon that has yet to be discovered by French butchers.

In fact, most of the items found on the breakfast table at Chalet Neige are imported, although I jokingly tell guests that all my ingredients are 'locally sourced' - which is technically true, because I buy them from COSTCO, my *local* wholesaler in Birmingham.

Preparing for a Bacon Run is a military operation. I create checklists of supplies: skiing kit, medicines, spare parts for Landie, tools, clothes, toiletries and food – in fact everything needed for a four-month expedition. It has been pointed out to me that there are supermarkets in France and, it being a reasonably civilised country, most of the essential items to sustain life can be obtained there. However this Englishman needs his home comforts and so, I think, do most of his guests.

The Bacon Run is more than an 850-mile grocery run. It's an emotional journey of self-reflection. It's a pilgrimage to the skiing version of Mecca – the Alps. In true pilgrim fashion, Landie provides the traveller with little comfort. The heater sometimes works but fails to compete with the drafts that whistle in from the gaps around the doors. There's no radio; that would be pointless because you wouldn't hear it above the wind and engine noise. Also, above 50mph most things rattle, including the occupants' teeth.

The journey out is always more exciting than the journey back because a new season awaits, although it used to be done under time pressure in order to get the pork products to the chalet's freezer before they went off. The installation of a chest freezer in the back, (not a standard Land Rover accessory I'll grant you) took the pressure off later runs, but it did mean the bacon was more cosseted than the driver and, being frozen, no use for sleeping on in an emergency.

The run back is generally more tortuous because the pilgrim's body, particularly his knees and liver, are hurting from overuse and usually done with a compound hangover from the end of season partying. Landie is often equally fatigued, overdue for a service, and usually nursing some major malfunction.

I have been on other equally uncomfortable road trips on a motorbike. What I love about travelling by motorbike is the way you experience the changing environment through all four senses. They make travelling in a modern air-conditioned car feel like you're watching TV. In a car, you sit in an armchair and listen to your music as the scenery floats past; on a bike, you feel and smell your environment and your engine's toiling is the gritty soundtrack.

When travelling by motorbike a relationship with your steed develops too. You feel its moods and offer it mental and sometimes audible encouragement. I often give my bike a pat on the tank when it successfully completes a tight bend or a steep climb. I hold the same unspoken conversations with Landie, which makes the Bacon Run feel like a bike trip. Or it could just be because it's an equally cold, noisy, smelly, drafty and uncomfortable experience.

The Bacon Run is best undertaken with a co-driver, if only to share the boredom. Those foolish enough to accept the ultimate endurance challenge - talking to me for eighteen hours - will get to know themselves, as well as me, very well. On the inaugural Bacon Run, my co-driver was a twenty-five-year-old Snowboard Dude called Alec, who'd signed up to be the chalet boy that first year.

Foolishly, we decided to make the journey in one big hit, stopping only for fuel, the call of nature and driver swaps, all of which we synchronised. We ate and drank, mostly Red Bull, on the move. Having reached the Jura Mountains, the foothills to the Alps, and having finished my fourth can of the stuff, I lost the plot so Alec had to steer Landie home. After that experience, all future runs include at least one overnight stop, sometimes in luxury Chateaus, often in lay-bys and, in one case, a hospital.

On that first Bacon Run we picked up an unwanted hitchhiker at Calais. A rain cloud hooked itself to the roof rack and we dragged it all the way to Morzine. After six hundred miles of torrential rain, one of the windscreen wipers, like me, lost the plot and fell off. Luckily it was on the passenger side and in Land Rover terms, non-essential so we didn't stop. I opted out of the Wine Run that year, paying Alec to drive Landie back for me, which was a mistake because, like any spurned female, she broke down once I'd left her.

Breaking down in France is something, unfortunately, I now know a lot about. The last place you want to breakdown is on a French toll road. The owner of these privately funded roads only allow the vultures they've franchised, to assist you. For instance, AA vans aren't allowed on their roads. With no competition, the fee for being towed off the hard shoulder seems only limited by the conscience of the tow-truck driver.

Despite Alec's impoverished appearance (a young lad in a beat up vehicle), the tow-truck driver's conscience was untroubled, judging by the bill I got. He towed Landie to a garage, which promptly shut for a two-hour lunch break. This is the other infuriating thing about breaking down in France, garages never seem to stay open long enough to get anything fixed.

To his credit, once he got the parts, Alec fixed Landie himself despite have only a 'gypo toolkit' as he described the collection of rusty spanners Landie carried. Like most Defender owners I do always carry a can of WD40 and at least one roll of Gaffa Tape, the theory being that all problems fall into two categories:

(1) things that move but shouldn't or (2) things that should move but don't.

Gaffer tape can be used to rectify the former and WD40 the latter, at least until you can get replacement parts delivered – often they're couriered to Morzine by friends in their hand luggage.

The second Bacon Run I undertook alone, due to a lack of willing co-drivers. This time leaving home was very emotional. It had been a difficult Christmas that turned out to be my last in the Loft. But on departure my wife handed me a box of turkey sandwiches and a flask of homemade pea & ham soup and bade me a tearful farewell despite me suspecting she might soon be changing the locks. Perhaps it was her way of saying a final goodbye. The journey down to Dover was an unbearably sad and lonely one, spent eating turkey sandwiches.

As usual, I was stopped at the UK border control. There must be something dodgy looking about Landie, or perhaps its driver, because we always get picked out of the line for closer inspection. The customs officer asked me if I knew they had pigs in France too? I forced a laugh, knowing it's always good to humour officials.

As the ferry left Dover I stood on the rear deck. I looked back at a vanishing England wondering how many others had previously stared at the famous white cliffs uncertain about their futures? (It reminded me of a favourite painting, *The Last of England*, which depicts emigrants leaving Dover.[52])

French customs were uninterested in me as usual and I headed south towards Lyon. I wasn't alone for long; I picked up another rain cloud at Calais and drove into the night drinking the lovingly made soup. After listening to every track on my iPod twice and feeling empathy with just about all the lyrics, I

---

52 *The Last of England*, *painted by Ford Madox Brown in 1855, hangs in a Birmingham art gallery.*

grew unbelievably weary and started looking for a motel. But none materialised and I pulled into a layby and constructed my unorthodox bed. As I crawled into my sleeping bag, my mood was lifted by an entertaining thought - if Bubbe (Jewish for grandma) could see me now she would be laughing in her grave.

I headed for Morzine really early the next day. It had snowed heavily and I was the first up the mountain road, my wheels cutting fresh-tracks in the snow, a good omen for the forthcoming season. Finally Landie was in her element. A procession of French cars followed in my tracks; one for the British, I thought.

The third Bacon Run was an altogether different experience. This time the expedition had its own medical officer, Debbie. She'd volunteered to be the co-driver, her judgment clearly clouded by love and the false notion of a romantic road trip. She soon realised that the co-driver's duties included managing a neurotic (me) and his tempestuous relationship with another female (Landie). Not to mention his idiosyncratic navigational requirements and anxieties about running out of fuel.

Debbie's reward was a night and dinner in an expensive Chateau en route. I foolishly ate seafood, including a dodgy scallop, which required us to unromantically visit just about every service station between Calais and Dijon the next day. I let Debbie drive the section past Reims for obvious reasons. The bottom had dropped out of my world since I was last in that city; now it was the other way round.

It wasn't obvious at the time, but Debbie must have enjoyed the Bacon Run much more than she let on, because she volunteered to do the Wine Run that year too. She flew out a few days before the end of the season and fully embraced the tradition of getting plastered on your last night in Morzine. Even though we decided to set off late the next morning, she was still suffering, so I volunteered to take the first driving shift. As we wound our way down the valley, Debbie began to twitch. Then I discovered she suffered from what I now know is called 'gephyrophobia' - a fear of crossing bridges!

It's always a relief to find out your phobia has a medical name. It means that it has been acknowledged as a recognised medical condition. It also means at least one other person suffers from it too so you're not going mad – well, not on your own. I'm not sure the latter applies to 'anatidaephobia', the fear of being watched by ducks! And hippopotomonstrosesquippedaliophobia', the fear of long words, is clearly just some psychology professor having a laugh.

My study of skiing phobias, including my own, had given me an insight into the human psyche. It looked like I had another complex mind to examine and plenty of time to do it too, as Debbie was effectively my captive for the next 18 hours. The alpine section of her inaugural Bacon Run had been done in the dark so the cliff hugging motorways and bridges we'd travelled over on the way into Morzine had gone unnoticed. But now, in daylight, the breathtaking viaducts and chasms they spanned looked impressive - she looked petrified.

This was more than a simple fear of heights. She said 'I'm worried that if I feel the urge to drive off the side of a bridge, I won't be able to stop myself'. 'You're not driving,' I replied. 'Even if I'm not driving, I might grab the steering wheel and force the vehicle towards the barrier,' she answered! I reassured her that I wouldn't let that happen while doubling my grip on the wheel. I made a mental note, not to let her near it until we reached the low country and briefly thought about asking her to sit in the back with the wine.

In order to distract her, I babbled on about my amateur studies of skiing phobias and that I'd found that the more intelligent the sufferer, the more bizarre the phobia seemed to be. I tried to reserve my place in that category by telling her of a desire to throw my keys in the water every time I walked down a canal towpath. Thinking I might have revealed too much and her primary concern might no longer be bridges, but the sanity of her new boyfriend, I told her about some of my more rational phobias.

I used to be afraid of contraflows and suffered extreme anxiety about not having access to a hard shoulder. My first car, a decrepit Fiat, used to overheat in traffic and I often needed to get to a hard shoulder fast, before it blew up. Long after I started driving more reliable cars, I still had panic attacks in contraflows. Now, thanks to Landie, I have a phobia of hard shoulders themselves rather than their absence, having spent so much time sat on them.

By 4pm, the worst of the bridges were behind us, and Landie was behaving well. Despite being at warp speed (65mph) for six hours, she seemed to be coping. No sooner had I articulated this thought, I experienced a brief loss of power. Initially I thought I'd imagined it. So many times, while driving Landie alone in the dark, my mind had played tricks on me. I'd hear new engine harmonics and assume them to be harbingers of doom, when nothing was actually wrong. But, after a driver swap, Debbie confirmed that the intermittent loss of power was happening to her too. Here we go again, I thought, it will soon be time to meet the French toll road vultures.

Like most of their owners, I'd been forced to learn a lot about Land Rover maintenance, but the intermittent nature of this problem proved hard to diagnose. I decided it was unlikely I could fix it with Gaffer tape or WD40. We were still rolling, so I decided to keep going and keep my fingers crossed until Landie actually came to a halt. We had a room booked at a Chateau, a mere three hundred miles away; we might just make it. We spluttered north, experimented with different speeds, gears and throttle settings, trying to diagnose or at least minimise the problem. The only consistency we found was that the loss of power always happened while overtaking a line of lorries – creating a few heart stopping moments.

It got dark and the road became empty as we poignantly passed Reims. It felt like we were nursing a badly shot up Lancaster bomber home to Blighty after a raid on Germany - not least because it was cold, noisy, drafty and damp. I mentally, and at one point audibly, willed Landie forward, counting each mile closer to our destination, a hot meal, a bottle of wine and a warm bed. We finally landed in the small hours – 'undercarriage intact'. I turned the engine off wondering if it would ever start again. I got out, patted Landie on the bonnet while muttering praise to the Land Rover gods. Debbie rationalised, 'There are worse places to be stranded' she said, while looking at the magnificent floodlit Chateau.

The next morning, after a restless night praying to the automotive gods and an underwhelming continental breakfast, I turned the ignition with trepidation. How much of Landie's problems where in my head? None of them – the engine remained lifeless; Landie had clearly not made it through the night. I turned the key again, but nothing stirred. Not even a whimper came from her bonnet. I thumped the steering wheel and blasphemed.

I then pleaded with her, promising endless oil changes and other pampering if she got me to the ferry. I turned the key again and she fired up - she had obviously forgiven me! I whooped with joy and affectionately kissed the steering wheel. I then furtively looked round the car park to check whether anyone had seen me talking to, and indeed kissing, my vehicle.

We set off for Calais, and found that the engine problem from the day before had miraculously vanished. I wondered what weird noise or intermittent malfunction would be today's entertainment and whether the reprieve from yesterday's one would last long enough to make it to the channel port – it did.

As the ferry left port, Landie safely parked in the hold, we stood on the rear deck, looking at *The Last of France* and, empathetically, it started to snow. To celebrate our success we ate in the boats posh restaurant. Now a Wine Run tradition, eating sit-down Fish & Chips on the Ferry symbolises a return to England and the end of the cheese and ham based Haute-Savoie diet. Afterwards we returned to the deck and, while the White Cliffs of Dover grew larger, I recalled my previous journey home – one that had ended in my own spare bedroom. This time I wasn't going home at all, but to Debbie's house. I realised that I would never be able to go 'home' - a deeply saddening thought. I had to make a new summer life in England, a daunting proposition for a 48-year-old.

By the time the fourth bacon run came around, I'd gone some way to building that new life. Debbie, clearly a glutton for punishment, was the co-pilot on that Bacon Run too. Landie started misfiring again, almost as soon as we hit French roads, but the protest didn't last long. I'd learnt to ignore such tantrums and concluded she just didn't like driving on the right.

The fourth wine run was a solo affair and despite almost running out of diesel, was an uneventful trip. For once, Landie and I were in great shape and made Calais in one hit. The mother of all traffic jams greeted us at Dover because the M20 was closed. While crawling through a 19-mile contraflow on the M25, I wondered why anyone would want to live in the South of England.

I'd coincidentally undertaken the journey on my wedding anniversary, a cause for much thought. But that is the great thing about long solo journeys, they give you time to think. The runs are always a great time to take stock and I don't mean as part of the cargo. I compare my current situation to that of the previous year's run. Have things got better or worse? Or am I just one year closer to death?

I'll continue to make the annual pilgrimage; for that is surely what it is. If only so that my chalet guests can continue to enjoy a proper breakfast, and have tea without any strings attached. Although whenever I see faddy guests leave bacon on their plates, I feel like shouting at them. 'If you had any idea what it took to get that rasher on your plate – you'd bloody well eat it!'

26. Half-Term Hell Week

No matter how old you get, sleeping in bunk beds is fun, right? That's what I thought until, one morning, I woke up in a bottom bunk to a horror scene I will never forget. For once my location was not in doubt, I was in the chalet's bunk room - but it smelt like the back of the Land Rover after a boys' trip, of stale alcohol and vomit. I went through the usual abduction checks: who, where, what … then I realised I'd not been out the previous night, this wasn't the Après Aliens work.

I heard the unmistakable sound of a trombonist coming from the top bunk and a sheet of sick fell past my face into a lake of the stuff already covering the floor. I rolled over to face the wall, hoping I'd soon wake up and the nightmare would be over. A second, more violent barrage cascaded down the bunk bed ladder. I pinned myself to the wall in disbelief, I was awake; it was really happening.

It was half-term week, the chalet was rammed and I'd ended up sharing the bunk beds with a friend's son, Tom, a polite well brought up sixteen-year-old who, apparently, was unaccustomed to drink. He had been on an extended après session with a female seasonaire he'd recently met, who was clearly a stoker. Later, as he cleared up the mess, apologizing profusely, I lectured him about the evils of drink and women, tongue firmly in cheek. He will not forget his first skiing holiday, and neither will I come to that.

February is a tough month in the Alps and not just because of the cold weather. There's a palpable malaise amongst the seasonaires. A sort of communal depression hits around the middle of the month. It could be that the novelty of living in the Alps has been replaced with the monotony of hard domestic work or, more likely, this malaise comes about because in the middle of February the Alps turn into a child-infested hell, where vomit is not always alcohol-related.

Each February three notable school holidays have to be endured: the Paris, UK and local half-terms. The UK half-term is the worst, followed by the Parisian one, but on a bad year the two coincide (usually on Sat 15th Feb). This is known as 'Hell Week' and many winter residents flee Morzine to escape it.

During Hell Week everything is fully booked, usually a year in advance, flights and accommodation almost double in price because property owners cash in, putting parents under additional financial stress. Many families bring cars to save on equally inflated airfares, so traffic jams are common and parking becomes impossible anywhere near the lifts.

Driving in Morzine can be very stressful, not just when the roads are covered in snow or ice. There are always dithering tourists blocking the road while trying to find their accommodation. There is general uncertainty at junctions, not helped by poor road markings and most foreign drivers are unclear who has right of way. Pedestrians meander all over the roads. Some like to walk a metre out from the gutter because the pavements are too slippery and therefore dangerous - apparently it's much safer to walk down the road. If you toot your horn they glare at you - apparently cars cannot kill you when you're on holiday. The French use a different version of the Green Cross Code – it's called 'Coming Ready or Not'.

During Hell Week, the beginner slopes become crowded and equally hazardous. Long lift queues start to appear on the lower slopes. The queues are exacerbated by a French ineptitude for organising boarding efficiently, letting chairs go up half empty, and by kids falling off, requiring the lifts to be constantly stopped.

French kids are generally better at skiing than British kids, however their reckless speed and lack of piste etiquette makes them more dangerous - and any collision will obviously not be their fault. Conversely, the off-piste is relatively quiet because all the good skiers (whatever that means) avoid Hell Week like the plague, either that or they're chaperoning their own kids on the baby slopes. I don't get to enjoy the empty off-piste though because the chalet is always full of mothers with young children, the most demanding type of guest.

I didn't realise that the Chalet Project would require me to cohabit with so many families. They tend to book early, take the entire chalet and are prepared to pay top price for the half-term weeks, so accommodating them makes good business sense. The project has unfortunately turned me into a self-appointed expert on parenting – one with some rather radical views. I admire parents who take their kids skiing, when it would be so much easier (and cheaper) to leave them at home. But giving kids the opportunity to learn while they are still young is a lifetime gift of winter fun, assuming they succeed. Unfortunately, the best age to start a child skiing is five, which is the worst age to take them on a skiing holiday, or indeed anywhere.

Skiing is a lot of hassle even for an adult. Getting yourself to the top of a snow-covered mountain suitably equipped takes a lot of personal organisation. Many adult males find it difficult to manage even with my help. Just getting to the mountains is an effort. The snow-covered ones are usually far from airports and require long transfers over winding roads, a vomiting opportunity most kids find hard to resist. The hassle increases exponentially with every child that is taken along. Parents who take on the ultimate logistics challenge (taking a young family skiing) deserve respect and possibly a medal. I wish my parents had attempted the challenge, but then skiing wasn't on our family radar. If they had, who knows, I might be holding an Olympic medal by now? (Unlikely).

The rich delegate the child-related hassle by bringing along a nanny, which isn't always good news for me because the chalet gets turned into a crèche. Some bring grandparents to do the job, which can be worse. Generally, having non-skiing guests, however nubile, is a pain because they hang around the chalet and, if I'm not careful, I end up looking after them all day. More importantly I can't slob around the place myself.

The most annoying thing about having toddlers and babies in the chalet is the noise. Not the noise made by the babies, but the noise made by the adults trying to entertain them. I've discovered that an inanely loud and permanently surprised voice is used by all nationalities when talking to their infants, although it is slightly less annoying in French because you can't comprehend the drivel. Whatever their nationality, it must confuse the kids who have to try to interpret this weird inflection. Even at two years old, not everything warrants complete surprise. I now catch myself doing it to my adopted dog, but then, he's not trying to learn to speak English so it doesn't matter.

It turns out that grannies are the same no matter what nationality. I spent one week with a scatty Dutch granny who couldn't find anything without my help. This included, at one point, her grandchild who'd decided to go into the garage and helpfully empty all my drawers. Another memorable week was spent with a French matriarch. She spoke no English so we had to rely on my French and mime to communicate. She wasn't too impressed with the equipment level of my kitchen. Where was my fondue set? Did I have a raclette machine? At least, that's what I think she was asking. 'I have no specialist devices for melting cheese,' I think I replied, 'apart from that' – I pointed at the grill.

There seems to be a widely held opinion amongst French skiers that an alpine chalet should have either a raclette machine or a fondue set. One French family, staying in the chalet opposite, were so bemused that their place didn't have either device, they knocked on my door and asked if they could borrow mine. I had to disappoint them.

The French matriarch who stayed with me decided to cook another traditional Haute-Savoie dish, tartiflette, one night. Or so I thought, until I discovered that one I'd made was missing from the freezer. I took it as the ultimate culinary compliment - she'd passed off my French cooking as her own.

Then there are the second-time-round dads, of whom I see quite a few. We've already discussed why skiers make poor first husbands, but why so many remarry and start another family is unclear to me. One inventive, recycled father paid his teenage son to be nanny for his newly arrived stepbrother while Dad skied with his trophy wife. Even though I was sleeping two floors away from the howler, it woke me up every night. I concluded that at fifty having a screaming baby was too high a price to pay for having a trophy wife.

I find myself studying second-time-dads like I would an alien life form; one that is radically different to my own. I've spent my life carefully avoiding becoming a dad and they seem to have blundered into the role twice over. I'll accept that I'll never know the joy of being a parent; I'm told it is very hard to explain and that I'll only really understand when I become a dad myself. But that is what the French call a '*fait accompli*' from which there is no going back.

One five-year-old I will never forget really hadn't travelled well. When I opened the front door to welcome his family, he projectile vomited into the hall. He'd managed to make the whole chalet smell of sick before he had even crossed the threshold - an impressive feat. The next morning he vomited over the breakfast table, putting everyone right off their porridge and subsequently turned the chalet into a scene from the Exorcist for most of the following week.

Another little Damien stole all my ski passes, leading me to question my own sanity while I tore the chalet apart trying to find them. I tactfully suggested to his mum that he might be the culprit although I think she already suspected he was the thief.

Some parents have clearly become desensitized and ignore their children's bad behaviour. I suspect they've come on holiday for a rest. Some are just choosing the battles they want to fight, ones they can actually win. Others have clearly lost the war of attrition that is making their kids behave. The main battlefield seems to be the dinner table and the rules of engagement seem unclear. What is considered good manners varies considerably between nations and parents although eating with your mouth closed and generally minimising mastication noise appear to be an internationally lost cause.

During Hell week, most teenagers either grunt through a blank expression or refuse to engage with their 'totally irrelevant' parents. Older teenagers are more entertaining because they use logic and ridicule to answer their parents back. Whenever I encounter a revolting youth, slobbed on the settee mining his nose, or a Smart-Alec being cheeky to his parents, I try and remember I was a teenager once too, although I was brought up with a much firmer hand and in much more fear of my mother. Often I'll see mums mollycoddling their kids while the dads are obviously counting the days until the ingrates leave home.

I've discovered that the phrase 'self-catering holiday' is really an oxymoron if you're a mum. Even twenty-somethings who have fled the nest revert to being children when they're on holiday with their parents. They expect Mum to run around after them and do all the work. The 'kids' probably do the same when they visit home for a weekend. Surprisingly, Mum often seems happy to revert to being their indentured servant. I now empathise more with mums and try to be more helpful with my own.

Of course, I've had some delightful and angelic kids stay too but I'm struggling to recall any entertaining anecdotes about them or even to remember their names – which is the highest compliment I can pay to any parents. I also meet some charming teenagers, who've been intelligent, eloquent, polite and respectful. I like skiing with youths too, as long as they're not snowboarders - or better than me.

Like most childless people, I think I would make a great parent. However, despite the obvious loss to the gene pool, I think I'll serve humanity better if I stick to criticizing other peoples' kids rather than having my own. Parents often tell me I've missed out on one of life's biggest joys. I tell them I can share their 'little joys' vicariously, if only for one all too short a week, but without the financial or emotional commitment.

Whenever the meaning of life gets discussed at dinner parties, a subject that usually come out with the brandy, people always tell me that the only true purpose of life is to procreate – to replace yourself then die. I tell them they really need to try skiing first.

27. Everything is Easier Second Time Around

I recognised the paisley wallpaper above the bed. The morning light, reflecting from the canal basin outside, twinkled on the ceiling. I recognised the steel girder embossed with the words 'Made in Middlesbrough 1805' above my head. It had been the first thing I'd read every morning for the last fifteen years. It always reminded me that I lived in a very special building steeped in history from the industrial revolution. But hang on a minute - had I not moved out the Loft two years ago? Had the entire Chalet Project been a dream or had the Après Aliens been playing with the space-time continuum again?

The lyrics from Crazy, the Gnarls Barkley song, started flooding into my consciousness. The tune was emanating from Debbie's iPhone - her alarm had gone off. I checked that it was definitely *her* beside me then looked up - the dancing spots of light and the girder had gone, replaced by a traditional cornice and curtains - I was back in Sutton Coldfield.

'Winter's lease hath all too short a date' (further apologies to the Bard) and once again it was time to 'return to reality' as the seasonaires put it. Season 3 had ended and summer in Sutton had to be endured a second time around.

But everything is easier a second time. The first time you go down the Wall for instance, you really don't know what to expect. The second time you're wiser, better prepared and, hopefully, you've chosen a better route. That summer I passed many milestones a second time round. The first birthday or Christmas without your ex is very difficult, in fact going to any annual event that you traditionally attended together is hard because everyone's acutely aware that someone is missing. The second time round nobody notices - except perhaps you.

The daunting task of starting a second life at fifty had already begun the previous summer and my new domestic partner was significantly lower maintenance than my last. Having already been house-trained by my wife, I felt I was doing a better job this second time round. I was determined not to make the same mistakes twice.

There were new challenges, like living with two teenage boys for instance. Unsurprisingly, they exhibited most of the annoying teenage behaviour I'd seen in the Alps, but these two were not going to leave after a week so I tried to build a relationship with them, which proved hard. To them, I was just an unwanted guest, a third person to share their servant (mother) with and so they were typically uncommunicative. It was undoubtedly hard for them too, having never had a man about the house. They were perhaps in need of a positive male role model, but I wasn't exactly a perfect choice for that, although I tried my best.

Like the kids that pass through the chalet, I had no parental authority over them, so I spent a lot of time biting my bottom lip. The summer school holidays proved particularly challenging. I was stuck in a protracted version of Hell Week. Worse actually, because during Hell Week, the kids go skiing and don't slob around in their pyjamas on the settee all day watching TV. But they were there before me - it was their home, not mine.

It reminded me of my student days. My flatmates then, like me, seldom cleaned themselves, let alone anything in the flat, and were completely undomesticated. On the positive side, I'd recently tried living alone and hated it, so I was glad to have some summer housemates, no matter how inflicted with domestic deafness and domestic blindness they were.

Moving in with your girlfriend or boyfriend is never easy even without kids. The truth is, no matter how considerate people are, eventually people get on each other's nerves. The great thing about chalet life is that most people leave after a week - before that happens. You can put up with anyone's foibles for a week and it helps of course if they're paying you.

I decided to extract myself from the scenario as often as I could that summer and planned lots of trips: walking, biking and bird watching. For distraction I made a study of Great Crested Grebes, the poster boys of British waterfowl, common in Sutton Park. I retook my BASI Level-1 course and this time I passed the dreaded snowplough test. Second time round I knew what to expect and didn't have a compound hangover, either.

I also honed my cooking skills that summer and expanded my culinary repertoire. I increased the number of dishes I could attempt with some certainty of a good outcome and significantly expanded the chalet's dinner menu. This also meant Debbie's kids could see a tangible benefit to having a strange man living in their home - better food at dinner time.

I needed to address my drinking problem too, the first step being to admit that I had one. Most unlike me, I sought help from a professional counsellor. She'd never been on a skiing holiday but, after a few sessions listening to me describing life in Morzine, she concluded 'I was in the wrong job.' No kidding, I thought, I could have told you that before we started. But using some of her advice I managed to rein in the drinking.

I was still angry at losing my home - my life's work up to that point. I felt like I was living in exile in Sutton Coldfield, a refugee from my own life. My home and most of my old life were still intact and just a few miles down the road. I don't know what real refugees call it, but there's a sort of homesickness that never goes away. Whilst outwardly grateful for sanctuary, you secretly wish you were in your homeland.

That second summer in exile, I'll admit I was a little over sensitive with our mutual friends. One friend, who had been round to my old home for a dinner party informed me that 'The wine had improved since I'd left.' One couple, invited my ex and me on holiday that summer - with our new respective partners! I understood, through their eyes, that it looked like I had ended up in a much better place (metaphorically – not Sutton) and that I had effectively won the lottery in meeting Debbie - which was true. However I don't think either of us were quite ready to forgive and forget and then, literally, go skipping off into the sunset as a foursome.

I tried to make myself feel more at home by turning Debbie's study into a 'man cave'. I hung my photos of the Alps and installed a TV and Sky Box. I liberated a few possessions and an armchair (a family heirloom) from the Loft. Like its owner, it looked rather dislocated in my man cave but I had a room that was all mine, somewhere to escape, to watch cricket and to write. I surveyed the meagre collection of artefacts from my former life. Not much of a haul, I thought, although there was a certain nomadic appeal in knowing that I could put everything I now owned into the back of Landie.

That summer I had reached the ridiculous age of fifty and I felt it was time to tick a few items off my Bucket List. It had been a childhood ambition to do Wainwright's Coast to Coast walk across Northern England and finally I had the time and a willing companion in Debbie. We walked through a heat wave, which required a lot of rehydration activity at night, turning it into the world's longest pub crawl. The trip reignited my love for the North of England and, having lost most of my connections with the Midlands, I wanted to reconnect with my older roots.

The Pennines are no match for the Alps when it comes to altitude, but they are their equal in beauty. I particularly love the Yorkshire Dales, a childhood holiday destination, possibly the only place in the world I love more than the Alps. I thought about setting up a summer business there (The Dales Project perhaps?) but the Dales folk have even less need of a ski instructor than the people of Sutton Coldfield, so I quickly dismissed the idea. Besides which, visiting places on holiday then deciding to live there, had got me into enough trouble already.

Unlike most people, I greet winter's first chill with a smile. Once the clocks go back and British Summer Time is officially over, my countdown to the skiing season begins. I start my marketing campaigns, which usually involve badgering anyone I've ever seen on a pair of skis to book a few days in the chalet.

By that November, my bookings diary for the forthcoming season was almost full. Many were repeat bookings, a sign I was getting something right and, apart from me, all the migratory birds had by then left Sutton Park.

In December, the Grebes change into their winter plumage and I knew it would be time for me to migrate south too. That second summer in Sutton, the dust had settled on my marriage and the post-mortem was completed – the marriage died through natural causes. Thanks to some extraordinarily good fortune in meeting Debbie, I now had a future. From then on, for this ski bum at least, in summer time the living would be easy.

28. The Big Brother Chalet

Sharing accommodation with strangers is not everyone's idea of fun, especially if communal dining is involved. But, unless you own one or have enough skiing friends to fill one, that is what a chalet-based skiing holiday involves. I wouldn't have said it was my idea of fun either, but I have always preferred staying in chalets to hotels when skiing.

It's not just that I have an unfashionable love of pine and like being in a building made of the stuff, although most do have a cosy, log cabin appeal. I also prefer the homely comforts that a good chalet can provide. I like sitting in a comfy armchair by a blazing log fire, the bitter weather safely locked outside. I like being able to walk around in my socks, to help myself to a drink and generally make myself feel at home. But what I like most about chalet holidays are the communal living spaces and the impromptu soirées that can occur in them with strangers and friends alike.

In my time, I have shared chalets with some very eclectic groups of people, all of whom have made for fascinating, if not always pleasant, company. I've made some lifelong friends too. You never know with whom you'll be sharing your holiday, when you first walk through the chalet door or, indeed, who they'll turn into during dinner, once they've had a few drinks. I've had a few nightmare scenarios too, sharing chalets with unpleasant people and I've been forced to dine with some seriously bombastic bores. But, no matter how unpleasant the general public can be, they were usually better behaved than the people I'd brought - my friends.

When taking bookings for the chalet I try and prevent too many obvious clashes. People with kids and those without, never really hit it off and I'd never allow a stag or hen party to share the chalet with anyone - for pretty obvious reasons. However, ultimately, I can't allow a room to stay empty, I'm running a business after all and, after suitable warnings, whoever wants to book an empty room, can.

I'm thinking of renaming it the 'Big Brother Chalet' although that would no doubt breach someone's copyright. Each week on changeover day, I feel like I'm preparing the chalet for a social experiment as well as giving it a good clean. Even if I know most of the guests about to arrive, I'm always a little anxious when introducing guests to each other. Surprisingly most will end up laughing and joking together around the dinner table that very evening, much to my relief. But then everyone has at least one thing in common, skiing, which gets the conversation rolling.

Sometimes it's not me, nor the random nature of Internet bookings, that has set up the social experiment. Some of the more radical experiments are inadvertently set up by the guests themselves, inviting friends of friends in order to fill the chalet. They assume that, because a person has chosen them, they've chosen their other friends wisely too. But the truth is, we only really like one side of a person. It might be that you like Mr Hyde but his other friends like Dr Jekyll. Just because you like someone doesn't mean you'll like their friends.

As usual, it's best to take Hemingway's advice. He said 'Never go on a trip with people you don't love.' He'd probably just come back from sharing a chalet with friends of friends when he wrote that.

If you don't have enough people you love to fill a chalet, or at least, not ones who want to go skiing, there are certain types of people you really want to avoid being in the Big Brother Chalet with. I have covered most of them in previous chapters, but here is a list for easy reference:

1. Other people's children. Children are like farts – you can stand the smell of your own. Remember, the younger the kids, the more annoying the parents will be.

2. Your own kids. No matter how old they are, they will expect you to wait on them and pay for everything. Remember, your teenagers are only on holiday with you because they can't afford to go skiing without you.

3. Lads or laddettes. Actual stag and hen parties will usually be made to book a chalet exclusively. Neither they nor the host want any innocent bystanders to get hurt.

4. People who wear beanies inside. This is usually the preserve of youths and snowboarders. They may think they are cool but we know only stupid people wear outdoor clothing inside.

5. White 'black' people (usually 18-24 year old males). They will play loud hip hop music and you'll end up telling them to 'turn that noise down, put your baseball cap on the right way round and pull your trousers up. You're not black, no matter how desperately you want to be, you're from Surrey, not Compton, so stop calling me bro – bro' – and then you'll feel bad about it.

6. People recently in or out of love. Those smitten or bitten by love seldom make good drinking companions and are either unbearably happy or unbearably melancholy. With the former, you may have to endure endless mobile-phone drivel on lifts and in other public places as they make and take calls from 'snuggle bum'.

7. People who don't drink. They're not safe to drink around because they will remember what an arse you were the night before and will remind you at breakfast.

8. Stokers. Anyone who likes drinking games or says, 'Eating is cheating'. They're in radio contact with the Après Aliens who will take you to the wrong chalet.

9. Equipment bores. I like talking about skiing equipment as much as the next man – which is around twelve minutes. There's only so much that can be said about two planks of wood, two poles, bindings, boots and warm clothes.

10. Skiing raconteurs who love the sound of their own voice. They will have been to every resort you mention and have skied every run you have – only backwards.

11. People who don't talk about skiing. I had a group of scuba divers stay in the chalet who talked about diving all week. I kept looking out the window to check I could see the Alps and not the Red Sea.

12. Drug dealers from Essex. Actually drug dealers from anywhere and anyone from Essex. Just trust me on this one.

13. Frustrated naturalists. Men who think it's okay to eat without a shirt on, both at breakfast and at lunchtimes. Even if you're outside and it's sunny, there's just too much molten cheese knocking around an alpine table to make topless eating safe. It also puts others off their food (don't make me show you why). Many people are also exhibitionists who like to wander around the chalet in their underwear. Note: this is totally okay for young women, but not men – of any age.

14. People who don't wear watches. Need I explain?

15. Snowboarders, who think everything is 'rad' or 'sick'. You'll end up telling them to 'take the beanie off and get some trousers that fit. You're not American, no matter how desperately you want to be, you're from Manchester, not NYC, so stop calling me man - man' and then you'll feel bad about it.

16. People on diets. Diets should start *after*, not before, a skiing holiday. It's the opposite of a beach holiday (unless you're a frustrated naturalist of course). Dieters will make you feel bad about your own indulgences and their 'My body is a temple' attitude will grow tiresome towards the end of the week, when you know they have a secret stash of Mars Bars in their bedroom.

17. Vegetarians. Luckily few make it to the Alps as the French do everything in their power to discourage *Les Cucumbers* from holidaying in their country.

18. Gastro skiers. People who care more about the eating than the skiing. Good food is a big part of a skiing holiday, especially in France, I will agree. Even though I now have a new interest in cooking, I still don't want to hear about every memorable meal someone has ever eaten or indeed cooked. I eat to ski; some people ski to eat and they are best avoided.

19. Fussy eaters of all ages. They will prevent the chalet chef from creating anything interesting. It's best if they stay in a hotel with an *à la carte* menu from which they will always choose the burger or the omelette.

20. People with allergies. Folk who will, or think they will, die if they eat nuts, gluten, dairy products or make eye contact

with a clove of garlic. They may exhibit extreme forms of attention-seeking behaviour, such as anaphylactic shock or death. This can really ruin the ambience in a chalet.

21. Ski Nazis. They'll make you eat breakfast at 7am and generally make you feel bad about your own tardiness. You'll forget you're on holiday and they'll make you think you're at skiing boot camp.

22. People who want a resort-off. They will tell you just how much better the skiing experience is in their favourite resort – usually not the resort you are currently in. One assumes they have been forced to try somewhere new by their friends. They will tell you how much better the service is in Austria or how it's all ski-in/ski-out. How it's so much higher than where you are, therefore more snow-sure (wrong). The lift system is better and 'more modern' and you'll never see a lift queue (what, not even in February – really?) If you're currently in *your* favourite resort you'll end up defending it all week in a ski resort version of Top Trumps.

23. Morning people. They may ask you what you do for a living and other difficult questions before you've had enough coffee to come up with credible answers.

24. Faffers. They are happy for everyone who does own a watch to sit in the Land Rover waiting for them to appear. Towards the end of the week, someone will shout 'For God's sake what are you doing, get your boots on, get in the Land Rover, everyone is waiting for you again.' Admittedly it's better coming from the faffer's spouse, rather than me.

25. Travel Bores. People who talk constantly about their *amazing* experiences on previous holidays. They come in two types. The back packer bores and the five- star bores. The former will have a better story to tell than you about any exotic location you may mention. They've usually stayed in a shack in Laos and it will only have cost a pound a day. They will have eaten rice with their fingers in Vietnam and drunk water buffalo milk with natives in Borneo. Most will have climbed Kilimanjaro for charity. The latter type, usually rich retired people, will have been to any city you care to mention, only stayed in a better hotel. In both cases it's best to pretend that you've never flown long haul; then they may eventually shut up.

I do realise that I fit into at least five of the above categories myself. And that is probably why, in the past, I have found it hard to get enough friends to stay in chalets with me. Now I don't have that problem because I advertise on the Internet for chalet mates, offering to cook and run around after them all week.

Most of the Big Brother chalet experiments are a success or, at least, everyone goes home with an entertaining story to tell. Some are so spectacularly successful that the participants arrange to return on the same week the following season. Some have even had a 'snowmance' and fallen in love.

Thanks to the Big Brother Chalet I've met hundreds of interesting people from many different walks of life: surgeons, pilots, air hostesses, farmers, astronomers, zoo keepers, barristers, architects, carpet fitters, generals, ex-special forces, bee keepers, property developers, pub landlords, TV presenters - to name but a few. It's allowed me to ski with some amazing folks and hear some entertaining life stories, no matter how embellished. I've dined with some complex characters and listened to some outrageous opinions. I heard some seriously unfunny jokes and I've had many a captive audience for my own.

29. No Change Without Loss

Most business plans never see the light of day once their authors have secured investors or indeed have decided to invest themselves. The Chalet Project's plan was no different. However it wasn't a sound investment I was after but a lifestyle change. Although the project does now make a small profit, it has yielded life changes in abundance.

The profit means the project can be declared a success and has silenced those who joked about my ineptitude at hospitality. They thought I was deluded – and I probably was. But running a chalet is all about logistics and I was always good at organising things. The real objective was to extract myself from the vacuous world of online marketing and to get as far away as possible from Sutton Coldfield. Well, I achieved the former at least, if not the latter.

My initial plan was simple: to ski for an entire season and get other people to pay for it. I'd pick up the necessary skills as I went along.

There were a few unexpected side effects not covered by the plan: getting divorced was definitely not in the original draft; neither was losing my home and becoming someone else's house husband; nor was spending my summers in Sutton. Frankly, if you had told me at the start that my destiny was to live with two kids and a dog, I would have said that it was you who was barking.

When old friends hear about my new domestic goddess act they wonder if a proper alien, never mind an après one, inhabits my body. Some also express concerns that I'm now officially classed as safe to leave with children, let alone licensed to teach them to ski. But, I haven't really changed that much, I've just parked some old prejudices and learnt how to do domestic tasks in order to live in the Alps.

What has surprised me is that I actually enjoy doing some of them, like cooking, mostly because they don't involve the use of PowerPoint and the audience is usually appreciative.

What has changed is my skiing. Jealous friends often say 'You must be a really good skier by now?' I always reply, 'What I am, is out of excuses.' But of course anyone who skis fourteen weeks a year is going to improve - even me. Importantly, I can now access the backcountry and ski with The Nazis. My attitude to skiing has also changed. I now regard skiing as a recreational activity and skis as practical transport devices for moving around snow-covered mountains.

My drinking habits have also changed. Despite being the perfect place for an alcoholic to hide, working in a ski resort has opened my eyes. Being forced to stay sober in après bars has proved to be a very successful therapy. My mission now is usually to stay relatively sober, when before it was to get drunk.

My attitude to the French has changed too. I now accept that a Frenchman cannot snack and needs a two hour lunch. That's why shops will be closed whenever you want to buy something and sandwich selections never go past cheese or ham. I know that the only thing the French take longer to prepare than food is paperwork. Before the project these things frustrated me, now I say *'vive la différence.'*

Some things haven't changed. Having observed many different parenting styles and lived with the resulting children, I'm still very glad I'm not a parent - although I've come to admire parents who take on the ultimate logistic challenge: a family skiing holiday.

Then there are the losses to account for and I don't just mean the financial ones. I cut short a lucrative career, although I think mine was coming to a natural end anyway. I lost a house and, more importantly, a home. However my idea of a dream home has changed and I never want to live in a city centre again.

More significant are the collateral losses. Detaching yourself from people you've spent half your adult life with is hard. I didn't just lose a wife but a family of in-laws too, although I do try and keep in touch.

I did gain a new family (Debbie's). Sometimes on family occasions, particularly Sunday lunch, I feel like I've turned up at the wrong house but I eat with the inhabitants anyway. It's like being an actor in a long-running soap opera. All the other actors, those playing grandparents, sisters, nephews and nieces, have all been replaced – only I have retained my original role as the son in-law. Oh, and the set has changed significantly.

I've lost a lot of good memories too. Twenty years of adventures undertaken with my ex. My old holiday photographs invoke large bouts of nostalgia and, for now at least, it's painful to look at them - nostalgia uses very rose tinted glasses.

Some things I'm glad to have lost. The Sword of Damocles for instance, hanging over my head, and I'm no longer burdened with an unhappy wife or the worry that a marriage will fail. The worst has already happened, and strangely it's a relief - no longer being responsible for someone else's unhappiness is liberating. I've lost a litany of crimes and been given a clean sheet. I was already a ski bum when I met Debbie - I wasn't going to disappoint her by turning into one.

One chairlift philosopher 'Scouse John', a Ski Club Leader known more for his profanity than his profoundness, enlightened me. He said, 'It's not possible to have change without loss.' When he said it, I almost fell off the chairlift his words rang so true. I'd wanted the change but hadn't anticipated the loss. I'd gained a wonderful new winter life but lost a lot of things I held dear.

30. THE BLUE JACKET

I landed at Lyon airport with one mission in mind, to return to England wearing a blue jacket. Not just any blue jacket, but a Ski Club of Great Britain Leader's jacket, the one that had eluded me on my last trip to Tignes.

It was late November 2014, two years since that fateful trip to the Espace Killy, one that had ended in failure, one that had marked the lowest ebb of the Summer of Discontent. I joked that 'I'd passed everything but the actual skiing,' but it was still unfinished business for me.

They had given me a 'D' grade. D stood for 'Deferred', which meant I had two years to return for a skiing reassessment. Two years had elapsed and this was my last opportunity to prove to them that I was now a 'good skier' (whatever that means). I was to attend the three-day 'Performance Clinic' that marked the beginning of the 2014 Leaders' Course, where my skiing would be re-scrutinised by those who had judged me before.

I had spent my last day of Season 4 skiing with Andy Jerram in Morzine, who thought my skiing had improved enough to give it another go. The truth was that, on that day, I'd skied near the top of my ability at the end of a season, rather than at the bottom of it at the beginning of one.

I'd deliberated for most of the summer whether to revisit the horrors of Tignes. Then, in late July after a Hemingway moment, I decided to 'Man up' and go for it a second time. I contacted the Club and after they'd checked with Andy that my skiing had 'improved', they made room for me on the course - which was all very encouraging. Not only would it be a shorter ordeal, but also, this time, I was better prepared. I was in a much better mental and physical state. My life was on the way up not on the way down, and I was as fit as I'd ever been since my twenties.

Then, like most young men, I had taken my physique for granted, but at fifty it had been hard graft getting into shape. Once again I found myself pounding the streets of Sutton Coldfield, driven by the fear of a second failure. Slowly I began to run faster and further each morning, until I was regularly running five kilometres a day. I ran around the periphery of the local golf course, occasionally peering over the fence at the golfers and wondering who had the most pointless pastime, them or me.

I downloaded and ran to music from my youth, mostly heavy metal and mostly dreadful. But it was good to be reunited with a few classics I'd abandoned decades ago. It was safe music because it predated meeting my wife and didn't invoke nostalgic thoughts - it was bloody good running music too. I also spent a significant amount of time that summer trying to improve my skiing technique at the Snow Dome, training with Andy Jerram and his merry band of Midlands based instructors.

This time I was doing things differently. I was flying out a week in advance to get 'Bambi Hour' well and truly out of the way whilst no-one was watching. I was going to take my trusty powder skis even though they were old and cumbersome on-piste. I knew they'd been correctly serviced and were the right tools for the job – the deep powder I was expecting.

Officially, the Espace Killy didn't open for another week and no transfer services were going to Tignes pre-season so I had to drive myself there from the airport. It was a warm sunny day in Lyon. But, expecting a drive into arctic conditions, I paid extra for a car with snow tyres, much to the bemusement of the Hertz assistant. I wasn't going to need them; unlike my last trip, the roads were dry all the way into Tignes. I pulled into Val Claret, the top station of Tignes that would be my home for a week, the sun was shining and the temperature was well above zero. I parked the car and surveyed the surrounding mountains - the pistes I'd seen so often in my nightmares were no longer white but green!

I could see the dreaded Tichot chair, (which wasn't running) and the Stade de Slalom, the place of my former exhaustion, looked incredibly benign. Initially, relief washed over me, my suspect deep powder technique wasn't going to be a problem this time I thought. The chance of anyone dying in an avalanche was going to be zero too. Then I felt embarrassed that such an easy red slope had caused me so much panic two years earlier. Then followed a feeling of disappointment - it was going to be hard to practise with no powder. Worse, if none came that week, it would be hard to prove to the Club that I was now a 'good skier' (whatever that means) without any snow.

But the Grand Motte was open. There's always snow up on the glaciers that slip down the side of the 3450-metre-high mountain peak, making Tignes a favourite for pre-season race training. The car park at its base was full of minibuses emblazoned with the logos of racing teams from all over the Alps.

So I spent the week training at altitude with dozens of athletes, most of them dressed in Lycra race suits. Each day, as the Lycra made its way to the slalom courses, I made my way to the limited off-piste areas between them. They had coaches and stopwatches to tell them if they were improving. I had no time metric to evaluate my performance, nor anyone to monitor my progress.

My apartment in Val Claret would have been ski-in/ski-out under normal circumstances - that's why I booked it. The apartment was very French. It had a fondue set and a raclette machine but no kettle. It had no Wi-Fi and only French TV for entertainment. It was very noisy, with building work going on next door until late each night.

However there was no snow in the village nor on the adjacent slopes, so each morning I had a long walk to the funicular that ascends the Grand Motte. The walk was especially painful in ski boots and by the end of the week both my big toe nails had turned black. The funicular, an underground train, had carriages not dissimilar to a London tube train apart from the fact that they sloped up. Each morning, while queuing with the Lycra people, including dozens of precocious kids, I mused about the similarity. I was effectively commuting to work on the underground to do a tedious and repetitive job.

Every day I'd get up early and catch the tube to work. I'd be on the first train up, spend the morning repeatedly skiing the same runs, have an hour for lunch, then ski the limited off-piste in the afternoon, while constantly checking the slow movement of my watch. Then, when the hour hand mercifully hit four, I'd catch the tube home. I would then sit in my lonely bedsit watching French TV and try not to eat or drink too much.

One night the builders cut the electricity to my apartment block forcing me out into a deserted Tignes to escape sensory deprivation. It was like a scene from a spaghetti Western, all I could hear was the wind howling and a dog barking. I half expected to see tumbleweed rolling down the deserted high street.

Only a couple of bars and restaurants were open. I ate in the same restaurant (funnily enough it was a Tex Mex) on several nights, mostly to gain some human contact. At least I was safe from the Après Aliens in this ghost town, I thought. By midweek, I'd started talking to myself. Luckily, other candidate Leaders turned up for some pre-course training too and I skied and socialised with them.

They were all intrigued about why I'd failed the course the first time, especially after they'd seen me ski. The fact that I looked like a reasonably 'good skier' (whatever that means) and yet I hadn't passed, was obviously worrying them. I played a few mind games, describing the horrors that lay ahead for them on the course.

Finally the 1ˢᵗ of December arrived and I said goodbye to Val Claret and drove down to the Le Lac area of Tignes, where the Ski Club hotel was located. When I walked into the hotel reception, it felt like I was revisiting the scene of a crime. I immediately bumped into Shep. He clearly recognised my face but couldn't put a name to it. He shook my hand and I explained - I was the guy back for a second attempt - and he wished me luck.

I checked in and got some very welcome news – I'd been allocated a single room. This time I'd come prepared with earplugs, assuming I'd be sharing a room with four snoring baritones once more, but I wouldn't need them, I would actually be getting some sleep during this stay.

It felt like I was in a dream that evening, sat in the conference room with the other hopefuls, listening to the welcome talk. I'd time travelled back two years – the room, the furniture, the presenters and their presentations hadn't changed. I noticed the projector was still plugged into the same blue, power extension block that had been a painful reminder of my fish tank's demise. Now it made me smile - it was just a bloody power block for heaven's sake - I'd build another reef one day.

With fewer candidates on the course this time round, there seemed to be a more relaxed atmosphere. I sat down for dinner with some friendly people, this time with a glass of wine in my hand. It was a more international mix, with skiers from Ireland, Sweden, and Australia intriguingly, all aspiring to be British Leaders. It generally seemed an older, less testosterone driven group. Having been through the mill once before, I was of great interest to my fellow diners and I enjoyed the attention. I continued the mind games telling them about and embellishing Roland's reputation. In contrast to before, I felt disappointed I wouldn't be skiing with him again this time.

It was the first day of the performance clinic and I was heading up the Motte with Phil Smith – it was good to see him again. I was more nervous than the others in the group because I was actually being judged whereas they were, notionally, being trained. I would spend all three days on the mountains; they would spend their afternoons playing 'team building' games at the hotel – I wasn't envious of that.

It did mean I had the benefit of hearing Phil's on-piste lectures twice - once with the morning group and once with the afternoon group. They were consistently delivered and hadn't changed much from two years ago, although my comprehension of them had. I made a point of sticking hard on his tail whenever he set off. I wasn't going to be T. E. Charlie this time. My fitness didn't seem to be a problem either – all that running I'd done had paid off. When I'd first ascended the very top of the Motte, a week earlier, I'd struggled with the altitude. Now I could see others gasping for oxygen but I had already acclimatised.

The next day I had double rations of Andy Jerram's teaching. It was like being in the Snow Dome, only with better scenery. His morning group was full of really fast skiers and not being T. E. Charlie took considerably more effort, but I succeeded. My confidence, that most vital of skiing commodities, was growing.

My skiing posture took a lot of flak over those first two days but the constructive criticism was welcome. Most importantly (in my mind at least), I didn't fall over once. There were many fallers in the hard-packed conditions and in nearly every session someone was injured and had to retire hurt. Having remained injury-free for four seasons, it would be just my luck to break something now.

The third day arrived and I had absolutely no idea how I was doing. I'd had a lot off criticism but no praise. I felt I was skiing as well as the majority of the other candidates, so surely they wouldn't be failing half the course?

We hadn't really skied anything especially difficult and I was a little frustrated that we'd not had more challenging off-piste conditions to show off in. However, on the final day, accompanied by qualified guides (Paul and Shep), Phil and Andy were allowed to take their groups deeper onto the glaciers away from the pistes and the skiing got harder.

Paul, who was shadowing Phil's group, was clearly on my side. He gave me a pep talk in the cable car. He told me I needed to stop 'mucking about and really go for it' – motivational, if not practical advice. I had been holding back a little fearing injury. I'd already had some motivational advice earlier that morning from Andy: 'If you don't cock it up today, you should get a result.' Although welcome feedback, his words had reinforced the battalion of butterflies in my stomach. I skied the morning with Phil and Paul and tried to 'go for it' without 'cocking it up'.

I'd becoming accustomed to spending my lunchtime in the mountain cafeteria with Andy and Phil while waiting for the afternoon groups to ascend – fresh legs for me to compete with. That day Paul and Shep joined us and I found myself sat at a table surrounded by Ski Club legends. It felt very surreal, like having dinner with the characters from your own book (literally). They discussed the merit of each candidate openly as if I wasn't there. They were deciding which group to put each candidate in for the next phase of the course. They must have had a similar conversation about the class of 2012 – I hate to think what they must have said about me.

I tried to eat my lunch without getting indigestion but I was too nervous to swallow. There was lots of banter, some of it at my expense, which relaxed me. Surely they'd not be taking the piss if they were about to fail me? It was decided, for my final afternoon, that I would ski with Shep's group because he had yet to see me ski. Being a pessimist, this change in schedule suggested to me that there was some sort of deadlock and he needed to see my skiing in order to cast a deciding vote. The battalion of butterflies in my stomach trebled its strength.

The fresh legs arrived and, after a chat from Shep, we did some piste skiing to warm up then headed off down one of the glaciers. Shep asked me to lead the group to the bottom. I'd been down the same route that morning so my confidence was high, I was skiing pretty well, but I knew this was my moment of truth. I led everyone to the bottom of the glacier without incident, although I was accused of going too fast by one of the group – excellent feedback. Then I weaved my way through the rocks at the bottom, diligently checking that everyone behind was OK. This was the sort of leading I did all season in Morzine and, surprisingly, I was enjoying myself. I successfully found the way back to the piste. Others took their turn and my moment in the spotlight was over.

Once everyone had had a go at leading, Shep decided to take us on an adventure into the unknown. Despite it being a week since the last significant snowfall, Shep, a true powder hound, found us some fresh-tracks. At one point we found ourselves perched on a rocky outcrop above an almost vertical, if short, slope. He turned and said, 'Don't feel you have to make turns down this. Sideslip it if you need to.' Needless to say I took this as a challenge and made a couple of turns, leading to several heart stopping seconds of free-fall until my trusty skis, taking me as a passenger, made a safe landing.

My reassessment was over. On the bus back to the hotel, I sat opposite Shep but not a word was spoken about my performance. I bumped into Mark, my roommate from two years ago, on the bus. He was delighted I'd returned for a second attempt. Initially

I took this chance meeting as a good omen, but Shep remained silent throughout the journey, despite the conversation being about everything being easier a second time around, which was worrying.

As we de-kitted in the boot room, in my case for the last time, I broke ranks and asked, 'Well Shep, when will you let me know if I've passed?' 'After the evening meeting' he replied (the instructors met every evening at 5pm to review the candidates performance). 'See you in the bar after that,' he added. I looked at my watch and cringed, it said 4pm - this was going to be the longest hour of my life. I went straight to the bar and ordered a coffee, despite really wanting a beer. However at about 4:30pm Shep wandered in to get a coffee too and I caught his eyes. I told him the waiting was killing me.

'Don't worry' he said, 'you're fine.'

Waves of relief flooded over me. If I'd got a verbal thumbs up from Shep I was bound to get the 'result' that Andy had alluded to that morning. I started an internal celebration whilst trying hard not to give anything away to the stream of candidates asking me if I'd passed. It seemed that everyone was rooting for me.

Later, I bumped into Shep in the corridor outside my room, unceremoniously he handed me my pass certificate. He smiled and congratulated me as I thanked him for my second chance. I went into my room and sent a triumphant text message to the Ski Nazis, while staring at the piece of paper. It had my new Ski Club grading written on it in black and white. I was now officially a Purple/Purple skier – whatever that meant. I phoned Debbie with the good news - it was thanks to her I'd got my act together - returned to Tignes and ultimately passed.

Frustratingly I didn't have anyone to celebrate with. My Tignes journey might have ended but my new friends were only at the halfway point, so I went to the evening's lecture with a large grin on my face. Andy was giving a talk about ski technology - fully clothed. Before I could sit down, he spotted me and announced to the audience, 'Here's Chris, the only qualified Leader in the room.' There was a pause, then a round of applause, followed by handshakes and hugs. Then, in the room where I'd spend the darkest hours of my life two years before, I proceeded to spend one of the most elated.

The lecture was an informative and entertaining one but I was keen to get to the bar. I had an appointment with the Après Aliens to keep. I did persuade Andy to go out for a drink after dinner and the rest of the evening became the usual blur. But the Aliens were reasonably kind to me and I woke up in my own hotel room – albeit wearing a new blue jacket.

I had a plane to catch and a long drive to the airport, but first I went down for my continental breakfast. While I was eating my self-boiled egg, none other than Roland sat down at the table in front of me. He had just flown in from Chamonix to play his annual role in the leaders' course (that of crazy French guide). He congratulated me and we chatted a little and I told him to give the new guys hell. I packed and left for Lyon wearing my blue jacket. Finally I had the validation I was looking for – I was officially a 'good skier'.

31. Living the Dream?

The Chalet Project was a classic midlife crisis. The actions of a depressed, middle-aged man, worried that he'd wasted the first half of his life and determined not to do the same with the second. And I'll admit that I was a perfect candidate for one: a selfish, deluded, malcontent, not to mention an impetuous fool, with a romantic notion of 'living the dream.'

Dream or not, spending four seasons in Alps has taught me more important things than just how to snowplough and cook. I found out the hard way, that you can't have change without loss and that following your dreams usually has a price. It's given me new insight into, and caused me to reassess, old prejudices – not to mention taught me a lot about Land Rover maintenance. I've learnt some valuable lessons too.

Never take the bottom bunk when sharing a room with a youth newly of drinking age; never stand next to anyone in a bar who is still wearing ski boots after 8pm; don't go skiing during the school holidays unless someone else is paying – like your parents for instance. Most importantly, that you never really know your friends until you've shared a chalet with them.

I've learnt the French may be fussy about eating but that *we* are a nation of fussy eaters which is a completely different thing, and that I made the right choice not becoming a parent, despite the obvious loss to the gene pool. I learnt a lot about our nation's drinking habits and indeed my own. I've learnt that you can drown sorrow but anger floats. I've picked up some useful skiing tips too:

- Never go to Geordie ski school.
- Ski with Nazis if you want to improve.
- Avoid being T. E. Charlie at all costs.

- Never go on a 'boys trip' once you're over thirty.
- Eat porridge for breakfast.
- Ski with a 'girlfriend' once in a while, even if you have to borrow one.
- Be confident - even if you're not.
- Remember 'Speed is your friend'.
- Imagine you're a Page Three Girl – strangling two chickens (© A. Jerram).
- Make sure your second wife can already ski – don't have kids.
- There are no 'friends' on a powder day.
- Don't trust anyone who wears a transceiver but doesn't carry a shovel.
- Always have a strategy for dealing with bad luck.

Unfortunately I'm no closer to defining what being a 'good skier' actually means other than, one who doesn't die. But I'm now convinced that skiing is *not* a sport – unless you want it to be.

I've learnt a lot about skiing with demons and how to deal with fear on the fall line, mostly my own. I've discovered that no matter how experienced we are, we all face similar fears; the more experienced skiers are just facing their ski demons higher up the mountain. Most importantly, I've learnt that *everything* in skiing, and life, is easier a second time around. I may not be living a dream, but I'm a much wiser man.

After being a chalet host for four seasons, the novelty has worn off and I find myself searching for the answer to the biggest question posed by The Chalet Project - am I now really 'living the dream?'

The pedantic will point out that it's not possible to live a dream. Living is mostly done awake and dreaming is mostly done asleep so, unless you're suffering from narcolepsy or taking hallucinogens, the phrase is a bit of an oxymoron. If you're living, you're not dreaming. So, before I claim the impossible, I must ask myself: 'Is my new life significantly better than my old one?'

Sometimes, when I'm sitting in a friend's fabulous house or their beautiful garden, looking at their expensive cars parked on the drive, I feel a bit jealous. If I had stuck to the straight and narrow I too would probably have the trappings of wealth and have a dream home. Well actually, I did and lost it, but that's beside the point. The point is, if you go chasing dreams you're unlikely to accumulate anything other than experiences, memories and a great set of photographs.

I've had some amazing, and sometimes gritty, experiences over the last four seasons and accumulated some extraordinary, and often bizarre, memories. I could have done without witnessing an avalanche death and a heart attack on the Wall. Few people have woken up with a horse in their bedroom and even fewer Jews have slept on a bed made of bacon. However, I've met some fascinating people and heard some amazing life stories. I've shared their elation, sometimes their terror, and often their remorse.

Then there are the skiing memories that my new life is still accumulating: the deserted pistes, the powder days, the bluebird skies, the spectacular clouds and the breathtaking views of the most magnificent of all mountain ranges – the Alps. Not to mention the friendships forged on them, the good humour, the camaraderie and the wild après sessions.

However, my new winter life is a Spartan one. My wages are poor, my accommodation is basic and my company car is drafty, uncomfortable and almost as old as me. My working day is long, albeit I often spend the middle part skiing, and

I seldom get a day off for four months. During that time I'm permanently at everyone's beck and call. What is really hard work is constantly meeting and living with strangers, continually answering groundhog questions and perpetually making small talk.

It may be a life of servitude but I'm my own boss and, unlike any of my previous jobs, annoying clients only have to be endured for a week. There is stress, yes, but it's more physical than mental. There's great job satisfaction too. Especially when I'm heartily thanked for making someone's holiday special or I see the joy on a person's face as they shout, 'Claimed it' at the bottom of a powder field.

Being a ski bum turned out to be much harder work than the term 'bum' implied but, even when I'm scrubbing toilets or washing up piles of pots, I never find myself wishing I was back in that brain-storming meeting at the agency. If I find myself getting a bit stressed, particularly on changeover day, I look out of the window, admire the view and I smile - because in the winter I live somewhere that most people can only visit on holiday one week a year.

While trying to live my winter dream I inadvertently ended up living the suburban one in the summer, which I'd previously have classified as a nightmare. I do often have to take a reality check whenever I find myself doing the family shop at the supermarket, walking the dog in the park, cutting the lawn at the weekend or dealing with recalcitrant kids - but suburbia no longer makes me scream.

The Chalet Project was a risk that almost didn't pay off, but then life, like skiing, is a sequence of calculated risks – without risk there is no satisfaction in triumph. Nothing ventured; nothing gained. Yes, I'm 'living a dream' - it's just not the one I expected.

32. The Final Descent

The Swiss Wall was looking at its intimidating best. The wind was howling and the drifting snow was being sucked over the precipice as the col channelled the wind towards its entrance. I turned to look at the debutants, the Wall virgins, who had requested that I took them down the wretched run. I turned to offer my usual witticism –'there's only one rule on the Wall – every man for himself' but there was just David standing there!

'What happened to Polly and James?' I shouted although he was only a couple of feet way. 'They changed their minds and took the chair down,' (the Chairlift of Shame). 'I don't blame them,' he added 'I don't fancy it today myself.' I couldn't believe my ears. Was David, my ski-father, wimping out of the Wall? For the first time ever, we swapped roles and I had to give him a little pep talk.

'We're off-piste skiers. This is a marked run for heaven's sake, we've done it hundreds of times before and, more importantly, the guests are now watching from the chair.' He agreed and we dropped in.

Once over the tricky edge, to our amazement we found the entire Wall covered with six inches of untracked powder – we were the first people down it that day. The snow conditions were perfect. We bounced down the slope a couple of metres apart, leaving fresh-tracks behind us. Twenty years previously, when David first took me down the Wall, I had gone-ostrich on him at the top. Now I was skiing it seemingly as his equal. As we joined the others at the bottom of the chair, we looked up at the parallel tracks – and they were a beautiful sight to behold. The Student had become the Master and The Wall was now just another black run.

I decided I would never ski it again – but of course I inevitably would.

Appendix – Ski Terminology

Below is an index of terms in common parlance around ski resorts. I have included it in order to make this book more understandable, for non-skiing readers, but also to clear up any confusion as to their meaning.

Skiing Term	Definition
Age-inappropriate evening	Spending the evening with people more than twenty years your junior or senior.
All-mountain skier	A skier who can successfully ski all parts of a mountains (on- and off-piste) in any conditions.
Après (Aliens)	Drinking done immediately after skiing. Usually done in ski gear near a ski slope. If you drink too much, the Après Aliens will come and abduct you and usually deposit you in the wrong bed. You'll have little recollection of the evening's events.
Backcountry	Areas of the mountain that are far from any piste or human habitation. Backcountry skiing requires the services of a mountain guide and usually involves a lot of hiking – but it's usually worth it.
Backmark (er)	Deliberately staying behind a group of skiers in case they need assistance. Usually, the guide appoints the role to the skier who is least likely to need assistance himself - or the person wearing the loudest jacket who will be the easiest to see in a whiteout.

Bambi hour	The first hour spent on skis after a significant period away from skiing (like summer). Usually occurs on the first day of a new season or after recovering from a protracted injury.
BASI (British Association of Snow Sport Instructors)	Note: the 'S' does not stand for 'Ski' but 'Snow Sports' as the organisation embraces all forms of sliding down a mountain. This includes Alpine skiing ('normal skiing'), Telemarking ('silly skiing'), Nordic skiing ('uphill skiing'), Adaptive skiing ('skiing sitting down') and Snowboarding ('not skiing').
Big mountain skiing	See 'extreme-skiing'.
Bluebird day	A sunny day with no clouds in the sky.
Breakfast zombie	People who are brain dead before breakfast.
Carving	Using the shape of a ski to make a turn while staying in complete control of direction and speed. The holy grail of modern on-piste skiing.
Catching an edge	Common, but meaningless, excuse for falling over, see also 'Equipment failure'.
Chalet host	Front of house chalet staff employed to look after the guests' every need. Often doubles up as cook, barman, cleaner, taxi driver and agony aunt.
Chalet night-off	The night guests have to eat out and seasonaires have to get drunk.
Chalet wine	Cheap complimentary wine served with dinner. Usually inexhaustible.

Champagne powder	Light dry snow that is commonly thought to be the most fun to ski on. A trademark of Steamboat California.
Changeover day	When one set of guests leave and a new set arrive, usually a Saturday. You have to learn a new set of names and answer the same questions the previous guests asked (the Groundhog Questions, see below).
Claimed	The first person down a fresh field of powder can be said to have 'claimed it'. Often shouted, while holding poles in the air.
Committed	Move into a position where there is no other option but to ski down the run below, the point of no return.
Cougar	A female sexual predator, that hunts for preferably younger men.
Crow skiing	Skiing as a crow would fly – in a straight line. Usually by those lacking the ability to turn or lacking interest in self-preservation. (See also 'kamikaze skier').
Dropping in	Starting a descent, usually by skiing over an edge or lip, from which there is no going back.
Drunk proof	A plan that can be successfully executed by inebriated personnel.
Edge	The sharp side of a ski - used to carve turns.
Equipment failure	A common, if not always legitimate, excuse for falling over.
Extreme skiing	Descending on extremely steep slopes that offer only a slight chance of survival. The French coined the term 'Le Ski Extreme' in the 1970s.

Face plant	Inverted burial up to the neck or deeper in soft snow. Usually a result of sudden and unanticipated deceleration.
Fall line	The route a ball would take down a slope if it was unaffected by forces other than gravity and wasn't wearing any skis. The more time a skier spends on the fall line, the better skier they are. Unless, of course, they're actually falling.
Freeskiing (Newschool skiing)	Involves performing tricks, jumps, and other aerobatics in a snow park using skis for take-off and landing equipment. Should not be attempted by anyone older than twenty if they don't want to spend six months in traction.
Fresh-tracks	Marks made by skis in un-ski'd snow.
Girlfriend Skiing (GF skiing)	Skiing to and from an expensive restaurant using blue runs.
Good Skier	Undefined.
Go-ostrich	Being paralysed with fear at the top of a slope and unable to turn.
Grey on a tray	An old snowboarder. Often, but not necessarily, with grey hair. Can also be bald headed.
Groundhog Day (Groundhog Questions)	A day in which a series of unwelcome or tedious events appear to be recurring in exactly the same way as previously. Such as on changeover day, when new guests ask the same questions (Groundhog Questions) that the previous guests did.
Hemingway oath	A promise to always do what you said you would the night before – no matter how drunk you were when you promised to do it.

Jägermeister	Cough medicine invented by the Austrians. Subsequently marketed as an alcoholic drink.
Kamikaze skier	A skier who mistakes speed for ability and has little regard for his own safety or that of those he shares the piste with. Usually hopeless off-piste.
Lad skiing	What men of all ages do when on a male-only ski trip.
Laddette skiing	What women of all ages do, when on a female-only ski trip — very similar to lad skiing, just involving less skiing.
Landie	My 1996 Land Rover Defender 110 - has both male and female properties.
Liftie	Lift attendant. Usually found listening to Bob Marley or Jimmy Hendrix while having a joint.
Manzine	Morzine's nickname in January when 80% of its inhabitants are male.
Manther	Male equivalent to a cougar — see above.
Moguls	Mounds of snow found on steep runs that are created by better skiers than you.
Morzinenois	French local whose family has lived in Morzine for generations - usually called Baud.
Off-piste	Everywhere on the mountain that isn't a piste and is covered in snow.
Park rat	A person, usually a snowboarder, who spends all day in the snow parks learning tricks. Repeatedly does 'park-laps'. Going round and round the park.

Piste	A run marked by poles that has been made safe by the pisteurs. The colour of the poles allegedly indicates the difficulty of the piste.
Piste etiquette	The unwritten rules for sharing a piste with other skiers safely. Despite being a French word, it is seldom taught to French children (or snowboarders).
Pisteurs	Keepers of the pistes. Employed by the resort to keep the piste flat and safe. Usually drink pastis.
Poling	Using ski poles to propel oneself forward across the flat or to 'pole up' slopes. A technique not available to snowboarders – who have to unclip and walk.
Pow	Abbreviations for powder – see below.
Powder	Light, fluffy snow.
Pow-pow	Abbreviation for powder, repeated to make it longer than the word it replaced. (Mostly used by snowboarders).
Powder day	The day after fresh powder has been dumped overnight.
Powder hound	Skier whose whole life is devoted to finding 'pow' and making fresh-tracks in it.
Powder skis	Wide skis designed to float in powder, but difficult to turn on-piste. The wider the skis, the more 'rad' and 'gnarly' you look when carrying them to the après bar.
Ragdolling	To fall down a slope with limbs flailing in all directions, tumbling like a ragdoll dropped down a staircase. Usually ends in a 'yard sale', see below.

Returning to reality	Going back to England after a ski season to continue with higher education, resume unemployment or work as a house husband in Sutton Coldfield.
Route one	Skiing straight down the fall line. Also known as 'crow skiing' or 'falling'.
Schuss	The gaining of momentum down one slope in order to get up an opposing slope without having to do any poling.
Schussing engine	Either a large 'beer gut' on a man or large 'wine belt' on a woman. The heavier you are the further you can schuss. It also helps if the mass is centralised around your waist. Having a large schussing engine hinders all other aspects of skiing.
Scottish powder	Sheet ice, sometimes with grass sticking through it. Also known as 'New England powder' or 'Californian concrete'.
Seasonaire	Gap year student working in a ski resort, usually of middle-class upbringing. Usually chooses to lie in bed on their day off rather than go skiing.
Shredding	Skiing the same off-piste slope many times until there is no untracked 'pow' left.
Sideslip	To ski sideways slowly. Technique used to descend from positions where turning is impossible due to lack of room or ability.
Ski bum	Person whose objective is to have zero responsibly and ski a lot. They are usually willing to take on almost any menial task for a poor wage as long as the job comes with free board and lodging and the all-important season pass.

Ski cronies	People you ski with of a similar ability both on the mountains and in the bar.
Ski dude	Young man born on skis, lives on skis, and will soon die on them too. Usually seen carrying wide powder skis.
Ski-faffer	Person who wastes time fiddling with equipment and clothes instead of skiing.
Ski Nazi	A skier who catches the first lift up every morning and the last one down every night, no matter what the conditions. Seldom stops for coffee or lunch - will normally eat porridge for breakfast.
Skinning-up	Walking up slopes after attaching animal skins to the bottom of your skis to make them grip. Favoured by people who can't afford a lift pass.
Snowmance	A romance that happens on a ski holiday
Snowplough	A painful, pigeon-toed stance taught to beginners and used occasionally in an emergency by everyone.
Snow park	Area containing skiing hazards such as kickers, rails, boxes, jibs, and other man-made obstacles. Inhabited by 'park rats'.
Snow sure	Having a reputation for consistently having good snow conditions.
Snow whinger	Person who complains about the type of snow currently available in the resort.
Spring snow	Ice in the morning and slush in the afternoon. Usually late season (March/April).
Tail End Charlie (T. E. Charlie)	The slowest skier in a group who gets to a resting point last. On his arrival everyone else will set off again.

Traverse — Skiing across the fall line for a significant distance, aiming for a position that is only slightly lower than the one you started in.

Whiteout — When visibility had been reduced to zero by driving snow or fog, it becomes impossible to see the contours of the terrain ahead, let alone the next piste marker. It can sometimes lead you to think you are stationary even though you're still moving.

Wife skiing — Skiing while being shouted at by a loved one.

Yard sale — The detaching and scattering of equipment around a prostrate skier.

The End